THINK
BIGGER

THINK
BIGGER

Developing a Successful Big Data Strategy for Your Business

MARK VAN RIJMENAM

AMACOM

American Management Association
New York • Atlanta • Brussels • Chicago • Mexico City • San Francisco
Shanghai • Tokyo • Toronto • Washington, D. C.

Bulk discounts available. For details visit:
www.amacombooks.org/go/specialsales
Or contact special sales:
Phone: 800-250-5308
Email: specialsls@amanet.org
View all the AMACOM titles at: www.amacombooks.org
American Management Association: www.amanet.org

This publication is designed to provide accurate and authoritative information in regard to the subject matter covered. It is sold with the understanding that the publisher is not engaged in rendering legal, accounting, or other professional service. If legal advice or other expert assistance is required, the services of a competent professional person should be sought.

Library of Congress Cataloging-in-Publication Data

Van Rijmenam, Mark.
    Think bigger : developing a successful big data strategy for your business / Mark van Rijmenam.
        pages cm
    Includes bibliographical references and index.
    ISBN-13: 978-0-8144-3415-4
    ISBN-10: 0-8144-3415-0
    1. Information technology—Management. 2. Big data. 3. Business—Data processing.
4. Database management. I. Title.
    HD30.2.V3647   2014
    005.74068'4—dc23   2013032722

About AMA
American Management Association (www.amanet.org) is a world leader in talent development, advancing the skills of individuals to drive business success. Our mission is to support the goals of individuals and organizations through a complete range of products and services, including classroom and virtual seminars, webcasts, webinars, podcasts, conferences, corporate and government solutions, business books and research. AMA's approach to improving performance combines experiential learning—learning through doing—with opportunities for ongoing professional growth at every step of one's career journey.

Printing number
10 9 8 7 6 5 4 3 2 1

To my parents and my sister

Contents

The History of Big Data

O f all the data in recorded human history, 90 percent has been created in the last two years. However, the need to use and interpret such Big Data has been around for much longer. In fact, the earliest examples of using data to track and control businesses date back 7,000 years, when Mesopotamians used rudimentary accounting to record the growth of crops and herds. Accounting principles continued to improve, and in 1663, John Graunt recorded and examined all information about mortality rolls in London. He wanted to gain an understanding of and build a warning system for the ongoing bubonic plague.[1] In the first recorded example of statistical data analysis, he gathered his findings in the book *Natural and Political Observations Made upon the Bills of Mortality*, which provides great insights into the causes of death in the seventeenth century. Because of his work, Graunt can be considered the father of statistics.

The nineteenth century witnessed the start of the information age. Modern data was first gathered in 1887, when Herman Hollerith invented a computing machine that could read holes punched into paper cards to organize census data.[2]

THE TWENTIETH CENTURY

In 1937, during Franklin D. Roosevelt administration, the United States created the first major data project to keep track of contributions by more than three million employers and 26 million employees under the new Social Security Act. IBM was awarded the contract to develop a punch card-reading machine for this immense bookkeeping task.[3]

The British developed the first data-processing machine in 1943 to decipher Nazi codes during World War II.[4] The device, named Colossus, searched for patterns in intercepted messages at a rate of 5,000 characters per second. This reduced the time required to perform the task from weeks to merely hours. It was a huge step forward.

In 1952 the U.S. National Security Agency (NSA) was created and, within 10 years, it had contracts with more than 12,000 cryptologists.[5] They were confronted with information overload during the Cold War, as they started collecting and processing intelligence signals automatically.

In 1965, the U.S. Government decided to build the first data center to store its more than 742 million tax returns and 175 million sets of fingerprints.[6] Employees transferred all those records onto magnetic computer tape that was stored in a single location. The project was later dropped out of fear of "Big Brother," but it represented the beginning of the electronic data storage era.

Then, in 1989, British computer scientist Tim Berners-Lee developed what eventually became the World Wide Web.[7] He wanted to facilitate the sharing of information through a "hypertext" system. Little could he know at that moment the impact his invention would have on everyone.

Beginning in the 1990s, data was created at an amazing rate as more and more devices were connected to the Internet. In 1995, the first supercomputer was built; it performed as much work in a second than a calculator operated by a single person could do in 30,000 years.[8]

THE TWENTY-FIRST CENTURY

In 2005, Roger Mougalas of O'Reilly Media coined the term "Big Data," a year after the company created the term Web 2.0.[9] He used the term to refer to a large set of data that is almost impossible to manage and process using traditional business intelligence tools.

In that same year, Yahoo! created Hadoop on top of Google's MapReduce.[10,11] Its goal was to index the entire World Wide Web;

nowadays, many organizations around the world use the open-source Hadoop to crunch massive data sets.

As more and more social network sites appeared and Web 2.0 took flight, more and more data was created daily. Innovative startups slowly mined this vast amount of data and governments also began Big Data projects. In 2009, the Indian government decided to take an iris scan, fingerprint, and photograph of all of its 1.2 billion inhabitants.[12] All this data is stored in the largest biometric database in the world.

By 2010, when Eric Schmidt, the Executive Chairman of Google, spoke at the Techonomy forum in Lake Tahoe, California, he put the information revolution in perspective by stating that "every two days now we create as much information as we did from the dawn of civilization up until 2003. . . . That's something like five exabytes of data. . . ."[13]

In 2011 the well-received McKinsey report on "Big Data: The Next Frontier for Innovation, Competition, and Productivity," concluded that by 2018, the United States would face a shortage of 140,000 to 190,000 data scientists, as well as 1.5 million data managers.[14] The job Big Data Scientist is therefore often coined the sexiest job of the twenty-first century.

In the past few years, there has been a massive increase in the number of Big Data startup companies. All are trying to help organizations manage and understand this explosion of Big Data. As more companies are slowly adopting Big Data, just as with the Internet in 1993, the Big Data revolution is still ahead of us, so a lot will change in the coming years.[15]

In fact, the amount of data is growing at such an explosive rate that we have gone past the decimal system. Today, U.S. agencies, such as NSA and the FBI, are talking about yottabytes when calculating the size of their files. In the (near) future, we will be talking about brontobytes regarding sensor data. Therefore, new terms have been created to describe the amount of data that is expected to be created in coming years (see Figure 1-1).

Big Data will completely change organizations and societies around the world. It is expected that the amount of data currently available will double every two years worldwide.[16] So, let's take a closer look at what Big Data exactly is.

Figure 1-1 Brontobytes Infographic

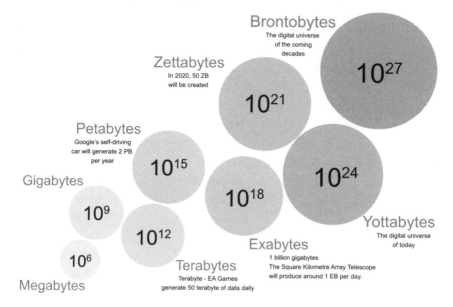

What Is Big Data?

2

As you know, everything that is digital is data. Nowadays, existing hardware and software cannot deal with the vast amounts of different types of data being created at such high speeds. Big Data has become too complex and too dynamic to be able to process, store, analyze, and manage with traditional data tools. The amount is so vast that we are not able to ask the right questions to find the right answers.

Fortunately, with the hardware, tools, and algorithms that have been developed, all that data can be turned into useful information. The insights provided by this information can be used to improve decision-making at your organization, improve your efficiency, decrease your costs, and increase revenue. The implications of the Big Data revolution are vast, and it will impact all industries and all types of companies.

EXPLANATION OF THE 7Vs

It is generally accepted that Big Data can be explained according to three Vs: velocity, variety, and volume. However, I would like to add veracity, variability, visualization, and value to better explain the impact and implications of a well-thought through Big Data strategy.

Velocity

Velocity is the speed at which data is created, stored, analyzed, and visualized. In the past, when batch processing was still common practice, it was usual to update the database every week or every evening. Computers and servers required substantial time to process the data and update the databases. In the Big Data era, however, data is created in real time or near real time. With the availability of Internet connected devices, wireless or wired, machines can pass on data the moment it is created.

The speed at which data is currently created is almost unimaginable: Every minute, we upload 100 hours of video to YouTube. In addition, over 200 million emails are sent every minute, around 20 million photos are viewed and 30,000 uploaded on Flickr, almost 300,000 tweets are sent, and almost 2.5 million queries on Google are performed.[1–4]

The challenges organizations have is to cope with are the enormous speed at which data is created and the need to use it in real time. We will discuss real-time Big Data in Chapter 3.

Variety

In the past, all data was structured data that fit neatly into columns and rows, but those days are over. Now, 90 percent of data is unstructured.[5] Data now comes in many different formats, including structured, semistructured, unstructured, and even complex structured.

Each type of data requires a different type of analysis and different tools to interpret. Social media, such as Facebook posts or Tweets, can provide insights in how your customers think of your brand, service, or product, while sensor data provides information on how a product or machine is used and provides insights about how you can improve the product.

Chapter 4 discusses the various types of analyses that can be performed on the different types of data and what tools can be used.

STRUCTURED DATA

Flat files in record format
A flat file can be a plain text file, usually containing one record per line. Single fields can be separated by commas. A .CSV files is a flat-file document.

GEO location data
Data about the real-world geographic location of an object.

HTML5 microdata
Microdata can include semantics in existing content to provide a richer browsing experience. The data can be extracted by search engines, crawlers, and browsers.

Legacy data
Information stored in old or obsolete formats or computer systems that is difficult to access or process.

Log files
Log files lists actions that have occurred in a standard format. Log files can give users a good indication of what is happening.

Microformats
A microformat reuses HTML/XHTML tags to convey metadata and other attributes.

Sensor data
Data collected by sensors that monitor equipment or products. Sensors can include RFID tags that store and send information.

Spreadsheets
A spreadsheet contains data in tabular format, meaning with tables and headings.

SEMISTRUCTURED DATA

Documents containing metadata tags
Metadata can include information such as author and time of creation; it can be stored easily in a relational database management system (RDBMS).

EDI documents
Electronic Data Interchange (EDI) documents imply a sequence of messages between two parties in a predefined format.

RSS feeds
Rich Site Summary (RSS) feeds are full or summarized text, including metadata, used to publish frequently updated work (e.g.,

blogs). RSS feeds are standardized xml file formats that allow the information to be published once and viewed by many different programs.

XML objects

Extended markup language (xml) objects are defined by a set of rules that allows formats to be readable by humans as well as machines.

UNSTRUCTURED DATA

Binary Large Objects (BLOBs)

BLOBS consists of binary data stored as a single file in a database management system. These BLOBs can be images, audio materials, or any other multimedia objects.

Business records requiring control

Documents, paper, or electronic files that are subject to business controls over storage, retention, disposition, and deletion to comply with legal, regulatory, or industry requirements or to support litigation and discovery.

Content management data

Data related to content management systems of online platforms. Wordpress or Joombla are content management systems.

Digital assets

Digital assets are documents that require specialized storage and transport to guarantee performance because they consist of large and/or special encoded files.

Dynamic content (multiple users)

Content that may be created, edited, reviewed, and approved by multiple people or groups. A good example is Google documents, which allows multiple people to work on the same document at the same time.

Email, text messages, chat

Data that represents correspondence or other communications between individuals, between companies and individuals, or between machines and individuals.

Intellectual property data

Data associated with intellectual property rights. Access to this data must be controlled. Property rights must be managed to avoid violation of contract or licensing terms regarding the use of the material.

Social data

Any data shared on social networks, such as Facebook posts, Tweets, YouTube movies, LinkedIn profiles, and so on.

Specialized content (web data)

Specialized content that requires special access, control, content entry, rendering, and other functions. A good example is online platforms.

Static documents

Documents in Word, PowerPoint, or ExCel that can be edited by one person at a time.

Taxonomies/ontologies

Ontology presents knowledge as different concepts (things, relations, or events), and it shows the relationship among these different concepts.

Voice recognition data

The translation of spoken words into text or data that can be understood by a computer. Voice recognition data includes Siri, podcast searches, speed-to-text processing, and voice-controlled systems.

COMPLEX STRUCTURED DATA

Hierarchically structured data (xml-based MISMO)
XML datasets related to complex financial products.

Volume

At the rate data is now being created, the amount will double every two years.[6,7] In 2011 we created a staggering 1.8 zettabytes of data. By 2020, the world will generate 50 times that amount of data, according to a 2011 study by IDC.[8] The sheer volume is enormous, and a very large contributor to the ever-expanding digital universe is the "Internet of Things," with sensors all over the world in all kinds of devices creating data every second.

Let's look at some examples. Airplanes generate approximately 2.5 billion terabytes of data each year from the sensors installed in their engines.[9] The agricultural industry generates and collects massive amounts of data from sensors installed in tractors. John Deere equipment uses sensor data to monitor machine optimization, control the growing fleet of farming machines, and help farmers make better decisions. Shell uses supersensitive sensors to find additional oil in wells and, if the company installed these sensors at all 10,000, approximately 10 exabytes of data would be collected annually.[10] And, that is absolutely nothing if we compare it to the Square Kilometer Array Telescope that will generate 1 exabyte of data per day.[11]

In the past, the creation of so much data would have caused serious problems. Nowadays, with decreasing storage costs, better storage solutions, such as Hadoop, and the algorithms to create meaning from all this data, storage is not such a big problem any more.

Veracity

The generation and collection of a lot of data at high speed is worthless if that data is flawed. Incorrect data can cause significant problems for organizations, as well as for consumers. If you want your organization to become information-centric, you need to ensure that your data and its analysis are correct. This is especially true in automated decision making, where no human is involved anymore. Shockingly, one in three business leaders do not trust the information they use in decision making.[12] Therefore, if you want to develop a Big Data strategy, you should strongly focus on the correctness of the data as well as the accuracy of its analysis. I will dive deeper into this important topic in Chapter 6.

Variability

Big Data is extremely variable. Brian Hopkins, a Forrester principal analyst, defines variability as the "variance in meaning"[13] He refers to the supercomputer Watson that won on the quiz show *Jeopardy*. The supercomputer had to "dissect an answer into its meaning and . . .

figure out what the right question was." That is extremely difficult because words have different meanings depending on context. For the correct answer, Watson had to understand the context.

Variability is often confused with variety. If a bakery sells ten different types of bread, that is variety. If, however, the same type of bread tastes and smells different every day, that is variability.

Variability is thus very relevant in performing sentiment analyses. Variability means that the definition is changing (rapidly).[14] In similar tweets, a word can have a totally different meaning. To perform a proper sentiment analysis, algorithms need to decipher the exact meaning of a word in its context. This is still very difficult.

Visualization

This is the hard part of Big Data. It means making that vast amount of data comprehensible in a manner that is easy to read and understand. With the right visualizations, raw data can be put to use. Visualizations, of course, are not ordinary graphs or pie charts. They are complex graphs that can include many variables of data while remaining readable and understandable.

Visualizing might not be the most technologically difficult task, but it certainly is the most challenging. The use of a graph to tell a complex story is very difficult, but also extremely crucial. Luckily, there are more and more Big Data startups that focus on this aspect of the challenge. In the end, visualizations will make the difference.

Value

All this available data will create a lot of value for organizations, societies, and consumers. Big Data means big business, and every industry will reap its benefits. McKinsey states that the potential annual value of Big Data to the U.S. healthcare industry is $300 billion, which is more than double the total annual healthcare spending in Spain.[15] The report also mentions that Big Data has a potential annual value of €250 billion to Europe's public sector administration. Further, McKinsey's highly respected report of 2011 states that the potential annual consumer surplus from using personal location data globally could reach $600 billion in 2020. That is a lot of value.

Of course, data in itself is not valuable at all. The value is in the analyses done on that data and how the data is turned into information and, eventually, knowledge and wisdom. The value is in how organizations use that data to create information-centric companies that base their decision making on insights derived from data analyses.

EIGHT REALITIES OF BIG DATA YOU SHOULD ALREADY KNOW

Now that we have defined Big Data, you need to know what the most important aspects of Big Data are that your organization should be aware of when developing a Big Data strategy. Big Data does require a paradigm shift, and knowing these realities will help your organization move forward. As they are so important, they will be discussed briefly here, but they are presented in greater detail in later chapters.

1. **Big Data requires a different culture.**
    To truly take advantage of Big Data, your organization needs to become an information-centric company. This culture shift will result in more data-driven decisions and will give your employees the opportunity to develop new operational, tactical, and strategic plans based on real data instead of calculated estimates. A Big Data culture requires that employees are encouraged to collect data at every point of customer contact. They need to ask the right questions and answer them with accurate data. Of course, changing a company culture is difficult and not easily achieved, but this book will provide guidance with a roadmap that will help in creating an information-centric culture.

2. **The real driver behind Big Data is the people within the organization.**
    Although a cultural shift is important to take full-advantage of all the possibilities of Big Data, development of a Big Data strategy comes from the people in an organization. In particular, managers and executives should be aware of what Big Data is and how it can be applied to their organization. The more decision makers are aware of the benefits of Big Data for the organization, the more likely it is that a successful Big Data strategy will be developed and implemented.

One of the most important facts to remember is that IT should not be responsible for a Big Data strategy. IT is merely a means to achieve your Big Data strategy, but it should not be responsible for overall strategic planning. There is a useful comparison to make here with the first years of social media. A few years ago, everyone thought that social media were the Holy Grail for marketing. Today, we see it, correctly, just as a means to achieve the marketing and strategy goals developed by the company. That's how Big Data should also be seen, as an important part of the overall strategy that is dealt with by the board or executive management.

To start to develop Big Data successfully, begin by finding the right sponsor within the organization, especially as the returns at first are uncertain and the costs can be high. The best choice is a senior manager or board member, as those individuals have the power to support the project even if the initial results prove to be negative.

3.   Big Data is everywhere, even at places you do not expect.

Everything digital is data. More and more items are digitized and connected to the Internet. This means your organization is receiving new data from completely new areas. The Internet of Things movement shows that any product or device can be connected to the Internet and therefore provide data.[16] Organizations should use this information and not be afraid to digitize products. Big Data literally is up for grabs; you only need to open your eyes to understand where you can find it and how to analyze and use it.

The Internet of Things even makes it possible to turn a cup of coffee into data! Just add a few sensors to the cup of coffee, and you can analyze when someone drank the coffee, how fast, where, for how long, with how many sips, what the temperature of the coffee was, how much coffee and water was used, and so on. If you collect and properly analyze the data about how coffee is consumed, you can turn it into information that can be used to understand the coffee drinking habits of your employees. This is of course a bit of a joke, as I doubt that any senior manager would be interested in such information, but it shows that to really incorporate Big Data into your organization, you should look out of the box.

But, you should also start looking in the public data marketplaces that are starting to appear everywhere. These data marketplaces collect free and paid public and open datasets from around the world. If your own data is combined with these new existing datasets, you will gain completely new insights and information.

4. Big Data engineers will be scarce, so you better start looking around.

McKinsey predicts a shortage of about 140,000 to 190,000 Big Data engineers in the United States alone in 2018.[17] The report also predicts a shortage of 1,500,000 Big Data managers who can supervise the Big Data engineers and can connect the IT aspect of Big Data with the strategy aspect. So, Big Data employees will be scarce in the future.

Big Data engineers and managers, however, are not the only personnel you should employ. Big Data analysts, Big Data solution architects, and, of course, the illusive Big Data Scientist should also be on your list. In particular, the Big Data Scientist will be hard to find and, therefore, expensive to employ. It is often called the sexiest job of the twenty-first century and, currently, only a handful of people around the world can truly call themselves Big Data Scientists.

For organizations to avoid missing out on future developments, they should start training their IT personnel in Big Data technologies, particularly if they want to develop Big Data solutions in-house. Universities are already creating Big Data engineering courses to prepare students for the future. In fact, more and more universities are already offering a Big Data study program, as well as courses on open online platforms, such as Coursera.[18,19]

5. Big Data does require big security measures.

Organizations that gather large valuable datasets need to protect that information from criminals whose goal is to steal the data and use it to their advantage. In recent years, a number of large, online companies and government organizations have been hacked, including LinkedIn, Evernote, and even Bitcoin.[20–22] Therefore, it is extremely important to protect all data that is collected. There are several ways to secure your data, the most common of which is to correctly encrypt the information. But, of course, there are many other ways to protect data, so security should always be part of your Big Data team.[23]

Every organizations should, however, also have a crisis plan ready just in case it is hacked. Surprisingly, many companies still have no idea what to do if they experience a security breach involving computers.[24] Such a breach can have disastrous consequences. Even more damaging is when a company lacks the security to even know it was hacked. Therefore, companies should plan for a possible attack either in-house or by using the services of an agency that specializes in this work. Not protecting the data of your organization and customers could very well mean the end of your company.

6.   A public debate about privacy issues in inevitable.

With Big Data come big privacy issues. In the age of Big Data, Big Brother will be watching everyone, whether online or offline. The PRISM leak by Edward Snowden in 2013 showed that privacy can and will be affected in this digital era. In addition, if the data is not correctly anonymized, the risk of reidentification becomes real. Although reidentification is difficult and expensive to achieve, it is not impossible. Furthermore, it is important to ensure that data is collected from reliable sources to ensure the correct ownership of the data. Therefore, you need to treat data correctly.

There are sufficient movies on the Internet showing the downside of Big Data. As more and more consumers become aware of the effects of Big Data on their privacy, the public debate about how far organizations should go in collecting that information will grow louder. Companies will need to establish clear guidelines.

Slowly, consumers are becoming aware of the amount of data that organizations are collecting about them on a daily basis. They are learning that companies often store the data for a long time, often two years or longer, and that they can sell that data if they want. Organizations will try to go as far as they can to maximize the use of this data. The payment provider Equens, for example, tried to sell transaction data to retailers in The Netherlands in 2013.[25] This immediately caused a stir with the public and the Dutch parliament. Within a few days, the company had to drop the plan.

7. **Governments all over the world are increasing their Big Data efforts.**

As with organizations, governments are also generating more and more data. Many governments are becoming digital. The Dutch government, for example, wants to become completely digital and scrap all paper correspondence by the end of 2017.[26] Imagine the amount of data 17 million citizens will generate when corresponding with national, regional, and local governments.

Other governments are also developing national Big Data strategies. In 2012, the U.S. government made $200 million available for research and development in the field of Big Data.[27] To store all the data that will be created, the National Security Agency (NSA) is developing a massive Big Data warehouse in Utah that is said to be capable of storing 12 exabytes of data, which is a lot of data.[28]

The European Commissioner Neelie Kroes is a supporter of Big Data, and she wants Europe to be in the front of it.[29] She sees the opportunities, and she urges countries to share their datasets with the public to develop applications that solve problems.

As a result of these initiatives, public datasets are becoming more widely available for organizations, and that drives innovation and new solutions for problems worldwide. More and more private initiatives are being launched as well. These marketplaces collect public and private datasets for organizations. Visitors can buy the datasets or download them for free. On some websites, organizations can also sell their datasets. In addition, Google and Amazon are developing Big Data marketplaces, although it is still on a relatively small scale.

There is still a long way to go, but it is clear that governments can also significantly benefit from the opportunities presented by Big Data.

8. **Big Data is not all about the amount of data.**

It is often thought that the term Big Data means a lot of data. Consequently, many think that a Big Data strategy is only possible when you have petabytes or exabytes of data. That is incorrect. Big Data is much more than just the volume of the data collected. Big Data is more about combining different datasets in different variances at different moments from different sources. In particular, it is the combining and subsequent analyzing of different datasets that will provide new and valuable insights.

This means that a Big Data strategy is also possible for small and medium enterprises. Even if your organization does not have petabytes of data, it can gain additional insights when that data is combined with, for example, public datasets or social data.

In addition, Big Data also refers to the analysis of available data in real time and the use of algorithms to predict behavior. Real-time insights can be extremely valuable to organizations, as can knowing what your customers will do in the near future.

This is part of Big Data, and such analyses can be done with less than exabytes of data. Don't be intimidated by companies that have massive amounts of data. Although more data does mean better insights, it does not necessarily mean more insights.

BIG DATA MEETS WALT DISNEY'S MAGICAL APPROACH

Walt Disney is one of the most admired companies in the world.[30] Annually, approximately 100 million visitors spend time in Walt Disney parks around the world.[31] These visitors generate a lot of data, and that is exactly what Walt Disney wants to capture. In 2013, the company announced the introduction of the wireless-tracking "MagicBand,"[32] a wristband that will make the visit to the Walt Disney World in Orlando a more magical experience while, in return, recording the complete data trail of the visitors.

The MagicBands, which are linked to a credit card, function as a park entry pass as well as a room key. They are part of the new MyMagic+ system that visitors are invited to join.[33] Membership offers many advantages, such as jumping the queues, pre-booking rides, changing reservations on the go via smartphones, being addressed with their names by Disney characters, and much more.

At the same time, the MyMagic+ system allows the Disney company to collect massive amounts of sensitive and valuable data about visitors, including real-time location, purchase history, information about riding patterns, and more. As such, Disney is building a gigantic database of every move of every visitor to the park. All this data is waiting to be analyzed and used by Walt Disney to make better decisions, improve its offerings, and tailor its marketing messages.

Although it is collecting massive amounts of data, Disney does respect the privacy of their visitors. The company allows visitors to completely control how much and what sort of data is collected, stored, and shared or to opt out completely.[34] Visitors can select via a special menu whether Disney can send them personalized offers during their stay or when they return home. Parents have to opt in before the characters in the park can use the personal information stored in the MagicBand.[35] However, even with the most restrictive selection, MagicBand does record general information about how the visitors use the park.[36]

To get the most out of the MyMagic+ system, Disney went to great lengths. Its 60,000 employees needed to be trained to use the system; for visitors, free Wi-Fi had to be installed across the 40-square mile park in Orlando. This free Wi-Fi allows visitors to use their smartphones more often while in the park, thereby adding to the amount of data that will be collected. Analysts estimate that the entire program cost approximately $800 million to establish.[37]

In order to store, process, analyze, and visualize all the data generated by the MyMagic+ system, Disney created a Big Data platform based on Hadoop, Cassandra, and MongoDB. It is complemented by a suite of other tools for specific uses.[38] The company moved from an RDBMS to its first Hadoop cluster in 2009, so that a Data Management Platform could by completed in 2011.[39]

Disney did start small, however, and built the Big Data platform as a startup builds a company.[40] The company began with a small and flexible team, made its mistakes early, and kept improving along the way. It began with open-source tools to keep costs down, but as the amount of data grew, the open-source tools used failed. Thus, Disney opted for paid tools that are more reliable in dealing with the large amount of data Disney processes. Today, Disney uses all the collected data to obtain valuable insights, using different forms of analysis, including, but not limited to, audience analysis, segmentation analysis, recommendation analysis and analysis of in-park traffic flows.

The opportunities for Walt Disney to use Big Data are enormous. The company is already experiencing great results from the MyMagic+ system in Walt Disney World in Orlando, so it is expected to expand to other parks around the world. The incredible volume of collected data will provide Disney with valuable insights that will enable the creation of an even more magical experience for visitors.

THE IMPACT OF BIG DATA ON SOCIETY

A lot has happened since McKinsey's well-known 2011 report, in which Big Data was referred to as the next frontier for innovation, competition, and productivity, but there is still a long way to go.[41] Tata Consultancy Services research from 2013 revealed that in 2012, 47 percent of the 643 companies surveyed were not using Big Data. In addition, 2013 Big Data research by the SAS Institute revealed that in 2012, 21 percent of the 339 companies surveyed did not know enough about Big Data, while 15 percent did not understand the benefits of Big Data for their organizations.[42,43] So, while more organizations are implementing a Big Data strategy, a large number still has no clue about its importance. And, when organizations do not understand Big Data, a large number of consumers probably also have no idea about its impact.

And, that is scary, as Big Data will have a gigantic impact on society, the way organizations are managed and operated, the way government is organized, and eventually, how the global economy functions.

Gartner predicts that Big Data development will drive up IT spending to $232 billion by the end of 2016.[44] Big Data has the potential to offer huge gains, but these only occur when all organizations and governments fully start to use Big Data and reap its benefits.

Obviously, what impacts the economy will affect society. Big Data will bring many benefits to consumers, such as better and more personalized products, improved services, lower energy bills, and more transparency. Thanks to the quantified-self movement, consumers are able to track and monitor their every move and thus gain a better understanding of their own lives (see Chapter 3). Big Data, however, will also affect the privacy of consumers. As society becomes more transparent for consumers it will also look as if big brother is constantly watching. There are many examples of organizations that did not respect the privacy rights of consumers or were not clear about how they dealt with the collected data. In 2012, for example, Path admitted to collecting data without permission; Twitter sold a multibillion dollar Tweet archive to a Big Data broker; and WhatsApp found itself in the firing line of a joint investigation by both the Canadian and Dutch data protection authorities.[45–47] In the future when this happens, these organizations probably will be punished by not only the governments or prosecutors but, more importantly, by consumers who could stop connecting with these organizations if there are better alternatives.

Slowly, consumers are grasping that their privacy is under fire with the new technology, which could lead to new legislation that will change the technology industry. If governments do not impose these changes, consumers could demand that organizations change policies, products, and the technologies they use. Therefore, in Chapter 5, I propose four ethical guidelines to help organizations do the correct thing with all that data now.

On a more positive note, society could also be the driver behind new technologies. A great example here is the rise of social media analytics, as consumers started to use social networks to connect with each other.

So, like any other disruptive technology, Big Data influences organizations. The innovators and early adopters are already working on their Big Data strategy that will change the way organizations are managed and operated. Organizations that have implemented a Big Data strategy already financially outperform their peers by 20 percent.[48] These organizations already reap the benefits of Big Data, and this impacts the global economy. Consequently, Big Data impacts many aspects of society; this, in turn, can affect technology.

This "technology-impact cycle" is ongoing (see Figure 2-1). Apart from its effect on Big Data, it can also be used to discuss the impact of other new technologies on organizations, the economy, and society.

Figure 2-1 The Technology-Impact Cycle

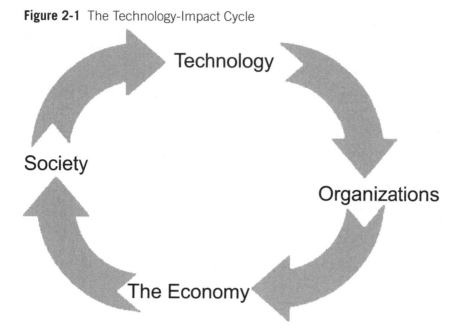

Generally, one rotation of the technology-impact cycle takes a few years. So, while O'Reily first coined the term Big Data in 2005, we are only now starting to understand its massive impact worldwide. However, it still unclear how society will impact Big Data.

TAKEAWAYS

The Big Data era is upon us. Organizations need to understand what Big Data is and how it can be used. The benefits and advantages are too big for organizations to ignore.

Big Data is often explained using the 3Vs: volume, velocity, and variety. However, to make it more complete, four additional Vs were added: veracity, variability, visualization, and, of course, value.

Big Data consists of many different types of data in different datasets that are combined to provide valuable insights that include better customer segmentation, a more efficient supply chain, or the reduction of risks. The combination of different datasets, such as company data, public data, and social data, will give even more insights.

In order to successfully move into the era of Big Data, a culture shift is required. Organizations should become information driven and ensure that all decision makers understand what Big Data is and how it can benefit the organization.

In addition, organizations cannot underestimate the security and privacy issues raised by Big Data. Such valuable data attracts criminals who want to steal that data. A company that does not have a crisis plan in place or the right privacy regulations can seriously endanger its future.

Big Data is changing how organizations operate and are managed. It also changes how society works and how consumers live. The impact of Big Data on society will be big, but it remains to be seen how society will impact Big Data.

Big Data Trends

Many different aspects of Big Data affect a big data strategy and how your organization should deal with it. As discussed in Chapter 2, each type of data affects what analyses you can perform and what tools you can use. Most of these factors involve the technical aspect of Big Data, but some trends will affect your strategy and also impact your organization as a whole. Therefore, it is important to look at them closely.

First, we will look at how the mobile revolution is affecting Big Data. The increasing use of mobile devices is driving growing sales for smartphones. Canalys, a global research firm, expects that in 2017 all of the 1.5 billion mobile phone sold will be smartphones.[1] In addition, the rise in tablet sales is enormous. Mobile devices require a different approach when dealing with Big Data.

Second, we will see that real-time Big Data provides the most value to organizations. The ability to analyze terabytes of data from various sources is interesting and can provide lots of insights, but analyzing terabytes of data the moment they are created anywhere in the world offers even greater possibilities. Data that is processed, stored, analyzed, and visualized in real time enables an organization to see what is happening among its processes, products, machines, employees, and customers anywhere in the world at any time. If you are able to respond to an occurrence in real time, it is more likely that the outcome will be positive.

The Internet of Things is probably the biggest trend within Big Data. In the coming years, the number of devices that contain sensors could grow to over a trillion. When we connect the unconnected, completely new possibilities will arise that were previously never thought of. In such an interconnected world, even the smallest things will have big implications. A great example of the Internet of Things is the city of Songdo. The smart city of Songdo, the world's first "City in a Box" will be available in 2015. Songdo will have smart innovations, such as streetlights that automatically adjust to the foot traffic. All houses in Songdo will be equipped with sensors, also known as domotics. Smart cities will have a major impact on the amount of data created on a daily basis. The Internet of Things will create a completely connected society. With trillions of devices connected to the Internet in the 2020s, brontobytes of data will be generated. All this data needs to be processed, stored, analyzed, and visualized for improved decision making. It will change our society and how organizations operate and are managed.

Another major trend is the rise of the quantified-self. The quantified-self movement is to consumers what Big Data is to organizations. Not only do organizations want to know what is going on, consumers also want to know what they are doing and how they can improve their behavior. The answer is first by tracking and understanding how you are doing at the moment. The quantified-self has resulted in applications that help consumers measure everything in their lives. From how they sleep to how much they eat to how many calories they burn. All this data is stored in the cloud, and it can give organizations valuable insights into how to improve their products. One company that fully understands the potential of the quantified self is Nike. It was able to turn a simple and individual sport into a social sport that generates massive amounts of data.

We will also dive into big social data, which focuses on the vast amounts of data created on social networks. There are hundreds of social network websites that continue to increase in membership. All those members generate massive amounts of data that can be analyzed by companies to provide additional insights. Clearly, the largest social networks are at the forefront of Big Data techniques. They have created algorithms that provide valuable insights. For example, LinkedIn could discern that something is happening at a public company when all senior managers suddenly update their profiles or link to certain other people. This sensitive data could, of course, be very valuable.

The availability of public data is a trend that cannot be underestimated. Governments around the world are seeing the advantages of Big Data. They are opening up datasets that were funded with public money. Sometimes, these datasets are given away for free or at cost. Organizations can use these datasets to gain additional insights and discover new markets or target groups. To find both free and low-cost datasets, go to one of the many upcoming online data marketplaces or data supermarkets.

Finally, we will look into the potentialities of gamification and how it can help organizations generate vast amounts of data in a user-friendly and engaging environment.

Normally, trends last only a few years. While Big Data is the megatrend, these seven trends form a crucial part of how organizations should address the challenge of Big Data. They will continue to exist in the coming decade and should form a important consideration in creating any Big Data strategy.

ON-THE-GO BIG DATA

The rise of mobile devices, which really took flight in the last few years, will have a major impact on Big Data, especially on visualizations. In 2013, over 20 percent of website visits was from mobile devices.[2] Mobile does not mean phone only; this includes tablets. Although a large percentage of mobile phones are still not smartphones, this is expected to change in coming years.

At the end of 2013, 1.4 billion smartphones were in use.[3] By 2015, Gartner predicts that more tablets will be sold than personal computers and, by 2017, 1.75 tablets will be sold for every personal computer.[4] The growth of the smartphones market goes beyond the Western world. Seventy-five percent of all new phones will be sold in Africa and Asia.[5]

On-the-go Big Data could have ground-breaking effects on some industries, such as healthcare. If doctors carry all important Big Data information about a patient on their smartphones or tablets so it is available while at a patient's bedside or in the operating room, it would certainly impact the way the healthcare industry operates.

The mobile era is upon us, and this will require a different approach by organizations. What is the effect on Big Data, and how can on-the-go Big Data add value to your organization?

The Mobile Revolution

Mobile devices are getting faster every day, and consumers are becoming less patient about waiting to connect to the Internet. Nowadays, consumers expect a reply in just three seconds.[6] They are willing to wait up to five seconds, but after that 74 percent abandon the connection.[7] Even more challenging is that 71 percent of mobile browsers expect web pages to load almost as quickly or even faster than web pages on their desktop computers.[8] This is regardless of whether the user is on 3G or Wi-Fi.

Fortunately, telecom networks are improving and 4G/LTE is well established in quite a few countries.[9] However, it will take some time before it is as widely available as 3G. 5G is also coming, and in 2013 European Commissioner Neelie Kroes made €50 million available to prepare Europe for the 5G era in 2020.[10] Still, as long as 4G/LTE is relatively expensive and 5G is still far away, consumers will have to deal with the slower 3G.[11] One thing is crystal clear: Data consumption will grow on mobile devices in the coming years. Ericson predicts that the average monthly data usages for smartphones will grow to 1.9 GB in 2018, as compared to 450 MB in 2012.[12] Tablet usage will grow to 2.7 GB from 600 MB in 2012. With 1.5 billion new smartphones and 1.1 billion new tablets in 2017, we are talking about approximately 6 exabytes of new mobile data consumption.[13]

What Is On-the-Go Big Data?

So, what exactly is on-the-go Big Data? Basically, it is making the results of Big Data analysis available on mobile devices. The analysis itself cannot be done on mobile devices, so on-the-go Big Data is merely giving consumers and organizations access on a mobile device to (visualized) results of analyses done elsewhere. This sounds simple, but it involves a lot of challenges.

Challenges of On-the-Go Big Data

First of all, the upcoming trend of "bring your own devices" is a challenge for IT departments. This means that employees are required to bring their own mobile devices to work instead of receiving one from the company. Increasingly, companies do not provide employees with mobile phones, tablets, and laptops. As more companies opt for bring your own devices, organizations will need to closely examine their security guidelines.

In Brazil, India, and Russia (three of the BRIC countries), about 75 percent of employees take their own devices to work. IT departments are getting tired of supporting devices that they do not manage or control.[14] However, because it decreases costs for organizations and increases conveniences for employees, it is a trend that is hard to stop.

Private mobile devices, however, are typically less secure and less controlled then (company) personal computers, laptops, or smartphones. Several organizations, such as Microsoft and IBM, are reaching out to help by developing company platforms that can be used by employees to securely download necessary apps and to secure the data that is transmitted on these personal devices.[15,16] IBM announced in 2012 "a risk-based authentication control for mobile users, integration of access management into mobile application development and deployment as well as enhanced mobile device control."[17]

Organizations that want to make company results from Big Data analyses available on mobile devices of employees will have to ensure a high security level. To achieve that, organizations have to start working quickly, as there is a lot to do. They should:

- Determine which employees will have access on their personal mobile devices to the data. In particular, sensitive company data should not be accessible to all employees.
- Document which data can be viewed via 3G/4G connection and which data can only be viewed via secured Wi-Fi connection. In the end, a public 3G/4G connection is always less secure than an in-company Wi-Fi connection.

- Train employees on how to keep data on their mobile devices secure. Just as organizations should train employees about how to deal with data on company devices, they should also train employees about how to deal with sensitive company data on private devices.
- Create, document, and communicate policies concerning how to deal with sensitive data on personal devices, and what to do in the event of a crisis.
- Prepare your IT department for a plethora of questions related to all kinds of devices.

Second, smaller screen sizes require a different kind of visualization. It might be a retina display or a full HD display, but it still is and always will remain a small screen (apart from a tablet, of course) that is used on the go and in public areas. With smart watches (with a projected screen size of 128 × 128 pixels) and Google Glass (with an expected display resolution of 640 × 360 pixels), this challenge becomes even bigger. It is not a problem; it just requires a different approach.

After all, the small screen only allows small portions of information to be shown at once. Programmers will have to think beyond the desktop. The Big Data startup, Zoomdata, clearly understands this, as it believes mobile devices are ideal because of their intuitive touch screens.[18] Zoomdata allows users to view its interactive graphs on tablets as well, while incorporating all the pros of tablets.

Third, mobile devices do have keyboards (except, again, the smart watches or Google Glass), but keying on them is a hassle for a lot of people. Entering a query on a mobile Big Data dashboard thus becomes difficult and takes a lot of time. In addition, it is also prone to errors, resulting in unnecessary queries and data transmission.

The Advantages of Mobile Big Data

With so many challenges, what are the advantages of on-the-go Big Data that justify spending so much time and money to overcome them? First of all, the availability of a large number of sensors opens up a lot of opportunities for data collection. The iPhone, for example, includes the following sensors, and this number will only increase in the coming years:

- The proximity sensor that determines how close an iPhone is to your face.
- The motion sensor/accelerometer that enables the iPhone to automatically switch between landscape and portrait modes.
- The ambient light sensor that determines the amount of available light in a space.
- The moisture sensor that detects whether an iPhone has been submerged in water.
- A three-axis gyroscope that enhances the perception of how the iPhone is moved.
- A magnetometer that measures the strength and/or direction of the magnetic field in the vicinity of the device.
- The GPS sensor that determines the location of the iPhone.

These sensors can increase the effectiveness of the visualizations shown on mobile devices. They can provide effects and tools not available on desktop computers and, therefore, increase insights into Big Data. When developing a Big Data startup or a Big Data strategy, it is therefore wise to take on-the-go Big Data into account and make the most of the sensors present in mobile devices. It will result in a better user experience, which in turn will lead to an increase in the use of the application.

Further, mobile devices simply make it possible to have access to all your data at any time and any place. This will increase employee productivity, as, for example, with a warehouse employee who has all necessary data on his or her tablet and does not have to walk back and forth to a desktop computer to get necessary information.

A third advantage of on-the-go Big Data is the availability of push messages that allow real-time data analysis to have the most effect. Whenever an event is triggered via data analysis, it can be pushed to users via mobile devices. This can result in an immediate response, otherwise users need to be in front of their desktop computers to acquire information. If the mobile device also allows the user to respond immediately, the efficiency, as well customer satisfaction, will increase dramatically.

Four Guidelines Organization Should Follow When Using On-the-Go Big Data

To be successful with on-the-go Big Data, organizations should follow the following four guidelines. These guidelines will help organizations make the most of their mobile Big Data strategy.

1. **Use simple but smart visualizations.**

Although the smaller screens of mobile devices require a different approach, the large number of sensors allows extremely smart visualizations. Organizations should remember that only the most vital information should be shown on a small screen, as too much information may confuse the user. This is particularly true on tiny screens, such as a smartwatch or Google Glasses. Give the user the vital information first. Then, provide the opportunity to dive deeper if wanted. Remember to limit the steps needed by the user to find more information; a small screen is not suitable for a lot of different steps.

2. **Enable voice recognition.**

The mobile Big Data dashboard should recognize voice input. Google Glasses, as well as smart watches, do not have a keyboard; they depend almost exclusively on voice recognition or simple touch gestures. Even with smartphones and tablets, entering a (large) query using the keyboard is generally a hassle.

3. **Ensure fast loading of visualizations.**

Users expect a mobile device to work lightning fast. Complex data analyses are done in the cloud, and the results are returned to the mobile device. Take this into account when giving the user the ability to access Big Data visualizations on their mobile devices while on a 3G/4G network. Data-intensive tasks could drain a monthly data subscription plan easily, while the user becomes frustrated. Focus on the most important analyses that a user needs to be able to perform while on 3G/4G network and allow the rest of the analyses and visualizations to work only on Wi-Fi.

4. **Secure your data transmission.**

On-the-go Big Data will require giving mobile devices access to (sensitive) data results, but only four percent of smartphones are protected with security software.[19] Therefore, you need to determine which data is sensitive and ensure that this data can only be transmitted when the user has a secure and acknowledged Wi-Fi connection. In particular, healthcare organizations should not send sensitive data through public Wi-Fi or 3G/4G networks.

The Future of On-the-Go Big Data

The future of mobile Big Data is difficult to see, as we are at the brink of a mobile revolution. According to Nathaniel Mott, a writer for *Pando Daily*, the future of computing will be a question of head versus wrist instead of desktop versus mobile.[20,21] In the near future, we will probably be flooded with new mobile devices currently unknown, and all of them will require a different approach to on-the-go Big Data. Organizations will have to adapt on time to meet the needs of the mobile future.

BIG REAL-TIME DATA

With so much data available, you will want to use it the moment it is created. Real-time analytics will see a huge growth in the coming years, as it offers many advantages. The ability to analyze the attributes of a visitor to your website and return a personalized homepage within a millisecond will increase your conversion rate. In the fast information age, access to real-time Big Data analyses can become the difference between your organization and your competitor. Therefore, more companies will look to base their daily business decisions on real-time knowledge.

Thus, the accumulation of data is one thing; the ability to store, analyze, and visualize that data in real-time is a whole different ballgame. Real-time insights will give your organization the ability to fully understand what is going on internally and externally. The questions remain: What are the advantages of real-time Big Data, what are the challenges, and which tools can be used for real-time processing of Big Data?

The Advantages of Real-Time Big Data

The advantages of processing Big Data in real time are numerous. They include the following.

Errors within the organization are known instantly. Real-time insight into errors helps organizations react quickly to mitigate the effects of an operational problem. This can save the operation from falling behind or failing completely. It can also save customers from having to stop using products because of an error. With real-time insight, problems can be fixed quickly.

New strategies from your competition are immediately visible. With real-time Big Data, you can stay one step ahead of the competition or be notified the moment a direct competitor changes strategy or lowers prices. Before the Big Data era, this could take a considerable amount of time.

Service improves dramatically, which could lead to a higher conversion rate and extra revenue. When organizations monitor the products that are used by its customers, it can proactively respond to avoid future failures. For example, cars with real-time sensors can notify a driver of a problem before something goes wrong. The sensor would let the driver know the car needs maintenance. Even better will be the ability of the car to anticipate an engine failure. In real time, the sensors identify the problem, determine if action needs to be taken, and, if so, search for the nearest garage by checking your agenda and identifying your location. Upon arrival, the mechanic would have already received the data analysis identifying the upcoming failure and can go to work instantly.

Fraud can be detected the moment it happens and appropriate measures can be taken to limit the damage. The financial world is very attractive to criminals. With a real-time safeguard system, you will be informed immediately about attempts to hack into your organization. Your IT security department can then quickly take appropriate action. In the financial industry, it is already common practice to track the massive number of credit card transactions. As soon as a suspicious transaction occurs, the appropriate bank is alerted to take action. The problem with the current technology is that the fraudulent action may have already occurred. With powerful real-time Big Data analytics, the fraudulent transaction will be discovered *before* it occurs and the bank will consequently not authorize the transaction.

Cost savings and increased revenue. The implementation of real-time Big Data tools may be expensive, but it will eventually save a lot of money. With real-time analytics, business leaders can obtain a complete overview of the organization instantly. Action can be taken immediately, if necessary, thereby saving money or increasing revenues. In particular, the stock market benefits from real-time analytics. The ability to analyze and identify a possible valuable stock one millisecond before the competition does can increase revenue substantially.

Better sales insights could lead to additional revenue. Real-time analytics keep you informed about exactly how sales are doing. If an Internet retailer sees that a product is doing extremely well, the company can take action to prevent missing out or losing revenue by adjusting stock levels or price depending on the real-time demand in a specific geographical location.

Keep up with customer trends. Insight into competitive offerings, promotions, and customer movements provides valuable information regarding customer trends. Real-time analytics enable a company to make faster decisions that better suit current customers.

The Challenges of Real-Time Big Data

Of course, real-time analytics is not all positive; it also presents some challenges. It requires special computer power. The standard version of Hadoop is, at the moment, not yet suitable for real-time analysis. New tools need to be bought and used. There are, however, some tools available to do the job.

Using real-time insights requires a different way of working within your organization. If your organization normally receives insights only once a week, which is common in many organizations, receiving these insights every second will require a different approach and way of working. Insights require action. Instead of acting on a weekly basis, a response in real time is now required. This will have an effect on the culture. The objective should be to make your organization information-centric.

Real-Time Big Data Tools

More and more tools offer the possibility of real-time processing of Big Data. Until Hadoop offers real-time analytics, the products listed below can be used.

Storm

Storm, which is now owned by Twitter, is a real-time distributed computation system.[22] It uses a set of general primitives for performing real-time analyses. Storm is easy to use and works with any programming language. It is very scalable and fault tolerant.

Cloudera

The Cloudera Enterprise RTQ tools offers real-time, interactive analytical queries about data stored in HBase or HDFS.[23] It is an integral part of Cloudera Impala, an open source tool of Cloudera. With Cloudera Impala, it is also possible to perform in real-time, ad-hoc queries in Hadoop.

GridGain

GridGain is an enterprise open-source grid computing made for Java.[24] It is compatible with Hadoop DFS, and it offers an alternative to Hadoop's MapReduce. GridGain offers a distributed, in-memory, real-time, and scalable data grid, which is the link between data sources and different applications.

SpaceCurve

The technology that SpaceCurve is developing can discover underlying patterns in multidimensional geodata.[25] Geodata is different from normal data, as mobile devices create new data quickly and not in a way familiar to traditional databases. SpaceCurve offers a Big Data platform, and its tool set a new world record on February 12, 2013 for running complex queries with tens of gigabytes per second.[26]

Of course, many more real-time tools are available but it would be a bit too much to describe all of theses tools here. The fact is that real-time Big Data is a trend that will increase substantially in the coming years and will thus have a large impact on any organization. Real-time Big Data is probably the ultimate usage of Big Data.

HOW ETIHAD AIRWAYS USES BIG DATA TO REACH ITS DESTINATION

Etihad Airways is the flag carrier of the United Arab Emirates, and it was founded just 11 years ago, in 2003. Based in Abu Dhabi, the United Arab carrier flies to 89 destinations in 55 countries all over the world, operating over 1,200 flights per week and carrying 10 million passengers annually. Its goal is to be a truly twenty-first century global airline, challenging and changing the established conventions of airline hospitality. To achieve this, Etihad turned to Big Data. It uses Big Data in several ways, ranging from maximizing income opportunities by optimizing its pricing strategy to forecasting maintenance and improving the traveler's experience while on board.

One of the most interesting applications of Big Data by Etihad Airways is that it taps into the Industrial Internet, which is actually the Internet of Things for machines and industrial equipment, such as aircrafts.[27] It uses complex algorithms to collect and analyze the vast amounts of data that are generated in real time by the sensors now present on every plane. Etihad Airways uses the tool from Taleris, a joint venture by GE Aviation and Accenture.[28] This tool helps Etihad keep real-time control over its entire fleet of Airbus and Boeing planes. The sensors help Etihad Airways to monitor planes in real time, as well as when in flight, to manage and predict maintenance, to spot problems before they happen, to reduce fuel consumption, and to shorten turn-around time at airports. This will save large amounts of money, as the airplanes of Etihad can spend more time in the air and less on the ground.

The data provided by the sensors is analyzed and turned into valuable information that Etihad Airways uses "to make rapid and informed decisions in relation to maintenance, while gaining technology leadership in diagnostics and prognostics health monitoring . . . to predict future faults and take proactive measures resulting in less unscheduled disruptions to our global operations," says Werner Rothenbaecher, Etihad's Senior Vice President on Technical Issues, on GE's blog.[29] The extensive tool will benefit the guests flying with Etihad Airways because they will encounter fewer flight delays and greater reliability, said James Hogan, Chief Executive Officer of Etihad Airways at the SITA Air Transport Summit in Belgium on June 20, 2013.[30]

To improve guests' experiences even more, Etihad Airways is also adopting the SITA CrewTablet, which will enable the crew to access any operational or passenger data via tablets, a great example of on-the-go Big Data.[31,32]

THE INTERNET OF THINGS

Within a few years, we will have to talk in brontobytes when discussing data derived from sensors. The Internet of Things refers to objects that can be uniquely identified via an IP-address, and all of them are connected to the Internet. Objects (which can be anything from a car to a chair or a bottle of soda) that are equipped with identifiers can be managed and inventoried by computers and algorithms. These objects contain sensors, and the data these sensors collect is shared with an Internet-like structure. The Internet of Things, or Machine-to-Machine (M2M) communication, will connect billions (or even trillions) of devices with each other and thereby generate an unfathomable amount of data. In 2020, 40 percent of all data in the world will be M2M data.[33] This data of course has to be processed, stored, analyzed, and visualized to have any meaning and to drive your business.

Sensor data, or M2M data, is data from readings made by machine sensors that measure conditions at regular intervals or in real time. This could be RFID tags or software that runs with a device to make it intelligent or any other sensor imaginable. Examples of the data that is collected include log data (especially Telco's), geolocation data, diagnostics (to alert you when maintenance is needed), CPU utilization, temperature, rules, and so on. This data can be linked to key performance indicators (KPIs) that send an alarm when a threshold is passed and an action is required.

The Internet of Things enables refinements in current business models; it can also open up entirely new business models. The Internet of Things is already all around us and is unstoppable. A few examples of products tapping into these possibilities are as follows.

- Usage-based insurance from Progressive in the United States.[34] The company uses Snapshot, a little device that users plug into their cars to keep track of customers' driving records.[35] The better you drive, the more you save on insurance.
- Glowcaps turns your prescription medicine bottles into devices that automatically notify you to take your medication.[36] A chip

inside the cap monitors when the pill bottle is opened and warns users when they forget to take their medication. Reports are visible on the Internet so family members can keep track of whether an elderly family member is taking pills.

- The connected toothbrush by Beam Technologies tracks how you brush your teeth, including which areas you covered and which areas you missed.

The Internet of Things Tracks the Earth's Health

All those sensors will collect massive amounts of data. Just look at the data created by planes, machines, and mobile devices. But a really extreme example of the Internet of Things is the Central Nervous System for the Earth (CeNSE), which was developed by HP Labs and Shell to make living on earth safer and more comfortable.[37] Billions of low-cost, self-powered nanosensors that are installed in all kinds of devices and machines will be able to monitor the Earth's health and the impact humans have on it. HP expects that by 2020, a trillion sensors will be needed to perform this task; this is the equivalent of 150 sensors per person.

Of course, the availability of so much data offers challenges and benefits. For example, sensors can reduce maintenance costs by telling you when a machine needs service before it actually breaks. This saves repair costs, as well as minimizes downtime of the machine. It also improves customer satisfaction.

Sensor data can also link observations that meet specific criteria to other datasets for additional insights. This combined information could result in knowledge that could be relevant in specific situations. SemSorGrid4Env uses environmental sensor data to manage and understand the environment; the company provides this information to emergency response teams in case of a disaster.[38]

As more and more systems are linked to each other, the challenge is to process, store, analyze, and visualize these massive datasets, preferably in real time. It does require high software and hardware costs to manage all this incoming data, but the benefits will outweigh the costs.

One advantage is that, in many cases, sensors provide high-volume, high-velocity data with consistent structures that are easy to manage. This enables organizations to combine different sensor data with business or public data to find new patterns, trends, or markets.

Getting Started

Start small with sensor data, as it can easily grow to massive proportions. Begin with a prototype, and build on it incrementally. Companies that are agile with the scope of the project and grow accordingly have the best chance for success. However, do plan from the beginning to eventually be able to support very large datasets so no unpleasant surprises arise later in the project. We will cover a roadmap for starting with Big Data and developing a successful Big Data strategy in Chapter 6.

As the Internet of Things emerges, the possibilities are endless. Earth will become a smart planet, where every item is instrumented, intelligent, interconnected, and online at all times. The potential is enormous, and the potential uses are vast.[39] To stay ahead of the competition and to keep customers satisfied, think about what the Internet of Things and the collection of big sensor data can do for your organization. Think about the products you have and how you can turn these products into data. As discussed in Chapter 2, even a cup of coffee can be turned into data—or a bottle of beer for that matter.

HEINEKEN BRINGS SENSORS TO A BEER BOTTLE THAT CAN DANCE TO THE RHYTHM OF MUSIC

A great example of the Internet of Things is the connected beer bottle that Heineken introduced during Milan Design Week in 2013. Heineken introduced Ignite, which used LEDs and wireless sensors to create a completely new experience for its customers. The smart bottles were developed to improve the social interaction of beer drinking using modern technology.[40] According to an article by Heineken, it used 8 LED lights, an 8-bit microprocessor, an accelerometer, a gyroscope, and a wireless transmitter with antenna.[41] It had fifty individual components that worked together and could fit underneath an ordinary bottle.

Each bottle lit up when during a toast they were clinked together. The LED lights would flicker rapidly when taking a sip, and leaving the bottle standing on a bar caused the light to enter sleep mode and slowly dim until it was picked up again. But, the sensors could also be remotely controlled to sync with the a musical beat, bringing a party to a completely new level.

Several organizations predict that the number of sensors will eventually reach into the trillions, but organizations differ about when this will occur and how much data these sensors will gather.

The Wireless World Research organization predicts that there will be 7 trillion sensors by 2017.[42,43] CeNSE is predicting a trillion sensors by 2020.[44,45] These trillion sensors will drive 50 zettabytes of data annually (that is, 50 billion terabytes!). According to IDC, these sensors will gather 40 zettabytes of data by 2020.[46] IBM expects that sensors for context-aware computing will reach a trillion sensors by 2015.[47] Although these predictions differ, it is clear that the growth of Internet-connected devices will be massive and that this growth will create a trillion dollar worldwide business. Cisco believes that by 2020, the Internet of Things will drive a $14 trillion business worldwide affecting all industries.[48] If we take into account that worldwide IT spending is currently approximately $3.5 trillion, it is clear that we are entering a very interesting era.[49]

Computing Industry

During the seventh annual "5 in 5" meeting, in 2012, IBM revealed a list of innovations that correspond to our five senses that have the potential to change the way people work, live, and interact during the next five years.[50] These innovations are:

- Touch: You will be able to touch through your phone.
- Sight: A pixel will be worth a thousands words.
- Hearing: Computers will hear what matters.
- Taste: Digital taste buds will help you eat smarter.
- Smell: Computers will have a sense of smell.

The "5 in 5" is based on market, technology, and social trends from around the world that can make these transformations possible. The presence of sensors in computing devices that will mimic our senses will change the way consumers deal with Internet-connected devices.

Healthcare Industry

The Sensor Era will have far-reaching effects on the healthcare industry. Changes will include personalized medicine, nutrition, and disease prevention, as well as real-time health monitoring of patients. By 2020, visits to doctors' offices may become less frequent, as doctors will potentially receive all the information needed from sensors the patient is wearing. By including nanosensors in a patient's medicine, doctors can also monitor its effect on the patient in real time.

Companies are encouraging the development of sensors that will be able to diagnosis diseases immediately For example, in 2011 Qualcomm announced a $10 million prize for the first Tricorder that will be able to capture key health metrics and diagnose a set of 15 diseases.[51] Registration has begun, and 16-year-old Jack Andrada claimed in 2013 to have already built a tricorder that almost met these requirements to win. However, he is not the only one trying to win this competition.

The implications of a sensor-based healthcare industry are enormous. When devices can measure all relevant patient metrics in real time, consumer healthcare will improve and costs will decrease.

SMART CITIES

The intial design of the smart city of Songdo, the world's first "City in a Box," began in 1996; it will be ready in 2015.[52] It is built on 1,500 acres of reclaimed land in South Korea and will be a revolution in city design. Located just 40 miles from Seoul and 7 miles from Incheon International Airport. Songdo will have commercial office spaces, retail shops, residences, and hotels, as well as civic and cultural facilities spread out over 100-million square feet. A consortium of partners consisting of Cisco, 3M, Posco E&C, and United Technology are the developers.[53]

Songdo will become a completely connected city, in which almost any device, building, or road will be equipped with wireless sensors or microchips. This will result in smart innovations, such as streetlights that automatically adjust to the number of people on the sidewalks. All houses will be equipped with sensors, also known as domotics, that can be managed via a large TV in the livingroom. These TelePresence screens will also be available in all offices, hospitals, schools, and shopping centers.

Work on Songdo started in 2000. With a projected cost of $35 billion, it was expensive to build. Cisco has ensured that every inch of the smart city is wired with fiberoptic broadband. By 2016, 65,000 people will be living in Songdo, while another 300,000 people will commute to the city daily. All these people will be using the many connected devices and connected services, thereby creating massive amounts of data that will be sent to the computer processors that keep Songdo operational.

In addition, traffic will be measured via RFID tags on cars. These sensors will send the geolocation data to the central monitoring unit that will signal black spots or congested areas. Since public transportation is completely wired, the location of all carriers will always be known. Sensors will even track when citizens throw away their garbage in the disposal containers, so in Songdo, even garbage creates data.

So do the climate, energy consumption, leisure activities, and water consumption. Special cameras will keep Songdo secure, while children will wear bracelets with sensors so they can always be located. The smart energy grid will ensure that energy is intelligently matched to accommodate supply and demand.

All this data will be collected, analyzed, and monitored in real time by the central monitoring hub. With so many citizens and workers using so many connected devices and services, Songdo will be a worthy creator of Big Data, bringing it to a whole new level. The data will provide valuable insights into how people work, live, and think within the smart city. This information can be used to improve the city.

Songdo is not the only smart city currently being developed. Masdar City in Abu Dhabi is another example of a truly connected city. Whether the behavior of people will change as a result of living in smart cities is still unsure. One thing is clear, however. Smart cities will have a major impact on the amount of data created on a daily basis, and it will change how cities operate and are managed.

Household Data

The domotics applied in Songdo are appearing in households throughout in the world. Household automation is gaining traction everywhere, and it will make our lives easier. Think of a home automation system that integrates all electrical devices and allows users to access those devices via smartphones or tablets from anywhere. Lights can be turned on or off through an app; the coffee automatically starts brewing when your alarm clock buzzes; and the fridge knows what's in stock. When you are not at home, you can give others access to your house using an app.

In past decades, such "homes of the future" were novelties; now, they are more widely available.[54] Eventually, sensors will be part of all electronic devices within houses, from kitchen equipment to bathroom fixtures and home security devices.

Retail Market

The supermarket is the perfect place for sensor-enabled products. In the United States, an average grocery store contains more than 50,000 products.[55] RFID tags will change how supermarkets function, as they will make it more efficient to track products. The Real Future Store, a concept store in Germany, is a playground for such new sensor initiatives.[56] Using RFID tags, supermarkets can provide a lot more information to customers. The RFID tags can contain information about the manufacturer, sizes, and prices of products. Discounts can be given automatically for products that are almost at their expiration dates. Shoppers would not have to place items on a conveyor belt for the cashier to scan, as all RFID tags would be scanned immediately on leaving the supermarket. The number of tags that would be necessary to accomplish this is huge. With more than 35,000 supermarkets in the United States alone, 1.75 billion RFID tags would be required on a daily basis just in the United States.[57]

How Should Organizations Prepare?

So, all those brontobytes generated in the sensor era will affect every industry. How should your organization prepare for the Great Sensor Era?

Organizations should start identifying those products that can be enhanced with sensors to deliver a better user experience. This improved experience could mean providing additional features (the quantified-self movement), giving additional insights (smart energy meters, for example), or decreasing maintenance. Start small by implementing sensors in a pilot product that will be carefully tested. Companies will then better understand how information is collected, how it needs to be stored, how it can be analyzed, and how it can be sent to the user and/or the manufacturer. Once the data is collected, it can be used to identify patterns, outliers, and errors, so that the product can be improved. Then, the changes can be implemented throughout the organization.

The Internet of Things will create a completely connected society. With trillions of devices connected to the internet by the 2020s, brontobytes of data will be generated. All this data needs to be processed, stored, analyzed, and visualized for improved decision making. It will change our society and how organizations operate and are managed. Although 2020 might seem far away, turning your company into an information-centric, sensor-based organization requires a lot of time and effort. Therefore, in order not to be left behind, start preparing now.

THE QUANTIFIED-SELF

Although Big Data is often referred to as being useful for organizations, it will also be relevant to consumers in their personal lives. More and more quantified-self apps will allow consumers to store, track, visualize, and interpret their own lives. Data about eating, sleeping, and exercising habits will be available, along with videos that record your entire life.[58-61] It is only a matter of time before there will be apps that combine all the data from these individual apps into one Big Data app about your life. They can then mash it up with geolocation data from your phone and social media activity. You will even be able to compare yourself to your peers. Such apps are already appearing on the market, although they are not this comprehensive.[62]

The quantified-self apps have the potential to generate massive amounts of data that will allow them to map information about entire population groups. Scary? Yes, maybe, but consumers have always longed for information about their own lives, so they are happy to join the pack.

The quantified-self movement has been around since the 1970s, but it only recently took off because of the Internet of Things and the availability of monitoring devices that connect to smartphones.

Today's smartphones carry all sorts of sensors that can track almost anything, The quantified-self means Big Data for consumers. What could this mean for your organization?

The quantified-self is especially aimed at improving health and behaviors. As such, many devices help consumers track their moods, sleeping patterns, activity levels, heart and stress levels, what they eat and drink, and even how often they walk the dog. Therefore, the movement targets people who are comfortable with having their personal data collected and, quite often, made visible to the public.

Growing Number of Quantified-Self Startups

Silicon Valley is taking particular interest in the quantified-self movement. New devices, or tracking software, are being launched almost on a daily basis. There are examples of how such devices are being used by consumers to improve their lifestyle, increase and improve their sleeping habits, and become sharper, more relaxed, and turned on, resulting in more effective and efficient employees.[63]

The number of these products and apps are growing steadily. Some require an additional device, such as a scale, a wristband, or a smartwatch, but some new apps do not even require a separate product. Some of the better known are:

- Withings has a Wi-Fi-enabled scale that measures several health conditions, including as heartbeat and weight, and can instantly share that information online with a friend.
- The Fitbit is a wireless activity-and-sleep wristband that measures different things, such as how many steps you walk, the number of calories burned, and how well you sleep.
- The HAPI fork tracks how fast you eat, how long it takes you to finish a meal, and the number of servings you eat per minute. It also vibrates the moment you eat too fast.
- Jawbone created a wristband that tracks and monitors how you sleep, along with other types of data.[64]
- Foodzy allows you to share on a social platform what you are eating to better understand your eating habits.[65]
- Moves is a free app that does not require a separate device to monitor how many steps you take or how far you have cycled or run.[66]

Although the business model for these apps may be difficult to find, the companies have no problems finding funding. The Moves app, for example, secured €1,2 million in venture capital in 2013; other startups have also secured millions in funding as can be found on the quantified-self section on Venturebeat.com.[67,68]

The Scientific Model

The quantified-self movement is also having a considerable impact on the scientific research model by enabling the collection of vast amounts of data that can validate research findings. PatientsLikeMe is a data-driven social networking health platform.[69] It enables users to share information about conditions, treatments, and symptoms to better monitor their health and learn from real-world outcomes. Tens of thousands of consumers are already sharing this information, which is producing insights that would previously have taken tremendous amounts of time to collect.

Another healthcare company is 23andme. It enables consumers to sequence their genomes and start exploring their DNA.[70] They can learn whether they are at increased or decreased risk for certain diseases. Consumers can, if they want, share their DNA information to improve medical research.[71]

Other products that are part of the Internet of Things help consumers better understand their lives. For example, the Delphi Connected Car device gathers data from sensors in cars.[72] Normally, such data was only available for car manufacturers, but now it can also be used by private car owners. This product is essentially a dongle that can be plugged into a car's diagnostics port (all cars built after 1996 have such a port). It monitors and tracks your trip times, where you drive, how fast you drive, the status of your vehicle, and engine fault codes. It can also remember where you left your car. All information is shown in an app for iOS or Android.

The Quantified-Self and Your Organization

Organizations from around the world are seeing the value of the quantified-self movement. As a result, they are including sensors in their products as a service to their customers, but also to understand how the consumer uses the product. This valuable information allows organizations to improve products faster, without extensive and expensive market research. As such, it will become easier to track our lives, as future products will almost all contain some sort of sensor that collects data. The only question is whether you want to start using all that data to better understand and improve your life. Organizations could push this movement and stimulate employees to start monitoring their lives, as a more aware employee is healthier and more productive.

The quantified-self movement has gained momentum, and we will see a plethora of connected devices in the (near) future to track, monitor, and analyze everything with do in our lives.

BIG SOCIAL DATA

The number of people who actively participate on social networking sites continues to grow rapidly. Let's look at some statistics from 2013: Facebook had more than 1 billion users, of whom approximately 850 million were active on a monthly basis.[73] Each day brought 2.7 billion new likes. In comparison, Twitter had 500 million users, and 180 million tweets were sent every day.[74] Approximately 100 million Twitter users were active on a monthly basis. LinkedIn had over 225 million users, and almost 175,000 users logged in every day.[75] Pinterest had over 10 million users, of whom 97 percent were women.[76] Instagram had over 5 million images uploaded every day, and Google+ received 5 billion +1s every day.[77] And, remember, these are only the social networks developed in the Western world.

There are numerous social networks in Asia that Westerners have probably never heard of, but that are as big or bigger than, for example, Twitter. Qzone, a website where users can create blogs, share photos and music, and do much more had 712 million users. The Chinese edition of Twitter, Tencent Weibo, had 507 million users. Sina Weibo, a hybrid version of Facebook and Twitter, had 500 million users. Wechat, a micromessaging app similar to WhatsApp, had 300 million users.[78] Social media are huge and drive massive amounts of data on a daily basis, worldwide.

For the last few years, companies have seen the value of big social data because it contains valuable information that enables them to better understand their customers. Using sentiment analysis, companies can learn what customers think of their services/product offerings/ latest commercials, and so on. Further, all available social data can be used to perform predictive analysis about what customers will want— and when. Based on the feedback customer post on social networks, companies can gather insights that would normally require expensive traditional research.

Companies that are using the data available on social media networks can begin hypertargeting customers. Thus, instead of just targeting (potential) customers by a certain age, location, or gender, companies can focus on customers based on their actual or latent needs. All of this information is derived from what customers say on social networks—the "like" or the "retweet" and its context.

Walmart uses the information consumers shared on Twitter to send personalized coupons to (potential) customers. It monitors what consumers are saying; the moment someone tweets about, let's say beer and pizza, Walmart sends a discount coupon for those products at their local store.

Another example of hypertargeting comes from the company MyBuys, which offers cross-channel personalization for consumer brands and ecommerce shops.[79] The goals are to drive conversion, engagement, and increased revenue by analyzing the individual behavior of about 200 million customers and 100 terabytes of data provided in real time, so decision makers know what to do when.

A third example is the Big Data startup Bluefin Labs, which has developed a social television analytics platform to inform television networks and operators about viewers' opinions in real time.[80] The product is so interesting that Twitter acquired it in 2013 for approximately $80 million.[81]

Big Social Data Pitfalls

However, big social data also has several pitfalls that could ruin the party. These include:

1. Not all Facebook and Twitter accounts are real. Facebook has around 83 million fake accounts; Twitter also hosts many fake accounts.[82] Decisions based on fake accounts can drive you in the wrong direction.

2. Unstructured messages on social media often lack context. If you do not take context into account, the data can be misinterpreted. However, technology is advancing rapidly, and Bluefin Labs already places Tweets in their context based on interactions, timing and location, followers, and friends.[83]
3. What is being said on social media is not always what is meant. Someone can really like a commercial because of the humor in it and Tweet about it, but dislike the product completely.
4. Narcissism flourishes on social networks, especially on Facebook.[84] Everyone wants to look his or her best, so bragging happens more often than not. How seriously can an organization take such information when deciding which target to focus on? More is not being said than is being said, so do not focus solely on what is being said.

Although social data has these pitfalls, it surely can help your organization better understanding its customer. If you start using big social data, watch for the following important items, as discussed in the VINT report.[85]

1. Is the data you use real time? The lifespan of a tweet is approximately one hour.[86] Social data appears fast and is gone in an instant. Real time is necessary to have valuable input.
2. Metadata helps interpret the data, especially from blogs, faster. Ensure that metadata is included in your analysis.
3. Ensure that the data is linked and integrated with other sources. The better integrated, the more relevant the data will be.

Social media gives companies an infinite source of data about customers and buying trends on an aggregate level. All this data can help your organization better address the needs and wants of your customers. Although some pitfalls need to be watch, the available tools and algorithms are becoming better, leaving a bright future ahead regarding big social data.

HOW NESTLÉ UNDERSTANDS BRAND SENTIMENT OF 2,000 BRANDS IN REAL TIME

Nestlé is a very big company, with 486 factories in 86 countries and employing over 330,000 employees worldwide. It has a portfolio of more than 2,000 global and local brands, and it is the leading company in nutrition, health, and wellness products. In 2012, the company had total revenue of 75 billion euros (98 billion dollars), serving millions of customers around the globe. All of these customers have something to say about the company's products and, with Big Data, Nestlé knows what.

Since the Kit Kat crisis in 2010, when 1.5 million people saw a Greenpeace YouTube video about Kit Kat and palm oil, Nestlé has learned a lot.[87] During the Kit Kat crisis, Nestlé did not reply to messages until it had received 200,000 protest emails. It even tried to delete messages and the video from YouTube. Consultant Bernhard Warner called it one of "the 50 greatest social media screw-ups."[88] With the help of Big Data tools, Nestlé learned from its mistakes and even went from #16 to #9 in the Reputation Institute's index of the world's most reputable companies.[89]

The company's objective was to get a better grip on customer sentiment, and it did not want to rely on surveys and other periodic customer testing.[90] Therefore, Nestlé created the Digital Acceleration Team, a 24/7 monitoring center that listens to all conversations about all of its products on social media. This enables Nestlé to understand in real time the sentiment regarding each of its 2,000 brands.

Although this is nothing new, any large organization from KLM to Danone to Unilever uses social media to understand what is going on online, Nestlé takes a different approach. It deliberately focus on mitigating any damage to its reputation that could appear. Employees are actively involved in listening to what is said, engaging with those who post any message online, inspiring customers and ideally transforming sentiment.[91] They have nearly 150 million fans across 650 pages on Facebook, and they produce 1500 pieces of original content on that platform every day. Together all messages that are analyzed reaches millions per day.[92]

Nestlé has 15 people working around the clock in the center. They have many screens available to them with real-time information. Each employee in the training program to become a marketing manager first spends eight months in this center to learn the ins-and-outs about online and social interaction using Big Data tools.

As Pete Blackshaw, Head of Digital Marketing, explains: "we believe that the web is becoming the world's largest focus group . . . to better understand consumers' unmet needs . . . and to figure out where to engage."[93] The company looks at the number of online conversations, the relationship and benchmarks to other players in the market, and the level of sentiment. This enables the company to understand what is happening online in real time regarding its vast collection of brands.[94] Nestlé takes full advantage of the Big Social Data trend, and its growth on the Reputation Index shows that its efforts have already paid off.

PUBLIC BIG DATA

In October 2011, Neelie Kroes, the Vice President of the European Commission, announced several proposals to legally unlock the data created and held by Europe's public institutions.[95,96] According to Kroes, opening these datasets to the public could double their value to around €70 billion, as when data is combined and turned into information, it can provide extra value to organizations and societies.[97] In addition, opening the data could lead to the development of new businesses, which would add value to the economy. The open data portal is all about transparency, open government, and innovation.[98] All available data can be reused, linked, analyzed, and visualized for personal or commercial use. This is a major step forward, as it can drive innovation and create new (business) opportunities.

Not only the European Union is considering opening massive datasets to the public. More and more governments are considering the same action. The Dutch Government, for example, has developed a portal on which open data sets that are funded by public means can be used by anyone.[99] The Dutch Government actively pushes local authorities and departments to share their open datasets on this portal to stimulate innovation and business opportunities. In the end this could lead to a more efficient, as well a more transparent, government.[100]

The United Stated is also studying the opportunities surrounding Big Data. In 2012, President Obama launched a Big Data initiative worth $200 million to investigate Big Data opportunities and technologies. The objective is to advance available techniques and tools to successfully access, process, store, analyze, and visualize the vast amounts of data created by the federal, state, and local governments.[101]

In 2012, Logica Business Consulting prepared a report on how to create a better supply-and-distribution process for open data.[102,103] The report describes different case studies about how the governments of the United States, the United Kingdom, Canada, and New Zealand are using and sharing open data. All four countries have the equivalent of a Freedom of Information Act that obligates governments to open data if requested under specific parameters.[104] The report details several lessons learned by these countries while opening up data to the public. The motivation for making their data public differed for each county, but, in general, they included increased transparency, stimulation of economic growth, improved government services, improved public relations and attitudes toward the government, and improved data quality. In other words, sufficient reasons exist for governments to create a portal to open their data.

Further, the Australian government has developed a Big Data strategy, with the objective of making data held by the national or regional authorities publicly available.[105] The Australian government developed the strategy to ensure that governments and organizations take full advantage of all the Big Data benefits while ensuring privacy is protected.

One new business opportunity that developed out of these government initiatives is the rise of data marketplaces or data supermarkets. Many new companies are building marketplaces where users can combine public data with all sorts of other (free) datasets for increased insights and discovery of new opportunities. Of course, Google joined this field and created a search engine that culls data from over 100 different datasets.[106] The same applies to the public datasets available on Amazon Web Services that can be easily integrated in different AWS applications.[107]

The usage of public and open data can really spur the application of Big Data. Therefore, I would like to share information about several organization that offer Big Data sets

InfoChimps is an organization that has developed a data supermarket. The platform hosts over 15,000 datasets from 200 different organizations and companies.[108] Visitors can combine these datasets with their own for additional insights.

DataMarket is another data supermarket offering more than 45,000 datasets from around the world delivered by, among others, 42 governments.[109] DataMarket's objective is to find all available (public) datasets and make them accessible and understandable.

Google Public Data allows visitors to delve search and download over 100 different datasets.[110] Visitors can upload their own datasets to visualize and explore it. Current available datasets include some from the World Economic Forum, Eurostat, and the IMF.

Amazon Web Services offers over 50 datasets to the public, including the 1000 Genome Project or the Common Crawl Corpus Project that makes data from over 5 billion web pages available to users.[111]

Enigma.io is a Big Data startup that offers access to public data sources. The New York-based company offers over 100,000 databases that can easily be searched or exported.[112] Users can download everything, including import bills of lading, aircraft ownership, lobbying activity, real estate assessments, spectrum licenses, financial filings, and patents.

Quandl is a public data set startup currently in beta testing. It offers more than 5 million financial, economic, and social datasets from all over the world for free.[113] Visitors can embed graphs on their own website or download the dataset via Python, Stata, Excel, or R.

Figshare is a platform designed especially for researchers, who can make their outputs available to everyone.[114] Figures, datasets, media, papers, posters, presentations, and filesets can be made public to everyone. All data is automatically published in a citable, searchable, and sharable manner.

Datahub.io is a community-run catalogue of useful datasets on the Internet.[115] Users can collect links to data found on the web or store data on the platform itself. They can also search the data collected by other users. The platform runs on the open-source software CKAN. Most of the data indexed is free to use or reuse because of the open license.

Open Science Data Cloud is a platform providing petabyte-scale cloud resources that enable users to easily analyze, manage, and share data.[116] The OSDC currently hosts about 450 TB of data and plans to increase this to the petabyte level.

Datamob is a website that shows how public datasets made available by governments can be used.[117] Datamob believes that good things happen when governments and public organizations make data available in developer-friendly formats. Therefore, Datamob currently lists 227 data sources, 165 apps, and 66 resources.

Freebase is a community-curated database of well-known people, places, and things.[118] The website offers almost 2 billion facts divided over 40 million topics and 76 domains. Every fact and entity is available as an RDF dump, which enables users to analyze the entire database on their own computers.

OpenData is a platform with a large collection of open datasets by Socrata.[119] Socrata provides social data discovery services for opening government data. It has collected over 200,000 datasets from around the world. The datasets are divided into five categories: Business, Education, Fun, Government, and Personal.

Thinknum is working on indexing all financial data and exposing it through a simple API. It has over 10 million data-series all of which can be downloaded for free. It uses the data to build applications that help strategists analyse financial markets.

xDayta is a marketplace to buy and sell data. xDayta is an open platform allowing anyone to sell any type of data to any buyer. It's free to list data on xDayta for sale. Anyone can register and sell data on xDayta. Anyone looking for data to buy can use xDayta. The xDayta exchange facilitates over-the-counter data trades, brokers transactions, indexes data pricing, and regulates trading.

GAMIFICATION

Much of this new data will come from gamification. The gamification of business is not just a tool for effective marketing campaigns. Gamification will revolutionize the way organizations connect with consumers, and it will create extremely valuable Big Data that can enhance a company's big database.

Gamification is the use of game elements in nongame contexts. It can be used externally to interact with customers and improve marketing efforts that lead to increased sales. Gamification is also used internally, where it can lead to improved employee productivity, as well as internal crowdsourcing activities. Finally, gamification can change the behavior of consumers. The quantified-self movement is a perfect example of the match between gamification and Big Data.

The game elements often used in gamification are points, challenges, awards, leader boards, levels, avatars, and badges. Gamification can motivate users to execute certain tasks. Moreover, it can be used to learn something, to achieve something, and to stimulate personal development/health. The goal is to improve real-life experiences and make people more willing to do something. Gamification is not a game; it is merely game elements in a different context.

Many different aspects of gamification provide a lot of data that can be analyzed. Users can be compared to see how they perform, and why some group is performing better than another group. When users sign in via the social graph, a lot of public data can be added to provide context around the gamification data. Apart from the different elements that provide direct viewable insights, gamification can also help better understand consumer behavior and how consumers perform the tasks at hand. For example, how long do different groups take to complete a challenge or how do they use certain products or services. This information can be used to improve products and/or services.

Gamification is all about motivating people to act, as well as motivating them to share the right information in the right context.[120] In fact, gamification should be viewed as a catalyst for sharing. The more engaged users are, the more they will share. This will result in more attention to the company, as well as more valuable data.

The success of a gamification concept depends on the quality and speed of the information that is returned to the user. The better this content reflects the user's interest, the more involved the user will be. The personalized content can be created using Big Data. Clicking behavior, the time required to perform certain challenges, and interaction levels at the platform with others can all be combined with public data, such as tweets or posts shared on social networks as well as the profiles of those users on those social network. When properly stored, analyzed, and visualized, this will generate a lot of insights. However, users do expect instant feedback and results. Thus real-time processing of the data is extremely important.

Gamification has the potential to become more and more integrated with the lives of consumers. When that happens, even more data will be generated. With Big Data, organizations will learn how and why someone behaves in a gamified context and, as such, it will provide insights into how a person behaves in real life. That information is very valuable for advertisers who want to reach (potential) customers with the right message in the right context at the right moment.

The right design of a gamification concept is very important if it is to deliver the desired results and insights. Gartner predicts that 80 percent of the gamification solutions will fail to reach their objectives because of poor design.[121] As with Big Data, poor design could lead to poor data quality and no insights.

Several advantages can be achieved when Big Data and gamification are combined.[122] Note, for example:

- Big Data provides transparent, real-time, and personalized feedback to the user. With this data, the user can receive various rewards.
- Personalized gamification elements will increase the involvement of the end-user with the product or service. More interaction could lead to more sharing and, thus, online reach for the company. Big Data enables the gamification elements to become more engaging and, importantly, more fun.
- Big Data provides insights into the behavior of users on an aggregate level, as well as an individual level. This valuable data can be used to improve products and services offered.
- Insights derived from the massive amounts of data should actually be used. Gamification can help make an organization information-centric by applying game elements in the dashboards that visualize the data.
- Roman Rackwitz, CEO and Founder at Engaginglab, states that gamification can transform Big Data into smart data.[123] Personalized and relevant feedback based on the choices made in the gamified context increases interaction with the user, who will be drawn further into the Big Data dashboard. This means more involvement and interest in data-driven insights and better decision making.

There are a lot of similarities between Big Data and gamification. One could even say that gamification is the friendly scout of Big Data, gathering data from literally thousands of potential actions that can be measured, but in a user-friendly and engaging manner. The insights that come from any good gamification platform are enormous and, if visualized correctly, can provide valuable insights to organizations as well as help to create an information-centric organization.

THE GAMIFICATION PLATFORM BY NIKE+ DELIVERS VALUABLE INSIGHTS

Nike turned the most uncomplicated sport in the world, running, into a data-driven social sport that gives users access to tons of data about their personal achievements. Runners can use this data to become better runners, which will result in a healthier lifestyle. In addition, Nike gives software developers open access to this data.[124] This Nike+ Accelerator initiative encouraged people to build companies to leverage the data generated from its digital products.[125]

Nike understands that its users want answers to simple sports-related questions. Put even more simply, as Nike's Vice President of Digital Sport Stefan Olander said, Nike+ ". . . thrives on the fact that people want credit for their athletic activity."[126,127] As such, the Nike+ platform gives runners answers to questions like:

- How fast am I running, and am I progressing?
- When do I lose momentum when I am running?
- How many calories do I burn while running?
- How are my friends performing, and what does it take to beat them?

As such, Nike has created an engaging, gamified platform where runners can interact with each other, share their data, and learn from the insights derived from it. Since its launch in 2006, the platform has built a user base of 7 million runners.[128] Think of all the data this generates and the insights it provides to Nike. It is a great example of how gamification is the friendly scout of Big Data.

Of course, building an engaging, beautiful, and full-fledged gamified platform requires a lot of investment and dedication, but the rewards are enormous for Nike. Nike benefits when so many users interact over a long period of time on different platforms while doing something they enjoy. By using Big Data, Nike managed to change the behavior of many consumers. In return, the company receives great insights that can be used to improve its products.

TAKEAWAYS

Big Data has many components, and all of these will influence your Big Data strategy. The mobile revolution does require a different approach to visualizing all the analyses performed on the data. The smaller screen size requires the use of simple but smart visualizations. It should be possible to perform queries using voice recognition, and the speed of loading visuals on mobile devices is even more important than on desktop computers. You should also not underestimate the security issues involved with Big Data on mobile devices, especially because many of them are poorly protected.

The need for real-time analyses will only increase in the coming years with the adoption of the Internet of Things. Devices that are enabled with sensors will be able to talk to each other continuously. Thanks to sensors, many objects will be turned into smart objectives that can proactively react to the environment, thereby saving organizations and consumers a lot of time and money.

Also the quantified-self movement is related to the Internet of Things. The need for humans to better understand their bodies is deeply rooted in our brain. With the many apps now on the market, we are able to monitor our behavior during the day as well as when we are asleep. All this data will be stored online for analyses and will provide organizations with vast insights. Gamification can help to make data collection a user friendly and engaging experience.

A large part of the data that is created through quantified-self applications is shared directly online through one of the many large social networks. The data created by a social network is very valuable to organizations, and social networks are growing rapidly. This is true not only in the Western world, but also in Asia, where many big social networks impact millions of consumers and, thus, organizations.

Organizations can enrich company and social data by combining it with data from public sources. These datasets are, in general, created by governments and are now being put to use through data marketplaces around the world.

Big Data
Technologies

4

The decision to move forward with Big Data is a strategic choice each organization has to make. It does, however, have significant IT implications, as Big Data requires the use of new technology. This technology ranges from different ways of storing and processing data to the various analyses that can be performed on the data, and a number of companies have developed the necessary technology. In 2013, worldwide IT spending on Big Data technologies exceeded $31 billion.[1]

The Big Data ecosystem is growing so rapidly that it is difficult to understand the market and to determine which players can solve what problems. Because Big Data promises so many benefits, many Big Data technology vendors are offering solutions to those problems.

There are the large players, such as Microsoft, SAS, IBM, HP, or Dell, that have made Big Data part of their total offerings. Most of these companies can deliver a complete solution. Smaller companies, however, do not need a total Big Data solution. They require a specialized solution to a specific problem, and many different Big Data start-ups can fulfill this need. I will discuss a few different categories that are on the market at the moment.

Next to paid solutions, there are many open-source tools that give organizations the possibility to use and experiment with free Big Data technologies. In this rapidly Big Data growing landscape, an open-source tool is available to solve almost any problem. One of the best known is Hadoop, without which Big Data would have taken much longer to reveal its potential.

HADOOP HDFS AND MAPREDUCE

Hadoop, which is named after the elephant toy of the child of the inventor of Hadoop, was developed because existing data storage and processing tools appeared inadequate to handle the large amounts of data that started to appear with the growth of the Internet. First, Google developed the programming model MapReduce to cope with the flow of data that resulted from its mission to organize and make universally accessible the world's information Yahoo, in response, developed Hadoop in 2005 as an implementation of MapReduce. It was released as an open-source tool in 2007 under the Apache license.

Since then, Hadoop has evolved into a large-scale operating system that focuses on distributed and parallel processing of vast amounts of data.[2] As is with any "normal" operating system, Hadoop consists of a file system, is able to write and distribute programs, and returns results.

Hadoop supports data-intensive distributed applications that can run simultaneously on large clusters of normal, commodity hardware. A Hadoop network is reliable and extremely scalable; it can be used to query massive datasets. Hadoop is written in the Java programming language, which means it can run on any platform and is used by a global community of distributors and Big Data technology vendors that have built layers on top of Hadoop.

What is particularly useful is the Hadoop Distributed File System (HDFS), which breaks down the data it processes into smaller pieces called blocks. These blocks are subsequently distributed throughout a cluster. This distributing of the data allows the map-and-reduce functions to be executed on smaller subsets instead of on one large dataset. This increases efficiency, decreases processing time, and enables the scalability necessary for processing vast amounts of data.

MapReduce is a software framework and model that can process and retrieve the vast amounts of data stored in parallel on the Hadoop system. The MapReduce libraries have been written in many programming languages and uses two steps to work with structured and unstructured data. The first step is the "Map-phase," which divides the data into smaller subsets that are distributed over the different nodes in a cluster. Nodes within the system can do this again, resulting in a multi-level tree structure that divides the data in ever-smaller subsets. At these nodes, the data is processed and the answer is passed back to the "master node." The second step is the "reduce phase," during which the master node collects all the returned data and combines it into some sort of output that can be used again. The MapReduce framework manages all the various tasks in parallel and across the system. It forms the heart of Hadoop.

With this combination of technologies, massive amounts of data can be easily stored, processed, and analyzed in a fraction of a second. If a top layer, such as Hortonworks or Cloudera, is added to it, real-time analytics becomes possible. Hadoop provides great advantages and makes Big Data analytics possible.

Although Hadoop, HDFS, and MapReduce offer many advantages to organizations, such as linear scaling on commodity hardware and a high degree of fault tolerance, it is not the Holy Grail, as was anticipated. Hadoop also has some substantial disadvantages. It is difficult to get Hadoop operational, it requires specialized engineers who are expensive, cluster management is hard, and debugging is pretty challenging. Organizations will need specially trained IT personnel to install a complete Hadoop cluster. Installing a Hadoop cluster on premises can be a daunting task and therefore companies, and especially smaller companies, should think carefully about whether to start with it. Especially because more and more Big Data startups develop Big-Data-as-a-Service solutions, taking away the need to build and own the Hadoop environment. These companies offer Hadoop clusters in the cloud instead.

OPEN-SOURCE TOOLS

Although Hadoop is the best-known open-source tool, many other open-source tools are available on the market, including some that offer extensive visualizations, drag-and-drop options, and easy-to-install scripts.

They have proven to be efficient and cost effective in storing, analyzing, and visualizing Big Data. Open-source tools are not as risky as they used to be, so more and more companies are adapting and implementing them.

An overview of the landscape can be found at http://bit.ly/16YR9zx. Among the advantages of open-source tools are:

- They do not require a huge investment to get started; just download and start working. It is a great way to try a product.
- The community around open-source tools is big and active, meaning that the product is developed and improved quickly when compared to closed tools that tend to have a longer time to market. It also helps when encountering problems, as someone else in the community might have had the same problem and already solved it. This prevents companies from having to reinvent the wheel.
- Open-source tools have a flexible, scalable architecture that is cost effective when managing huge quantities of data. This is especially desirable for SMEs.
- Open-source tools are developed in such away that they operate on commodity hardware, making it unnecessary to invest in expensive equipment.

That open-source tools are gaining importance is also shown by the fact that more and more vendors who traditionally relied on proprietary models are embracing this technology. For example, in 2012, VMware launched a new open-source project called Serengeti that is designed to let Hadoop run on top of VMware vSphere Cloud.[3] In addition, EMC Greenplum made its new Chorus social framework open-source last year.[4]

However, just as with Hadoop, open-source tools have some disadvantages. First of all, free open-source tools do not come with support from the developer; companies need to purchase an enterprise edition to receive that service. Community support cannot be assumed and, in some instances, may not be taken as granted.[5] Although an open-source tool can be useful experimenting with new tools, it usually does require trained IT personnel who understand the open-source tool. Finally, the original developers of the open-source tool may move to other companies or lose interest in further developing the tool. The result is outdated software that is less well equipped for future Big Data challenges.

So, the decision to use an open-source tool has to be made carefully. Organizations should consider not only the low cost of open-source tools, but also have a detailed understanding and analysis of the pros and cons of the different open-source tools as compared with commercial Big Data technology.

BIG DATA TOOLS AND TYPES OF ANALYSIS

Many commercial Big Data technologies have been developed by startups that have found a way to deal with vast amounts of data. They have developed disruptive technologies that organizations can use to obtain valuable insights and turn data into information and eventually wisdom. Of course, large existing IT players have also created substantial amounts of Big Data technology in recent years. Particularly large corporations that want an all-inclusive Big Data solution use those technologies. In addition, many different types of analysis can be done using these technologies, and each will have a different result. As there are Big Data startups for almost every need and any use in any industry, we cannot discuss them all. Therefore, the focus will be on some of the most important areas. For a larger overview of Big Data startups, go to BigData-Startups.com/Open-Source-Tools

As already mentioned, a disadvantage of Hadoop is that it works with batches and cannot deal with vast amounts of data in real time. However, real-time streaming and processing of data provides many benefits to organizations. Some Big Data technology vendors have built a layer on top of Hadoop or have built completely new tools that can cope with real-time processing, storing, analyzing, and visualizing of data. These tools can analyze unstructured and structured data in real time, significantly improving the functionality of Hadoop and MapReduce.

Some technologies integrate data from different sources directly into a platform. Thus, they avoid the need for additional data warehousing, but still delivering real-time interactive charts that are easy to interact with and understand.

Some Big Data technology vendors focus on delivering the optimal graphical representation of Big Data. Visualizing unstructured and structured data is necessary to turn it into information, but it is also very challenging. New Big Data startups, however, seem to understand the practice of visualizing and have developed different solutions. One is visualization based on the cortex of the human eye, which maximizes the ability of the human brain to recognize patterns. It makes it easy to read and understand massive amounts of relational data. The use of color and different thicknesses perceived within the cortex allow users to easily recognize patterns and discover abnormalities.

Another way of visualizing is a technique called topological data analysis, which focuses on the shape of complex data and can identify clusters and statistical significance. Data scientists can use this to reveal inherent patterns in clusters. This type of analysis is best visualized with three-dimensional clusters that show the topological spaces and can be explored interactively.

It is definitely not always necessary to have complex, innovative, and interactive graphical representations. Infographics are graphic visual representations of information, data, or knowledge that can help make difficult and complex material easily understandable. Dashboards combining different data streams showing "traditional" graphs (column, line, pie, or bar) can also provide valuable insights. Sometimes, real-time updated simple graphs showing the status of processes will actually provide more valuable information to improve decision making then more complex and innovative visualizations. On mobile devices, visualizations get a completely new meaning when a user is able to play intuitively with the data while swiping, pinching, rotating, or zooming.

Although the ability to visualize real-time analyses in a great way is important, it is even more valuable for organizations to be able to predict future outcomes. This is hugely different from existing business intelligence, which usually only looks at what has already happened using analytical tools that say nothing about the future. Predictive analysis can help companies provide actionable intelligence based on that same data.

Therefore, many Big Data startups focus on predictive modeling capabilities that will enable organizations to anticipate what is coming. Collecting as much data as possible while a potential customer is visiting a website can give valuable insights. Information such as products browsed and considered, transactional data, or browser and sessions information can be merged with historical and deep customer information about previous purchases and loyalty program records. This provides a complete picture about the visitor and can help predict the likelihood of the visitor to become a high lifetime value customer. With such information, organizations can take corresponding actions if required.

Predictive analytics is also used in the ecommerce world to help consumers buy electronics, reserve hotel rooms, or purchase airline tickets. These services can help consumers purchase products at the right moment at the right price by telling consumers when prices will drop or what the best period in the week is to buy.

Predictive analytics can be used in any industry, but a great example is the insurance industry. which uses it to determine which policyholders are likelier to make claims and to predict the risk the company is facing. This type of analysis works better as more data is collected because the algorithm can take more variables into account when making its predictions.

Profiling is used to better target potential customers. The ultimate goal is to develop a 360-degree view of each customer, so that a segment of one can eventually be created. Behavioral analytics can be used to discover patterns in (un)structured data across customer touch points, giving organizations better insights into the different types of customers they have. Consumer patterns derived from data, such as demographic, geographic, psychographic, and economic attributes, will help organizations better understand their customers. Sales and marketing data, such as campaign information, operations data, and conversion data, will also provide organizations with accurate data about customers that can be used to increase customer retention and acquisitions, grow upselling and cross-selling, and increase online conversion.

Profiles can also be used in systems that make recommendations. These recommender systems are one of the most common applications of Big Data. The best-known application is probably Amazon's recommendation engine, which allows users to get a personalized homepage when they visit Amazon.com. However, etailers are not the only companies that use recommendation engines to persuade customers to buy additional products. Recommender systems can also be used in other industries, as well as have different applications.

Recommender systems can be based on two different types of algorithms, which are often combined. The first analyzes vast amounts of data about past choices/purchases of customers and uses this information to suggest new products. This is called collaborative filtering, a system recommending other products based on what other users with the same profile have bought. For example, a user bought A, B, C, and D and another user bought A, B, C, D, and E. The system will then automatically recommend product E to the first user, as both users have the same buying profile. The second approach is content-based filtering, in which the system uses a detailed profile of what a user has previously bought, liked, searched for, tweeted about, blogged about, visited, and so on. Based on that information, a profile is created and products are recommended that best fit that profile based on the attributes of that product.

Most consumers know recommendation engines from online shopping, but recommendation engines can also be used B2B, for example, to recommend potential prospects to salespeople. In a post, Ellis Booker from InformationWeek explains that public data sets, such as credit bureaus company data information, can be combined with a company's own sales and customer database to find new relationships that a salesperson might have missed.[6] As such, recommendation systems are becoming common in finance and insurance companies, where they are used to suggest, among other things, investment opportunities or sales strategies.

In fact, recommendation engines can be used anywhere users are looking for products/services or people. LinkedIn uses recommendations to suggest people, jobs, or groups you might want to connect with.[7] The "you may like this" functionality on the platform blends content-based and collaborative filtering and uses a algorithmic popularity and graph-based approach for the recommendations. Building a virtual profile of each group and extracting the most representative features of that group's members creates "Groups you may like." LinkedIn recommends jobs by combining different profile features, such as behavior, location, and attributes, of people similar to you.

Recommendations has become a standard feature for most large, online players, from retailers to online travel websites. For any company working with recommendations, the trick is to deliver relevant recommendations.[8] This will improve the buyer experience and increase the conversion rate.

With the ever-increasing amount of data, recommendation engines will only become better in the future. For organizations, this will mean better targeting of products to the right person and, as a result, probably an increase in the conversion rate. For consumers, it will become even easier to find the product they are are looking for. However, this could also have a downside. If the recommendation engines become so good and recommend products/services before you are aware that you need them, how will this affect the possibility of a consumer discovering new products/services that are not in line with his or her profile? Organizations should be aware of this, as otherwise it could backfire.

HOW AMAZON IS LEVERAGING BIG DATA

Amazon has an unrivaled databank about online consumer purchasing that it can mine from its 152 million customer accounts.[9] For many years, Amazon has used that data to built a recommender system that suggests products to people who visit Amazon.com. As early as 2003, Amazon used item–item similarity methods from collaborative filtering, which at that time was state of the art. Since then, Amazon has improved its recommender engine and, today, the company has mastered it to perfection. It uses customer click-stream data and historical purchase data from those 152 million customers; each user is shown customized results on customized web pages.

Amazon also uses Big Data to offer superb service to its customers.[10] This could be the result of its purchase of Zapos in 2009. It ensures that customer representatives have all the information they need the moment a customer requires support. They can do this because they take all the data collected to build and constantly improve relationships with its customers.[11] Many retailers could learn from this example.

But Amazon is expanding its use of Big Data because the competition is closing in. As such, Amazon added remote computing services, via Amazon Web Services (AWS), to its already massive product and service offering. Launched in 2002, AWS recently added Big Data services, and it now offer tools to support data collection, storage, computation, collaboration, and sharing. All are available in the cloud. The Amazon Elastic MapReduce provides a managed, easy-to-use analytics platform built around the powerful Hadoop framework that is used by large companies, including Dropbox, Netflix, and Yelp.[12,13]

However, there is more. Amazon also uses Big Data to monitor, track, and secure its 1.5 billion items to be found in its 200 fulfillment centers around the world.[14] Amazon stores the product catalogue data in S3.[15] This is a simple web service interface that can be used to store any amount of data at any time from anywhere on the web. It can write, read, and delete objects up to 5 TB of data. The catalogue stored in S3 receives more than 50 million updates a week, and every 30 minutes all data received is crunched and reported back to the different warehouses and the website.

At AWS, Amazon also hosts public Big Data sets at no cost.[16] All available Big Data sets can be used and seamlessly integrated in AWS cloud-based solutions. Everyone can now use this public data, such as data from the Human Genome Project.

MIT Technology Review reported in 2013 on a new Amazon project to package information about consumers and sell it to marketers who can use it to advertise products tailored to what people really want.[17] In contrast to Google and Facebook, which might have more overall data about consumers, Amazon has a clearer understanding of what people actually buy and therefore what they are looking for and what they need. This is much more valuable information, and this could definitely grow Amazon's advertising revenue in the coming years.

In the past few years, Amazon has definitely moved away from a pure ecommerce player to a giant online player. It focuses massively on Big Data and is changing from an online retailer into a Big Data company.

When websites start using machine-learning systems for real-time recommendations, the recommendations will improve, as the system will learn from unsuccessful recommendations. The many social networks on the web also generate a lot of data about consumers. Tweets, Likes, blog posts, and check-ins can give companies answers to important questions, such as, What is the sentiment in the market?, How are (new) products/commercials received and perceived?, and How can products or services be improved to suit the needs of customers?

Organizations that use deep machine learning and natural language processing will be able to interpret the meaning of comments placed on social networks and place generic statements into the right context. Such social media analytics help organizations better understanding their customers. When integrated with other tools, such as sales data, surveys, support tickets, usage logs, and other sources of customer intelligence, social media analytics can turn customer retention into a data-driven process that will increase conversion and decrease churn.

Clustering analysis and segmentation is a data-driven approach to look for patterns within Big Data and to group similar data objects, behaviors, or whatever other information can be found within the data. This goes much further than human-created segments, which are mostly based on easily identifiable traits, such a location, age, and gender.

Big Data driven clustering and segmentation performed by algorithms can find segments and patterns that would otherwise remain hidden. When using self-learning algorithms, the segmentation is improved; while doing the segmentation, the algorithm learns about the segmentation it creates. It can, for example, come up with clusters of consumers who are becoming parents in a geographical location in a certain age group and with a certain type of job. The result can be used to drive personalized and targeted marketing efforts. Whatever can be found in the Big Data can be turned into a segment, and this can help companies to better serve their customers.

Where clusters can be found, outliers can also be shown. By finding the outlier within Big Data and identifying the unique exception, an organization can discover unexpected knowledge. Although finding an outlier can be like finding a needle in a haystack, it is less difficult for algorithms. Such anomalies can have exceptional value when they are found. A good example is fraud detection or identifying criminal activities in online banking. With machine learning and self-learning algorithms, outlier detection can find correlations that are too vague for humans to discover because of the huge amount of data necessary to identify the pattern.

In a similarity search, an algorithm tries to find an object that is most similar to the object of interest. The best-known similarity algorithm is the app Shazam, which can find a song in a database of more than 11 million songs after listening for just a few seconds.

In the past, SQL queries were performed to find components that matched certain conditions, such as "find all cars within a certain age range from a certain brand." Similarity searches can be more like "find all cars like this one." As these algorithms use Big Data to find similarities, there is a far better chance of success in finding what you are looking for. Most of the time, algorithms can also perform thousands of searches simultaneously in a split second, thereby locating what you are looking for in an instant.

Finally, some Big Data startups focus on the human capital aspect. McKinsey already forecasts that in 2018 there will be a shortage of 140,000 to 190,000 Big Data Scientists in the United States alone. If Big Data is made easier to manipulate and rearrange, this problem can be solved by removing the need for expensive Big Data Scientists.

Accessing and exploring heterogeneous data can be made so simple that users would be able to mix Big Data sources that are stored, for example, on Hadoop with traditional sources and perform analyses on them without the need to be a data scientist. Tools already on the market are especially designed for smaller organizations that want to start discovering the possibilities of Big Data without spending large amounts of money on IT and personnel. The tools provide these organizations with a single platform that incorporates data from any source in any environment and allows them to conduct analyses or create integrated data views. However, the problem is that it is difficult to adapt the solutions to personal needs. For extensive Big Data solutions, Big Data Scientists and engineers will always be necessary.

TAKEAWAYS

Without technology Big Data is just an empty shell. The tools available in the market help organizations turn their Big Data strategy into reality. Many different technologies are available on the market that address different problems in different industries. Therefore, finding the right tool for the right job will be a challenge.

This chapter discussed the best-known Big Data tool, Hadoop, which processes and stores massive amounts of data in a distributed file system. However, many different solutions exist for different tasks. Although Hadoop is the best known, it is definitely not the only storage tool available. For example, NoSQL databases solve some of the problems common with Hadoop. These databases offer scalability, agility, real-time analytics and flexibility. Although it has not yet reached the hype of Hadoop, thanks to these features the NoSQL movement is drawing a lot of attention. In addition, many cloud-based Data-as-a-Service solutions are appearing on the market. Therefore, small or medium-sized enterprises do not immediately have to build a Hadoop cluster on their premises if they want to start using Big Data.

The open-source landscape is also growing rapidly. By 2013, there was an open-source alternative for almost any paid solution. Although open-source tools are free and have the support of a large community, they also have disadvantages, such as the need for technically trained personnel. Organizations that want to start using open-source tools should be aware of the different pros and cons before they dive into the open-source world.

Further, organizations that would rather use a commercial solution that is easier (sometimes) to install and use will find many different options. The Big Data startup scene is growing rapidly. The investments made in this sector have exceeded $2.5 billion. and new Big Data startups are being launched on a daily basis.[18] With so many options available, organizations need to choose wisely when moving ahead with a Big Data startup and understand the benefits and the costs of the selected Big Data technology vendor.

Big Data Privacy, Ethics, and Security

5

With every new disruptive technology comes new issues. With Big Data, these issues are privacy, ethics, and security. As more and more data is collected, stored, and analyzed by companies, organizations, consumers, and governments, regulations are needed to address these concerns. Big Data brings big responsibility.

In a TED talk at TED Global in 2012, Malte Spitz stated that if the Stasi had known about people's activities what our governments know today, the Berlin Wall might never have come down.[1] With the information now available, governments can find the mavens and leaders within society. With this information, you can control a society.

The PRISM leak by Edward Snowden in the summer of 2013 showed that privacy in the Big Data world is indeed an endangered species. In the United States, the National Security Agency (NSA) used PRISM as a source for raw intelligence in its analytics reports. The NSA had direct access to information on the servers of many sites, including those of Google, Apple, and Facebook. In addition, Snowden showed that the U.S. government had access to over millions of private text messages from Chinese citizens, that British Intelligence spied on its leaders during the G20 summit in the United Kingdom in 2009, and that British Intelligence has secretly gained access to the fiber-optic cables that connect Europe with the United States.[2,3,4] On a daily basis, this adds up to 39,000 terabytes of data.[5] These scandals woke up the public, and privacy suddenly had a whole new meaning.

No matter how many advantages Big Data brings to organizations and governments, business cannot overlook the privacy factor involved in collecting all that information. They will have to map their Big Data privacy needs on time and ensure that they are addressed before any problems arise. In terms of privacy, the problem is not so much the technology or the possibilities it offers, but rather the vast amounts of (anonymized) data. By nature, Big Data is not privacy friendly, as even anonymized data can reidentify individuals as long as there is enough data available.

Traditional privacy regulations will prove not sufficient for protecting the consumer in the Big Data era. New policies related to privacy, security, intellectual property, and data ownership will need to be developed to meet the changing needs of businesses that are developing a Big Data strategy. Companies and governments will have to develop such Big Data policies to protect consumers and ensure organizations are not vulnerable to serious data breaches.

Closely linked to privacy is the ethical side of Big Data. Everyone creates data using a plethora of different devices, products, or applications. Who owns your data and what is done with that data are important areas of discussion. Most of the time, consumers are not aware of what organizations do with their data, and this can have disturbing consequences for both consumers and companies. To ensure that consumers understand what is done with the data and what they can expect, I will propose four ethical guidelines for organizations to adopt.

Finally, security issues are another important aspect of Big Data. Such Big Data can keep a country safe, as the U.S. government claimed regarding the PRISM program or prevent customers or employees from performing fraudulent actions, but Big Data can also in and of itself be a security threat.[6] When massive amounts of data are created, stored, and analyzed, criminals will want to illegally obtain that data for various reasons. In 2013, many large organizations experienced distributed denial-of-service (DDoS) attacks and went offline for some time. Even more serious, some had their customer data stolen. Organizations will have to implement the necessary security measures and have a crisis plan ready in case they do get hacked.

BIG DATA PRIVACY

The 2006 Data Detention Directive of the European Union states that all telecom and Internet service organizations need to store data from their customers for a minimum of six months to a maximum of two years.[7] This includes who calls whom, who texts whom, who sends whom an email, which websites are visited, which apps are used, and where you are. They know where you sleep. They know everything about you.

So, will Big Data mean the end of privacy? In an interview in 2009, ex Google CEO Eric Schmidt said: "If you have something that you don't want anyone to know, maybe you shouldn't be doing it in the first place."[8] He meant that in the future, privacy as we know it might cease to exist. Already, Big Data is causing some serious privacy issues that are important to address. I want to focus on how Big Data affects the privacy of consumers and how organizations have to deal with these issues to survive. How governments can and will deal with our privacy is beyond the scope of this book.

Big Data is everywhere and, as more products incorporate sensors, even more data will be collected. Thanks to the quantified-self movement, many (free) apps are already collecting a lot of information about users. It is estimated that 60 percent of Americans track their weight, diet, or exercise routine.[9] However, in the world of Big Data, nothing is "for free." Individuals who use free products or services pay by giving out data about themselves; for many consumers, it is unclear who owns that data.

Many services consumers use today began as free and innocent. Consumers did not see any harm in using services like Google or Facebook or other online applications that appeared in the last decade. Consumers are so used to the idea that everything online is "for free," that they are unwilling to pay for these services. They are so addicted to these services that they cannot relinquish them despite potential security issues.

In the past decade, however, organizations have slowly but surely moved to storing and using more and more data to profile consumers, while constantly adding additional "free" services. So, organizations that consumers thought were connecting them to their friends and providing information as a free utility are now targeting them with highly personalized advertisements using data collected about them from these very services.

The effect on privacy or ethical issues is still unclear. Consumers are becoming aware of the problem. The result is a movement in which users prefer to pay for a service with money instead of data. A great example is App.net, where users pay a monthly fee to use the services without advertisements.[10]

What can/do organizations do with all that data? Each field filled out, each click, each piece of information on how often consumers use a product/service, when they use it, or how they use it gets translated into data-driven product/organization improvements or is used to serve up increasingly targeted advertisements. As services are becoming more expensive to maintain or build, the advertising becomes bigger. Investors expect a return on their investments, especially in the case of public companies. A good example is Facebook, where the advertising space in the news feed is becoming larger and larger.[11] As long as users do not feel that this is an intrusion into their private space, Facebook can continue to show more advertising. Facebook's Graph Search will use even more personal information from its users and buys information from third parties to improve its targeted advertising.[12,13]

It is fine for consumers to pay for a service with data. It is a valid business model that has been used by many organizations for decades. As consumers become more aware of it and are able to protest against it, organizations need to educate customers about how the data is used. Consumers have to become more careful about their online Big Data footprints. They need to understand the costs of these "free" services.

Consumers should actually start to think of each data point as an economic transaction between the user and the service provider, and organizations will have to be transparent about this. They need to pay more careful attention to the terms and conditions and privacy statements of each website. They should also check their privacy settings on social networks on a regular basis.

Fortunately, an increasing number of websites are advising users about how to adjust privacy settings to appropriate levels.[14,15] Still, on the other hand, many organizations make it difficult for consumers to understand what happens with their data. Some companies may think that having a privacy policy is sufficient, but many consumers do not understand what a privacy policy actually means, if they read them at all. Organizations should not only inform customers of their rights, but should also protect these digital immigrants from ignoring or signing the privacy policy without indicating an awareness of its meaning and an acceptance of its terms.

Therefore, organizations should be very clear about what data is collected and what they do with it. They should educate their customers in a clear and concise manner. Who reads a privacy statement of 11,000 words that requires about 45 minutes to read?[16] Even the average privacy policy, which is only 2,500 words long, is almost never read.[17] Companies need to be transparent about what data they collect, why they collect it, and what they do with it, so that users can decide whether they want to use the service or the product.

In addition, companies could give users the opportunity to use a service without any data being collected or stored. In that case, the user would pay for the service with money instead of data. This is a validated approach, as shown by the success of App.net, which had over 100,000 paying users in 2013.[18] Give consumers a choice, and they will chose your organization.

Reidentification of Anonymous People

Another threat that Big Data poses for consumers is reidentifying individuals using anonymous data. This could drive people away from your organization if not addressed correctly. To reidentify individuals in large datasets, all you need is a laptop, Wi-Fi, and various datasets linked to each other. With these tools, anyone can start digging for personal identifiable information (PII) hidden in the dataset. It looks simple; it is, however, rather difficult but unfortunately not impossible, as research from the Whitehead Institute showed[19] when it reidentified 50 individuals who had submitted personal DNA information to genomic studies such as the 1000 Genomes Project.[20]

The researchers of the Whitehead Institute noted that both surnames and the Y chromosome are passed on from father to son, so they started analyzing public databases that housed Y-STR data and surnames.[21] They linked public datasets to the dataset collected by the

Center for the Study of Human Polymorphisms (CEPH) to identify 50 men and women out of data that was deidentified.[22] With more and more public datasets becoming available, could the reidentification of individuals pose a real threat to the use of Big Data and open datasets? What does it do to your organization if anonymous persons are reidentified using datasets from your organization?

Reidentification of individuals could lead to privacy issues because information that should not have been released can become publicly available. The reidentification of Massachusetts Governor William Weld, who collapsed on stage while receiving an honorary doctorate from Bentley College, caused a stir.[23] In 2010, using a dataset released by the Massachusetts Group Insurance Commission to improve healthcare and control costs, MIT graduate student Latanya Sweeney was able to reidentify Weld using some simple tactics and a voter list.[24,25] Eventually this study led to the development of the deidentification provisions in the American Health Insurance Portability and Accountability Act (HIPAA).[26]

Reidentification of individuals can have serious consequences if, for example, private health information is recovered that could lead to discrimination, embarrassment, or even identity theft. Or, imagine how medical records could influence a child custody battle. That is why the HIPAA includes 18 specific identifiers that must be removed prior to data release. Unfortunately, it does not stop people from trying to re-identify individuals in large datasets.

Another well-known example is the reidentification of a dataset from Netflix done by Arvind Narayanan.[27] The study used public datasets as part of a contest that was organized by Netflix to improve its movie recommendation engine.[28] Narayanan and his team were able to reidentify people in the anonymous database. This study lead to a privacy lawsuit against Netflix that subsequently canceled a second contest in 2010.[29] Additional examples are available of researchers reidentifying individuals in large datasets.[30] As long as it is done by researchers with good intentions, it seems right. Imagine, however, if hackers with bad intentions start doing the same thing? It could be very harmful for your customers and catastrophic for your organization.

Organizations would do well to perform a threat analysis on a dataset before releasing it to the public; that means checking for datasets available online that can be used to reidentify the people included. However, as Narayanan explains, it is not a 100 percent secure solution, as future datasets could still cause a problem for anonymity.[31] In order to solve this problem in situations such as the Netflix contest, Narayanan proposed two rules: (1) use of a fabricated small set of data for the first round for contenders to develop a code and algorithm that protects anonymity, and (2) have the finalists sign a nondisclosure agreement (NDA) before releasing the full dataset to them.

With all this said, however, how likely is it and how much effort does it take to reidentify individuals in so many datasets? Dr. Latanya Sweeney reported in 2007 that 0.04 percent (4 in 10,000) of individuals in the United States who appear in datasets that have been anonymized according to HIPAA standards can be reidentified.[32] If put in perspective, this risk is slightly above the lifetime odds of being struck by lightning (1 in 6,250).[33]

So, perhaps consumers should not worry too much about reidentification, as long as the necessary precautions are taken into account as defined by the HIPAA. Perhaps consumers should see it as a risk that is part of life. If we do not want to accept this risk, we should perhaps abandon the use of public datasets completely? However, as Daniel Barth-Jones (an epidemiologist and statistician at Columbia University) explains: "If we stop using and analyzing deidentified data, important social, commercial, and educational benefits, as well as innovation opportunities, might be lost."[34,35]

Apart from the small risk of being reidentified, it is also rather difficult to determine the characteristics of individuals in public datasets. As Barth-Jones wrote in a study in 2011, "each attack must be customized to the particular deidentified database and to the population as it existed at the time of data-collection."[36] In addition to that, Paul Ohm, associate professor of law at Colorado Law School, assures us that trustworthy re-identifications is labor-intensive.[37,38] It is time consuming, requires serious data management and statistics skills, and simply lacks the easy transmission and transferability seen in computer viruses.

Of course, this does not mean that organizations should stop paying serious attention to reidentification risks. Technology is always improving, including techniques for reidentification. As consumers leave more data traces online, it will become easier to reidentify individuals if measures are not taken accordingly. Measures, such as forcing Facebook to shut down its facial recognition feature as imposed by the European regulators in 2012, will be necessary.[39] There will always be companies trying to push against privacy regulations, and hackers will always do their best to find information they can use. Therefore, organizations should constantly reassess and strengthen de-identification and reidentification management techniques to ensure that public datasets can also be used in the future to drive innovation and develop great services for the public.

Why Big Data Privacy Will Be Self-Regulating

Technological progress has always led to heated discussions about the threats it poses to society.[40] When the printing press was invented in the fifteenth century, monks viewed easily available books that were unapproved by the church as a threat to their control over learning. The esteemed Swiss scientist, Conrad Gessner, feared that the information overload caused by the printing press could confuse people and prove harmful to them.[41] Comparable worries were expressed when newspapers became more available in the eighteenth century.[42] The French statesman Malesherbes feared that newspapers would isolate readers.[43] When in the nineteenth century, education became more generally accessible, some saw it as a risk to mental health.[44] Similarly, critics thought radio would distract children, while television was expected to hurt radio, conversation, reading, and the patterns of family living.[45]

Since the appearance of the Internet, we heard more of such doubts: Email would damage our intelligence, Twitter could harm our moral values, Facebook might even increase the risk of cancer, and Google would make us stupid.[46–48] Now, the era of Big Data brings fears that we will lose our privacy.

Although Big Data technology unquestionably makes it possible to follow our every move at any time and place, it does not mean that organizations can do whatever they want with that data. We know that Gen Xers and baby boomers are very careful about their privacy. Gen Y is also conscious about privacy; "just because they want to be in public, does not mean they want to be public," as stated by Dana Boyd in her talk at the TechKnowledge conference in 2013.[49,50]

So, how can the privacy of consumers be protected? Well, three different groups are needed to achieve this goal: governments, organizations, and consumers. Let's first look at governments. In most countries, existing privacy laws date from the 1970s and 1980s, when the World Wide Web did not exist, and we were still using landlines to call each other.[51] These outdated privacy laws contain many ambiguities, so governments around the world are in the process of updating them.[52] This is a positive step, but unfortunately writing new laws takes time and, more often than not, they do not achieve their goals. A good example is the cookie law in The Netherlands, which completely missed its goal and had to be amended within one year.[53] The original law prohibited companies from placing cookies on a visitor's computer unless the visitor had explicitly agreed to it. Many companies did not adhere to it, and consumers got tired of the number of additional clicks needed to enter a website. Understandably, governments cannot keep up with the speed at which technology changes. As such, laws are outdated the moment they are passed. Still, we also cannot, and should not, stop technological progress to match the speed of law making. In addition, PRISM has shown us that governments themselves do not protect consumer privacy very strictly.

So, we cannot rely on governments, but fortunately two other options are available for regulating Big Data privacy. Organizations cannot survive without consumers, but consumers can survive without organizations. People are becoming increasingly creative and independent of organizations as shown by the website instructables.com, which enables users to create their own products.[54] In addition, the 3D-printing market that is developing will eventually enable consumers to print whatever they want in their living rooms. Therefore, organizations will have to observe certain guidelines that promise to ensure the privacy of consumers or consumers will simply walk away.

An organization that decides not to play by the rules and respect the privacy of its customers could go bankrupt if things go wrong. The power of consumers increased with the growth of social media networks because a protest can be so easily organized. Within days, a large group of consumers can become connected and decide to boycott any organization that does not abide by the rules. Switching costs are low nowadays, so consumers can simply change to companies that better protect their privacy. If no alternative is available, there will always (eventually) be an entrepreneur who will fill that gap.

The real problem is organizations that misuse collected data and are not caught, because they can continue to invade the privacy of their customers. This could result in major catastrophes that cause damage to the lives of consumers. However, the moment a catastrophe occurs and an organization does not respond correctly, it is likely that the organization will be out of business rather soon. In the end, it is up to the consumers to control organizations and demand that they stick to ethical guidelines.

New technologies are always the result of trial and error, so we will unfortunately face a few catastrophes in the future. The challenge is to limit these as much as possible. Consumers and organizations should ensure this and governments should assist with regulations when needed. In the end, however, consumers will decide how society looks and which organizations are allowed to participate. The first organization that goes out of business due to privacy issue violations will serve as a warning for others. It will have a self-regulating effect on other companies. So, if an organization wants to survive in the future, it will have to adopt some ethical Big Data guidelines.

BIG DATA ETHICS

Big Data enables a company to check, control, and know everything. But to know everything entails an obligation to act on behalf of and to protect the customer. Such an obligation requires that organizations do everything possible to protect (sensitive) data sets and to be open and clear about what is done with that data. And, although it is possible to know everything, not every person within an organization is entitled to have access to sensitive information. In The Netherlands, it became clear that sensitive electronic health records could be accessed by anyone in a hospital, even administrative clerks, who could therefore check what his or her neighbor was doing in the hospital, or by an intern interested in why a fellow student was treated in a psychiatric institution.[55] These important privacy breaches should be prevented if the right ethics are in place within an organization.

Big Data Ownership

With the digital universe expanding so rapidly, such issues become even more apparent. We need to know how the data is protected, as well who owns the data. Everyone is responsible for this growth; every day consumers like, tweet, comment, share, blog, and publish information on the web. They do this via smartphones, tablets, laptops, and computers. Often, they are unaware that the information is shared.

Many people use apps that automatically share data on social networks, such as data on exercise, sleeping, and diet.[56–58] However, not many people ask about who owns all that data. The same goes for everything shared on Facebook, Twitter, Foursquare, or any other social network, or in e-mails using Google or Live, or in personal documents in the cloud.

The moment something is placed online, be it in the cloud or on social networks, it is copied, re-tweeted, cached, backed up, and almost impossible to remove again. It will remain there forever and, over time, the ownership of that data fades. And, although Google gives users the option of deleting data, it still owns that data or, as is the case with Facebook, might not really delete the data at all.[59]

Big Data is often described as the oil of the future. If that is the case, we can make a comparison with the "old oil." Most countries with large oil deposits have earned a lot of money by bringing that oil to the surface and selling it to the world. They own the oil that is within their boundaries. The same might be said for data collected by large companies, such as Google, Facebook, or Twitter, that store data in their own data warehouses and, thereby, own that data. Consumers may forget that they gave all that data to these companies voluntarily. After all, nothing in this world is free, and users pay for these "free" tools with their data.

Do consumers nowadays know exactly who accumulates what data? Do they know what it is used for? Are they told explicitly when this data is sold and to whom? Do they know who has access to all this data? Although it might be stated in a company's terms and conditions, these are hardly read.[60] So, consumers have no clue about what happens with their data. As a result, international laws, guidelines, and awareness campaigns are necessary to protect consumers.

The Data Portability Project is about this approach.[61] Its objective is to give consumers the ability to reuse their data across interoperable applications, while controlling their privacy and respecting that of others. The project aims to make consumers aware of what happens to their data and to direct them to organizations that respect data rights and privacy.

Perhaps, the big question is not so much who owns the data, but who has the capacity to analyze, visualize, and resell it. Raw data is, after all, not very usable. The ability to turn data into information and knowledge is the crux. It is all about who can put data to work.

Much is still unclear in the world of data and information ownership. Unless international standards and laws resolve this, organizations have to ensure that consumers know what they to expect. Clearly, we need some ethical guidelines.

Ethical Guidelines

The possibilities of Big Data are enormous, but a company that moves into the Big Data era carelessly will have massive ethical and privacy issues. Organizations should be master of the technology—not the other way around. The goal is to develop better ways to use the unprecedented computing power to our advantage without intruding on the privacy of others or violating ethical standards

Ethics, however, is not the only concern that needs to be discussed and resolved. According to Kord Davis, a former analyst at Cap Gemini and author of *Ethics of Big Data*, it is important that we also understand and agree on rules regarding privacy, identity, ownership, and reliability of Big Data.[62,63] Davis believes that it will be a long and evolutionary process of trial and error. Companies will push the boundaries, and governments will also go too far (think PRISM).

In addition, another problem is that each government will create its own laws regarding Big Data; some will be stricter than others. These different regulations and privacy laws in countries will become an expensive hassle for organizations.[64] Some countries may have no restrictions, while others will impose strict restrictions.

The best solution would be a broad-based, global set of privacy and ethical Big Data guidelines, but this will be a difficult and long process. So, together, organizations will have to learn the limits and understand how much privacy consumers want to keep and how much they want to give up in exchange for the free stuff.

Therefore, I am proposing the following four Big Data ethics guidelines

- Radical Transparency
- Simplicity by Design
- Preparation and Security
- Privacy as Part of the DNA

Radical Transparency

Organizations should tell their customers in real-time what sort of data is being collected and stored, and what they will do with it. Consumers want to be kept informed and to have at least the feeling of being in control. Always allow customers to delete data if it is not stored anonymously or if they simply want to remove it. If you want to offer a free service, be honest and transparent about it, so that your (potential) customers know what they can expect and what happens when they use the service. If possible, also create a paid version that does not collect any data but still provides access to the service. It could even mean an additional revenue stream for your organization.

Simplicity by Design

Customers should be able to simply adjust privacy settings, so they can determine what they want to share, when they want to share it, and with whom. This process should be simple and understandable, even for digital immigrants.[65] Do not hide the information about how to change privacy settings; instead guide consumers on how to adjust them to their liking—instead of to yours. Privacy regulations should be simple, straightforward, and understandable. A good example of how *not* to do it is Facebook, which changes its privacy policy every few weeks/months. Although any setting can be adjusted, it is not always easy to find your way around it. In addition, in 2013, Facebook's privacy policy contained more words (5,830) than the U.S. Constitution (4.543, not counting the amendments).[66]

Figure 5-1 Privacy and Ethics Framework

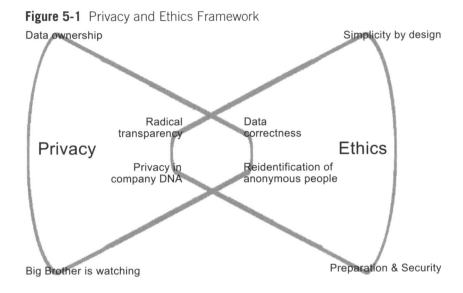

Data ownership

Simplicity by design

Radical
transparency

Data
correctness

Privacy

Ethics

Privacy in
company DNA

Reidentification of
anonymous people

Big Brother is watching

Preparation & Security

Preparation and Security

As more data is collected and stored, your organization becomes more valuable to criminals, who want to have a share of it for illegal purposes. Organizations need to develop a crisis strategy in case the company gets hacked and data is stolen, which seems to be happening quite regularly lately. Just look at how Facebook, Evernote, and LinkedIn were hacked in 2013.[67-69] Or, even better, test your data scientists and IT personnel with fake hacks, as explained in the next section.

Privacy as Part of the DNA

When your organization embraces transparency, simplicity, and security, your customers will embrace you. Ignore these principles, and your customers will eventually ignore you. It is a simple fact. So hire a Chief Privacy Officer or a Chief Data Officer, who is responsible for data privacy and ethics. Make this CDO accountable for whatever data you collect, store, share, sell, or analyze, as well as for how you collect it. Big Data privacy and ethics are too important not to be discussed at the C-level.

Proper usage of Big Data strategies, including combining and analyzing the correct datasets and using them in decision making, will help grow your organization. Doing it the correct way will help you sustain that growth for the long term. Therefore, when starting to develop a Big Data strategy, devote a large part of your time and energy to these four principles, and it will pay off in the end.

If we review all the different aspects of ethics discussed, we see that they are all connected to each other. If you want to take Big Data privacy and ethics seriously, they cannot exist independently (see Figure 5-1).

BIG DATA SECURITY

In the book *SuperFreakanomics* by Steven Levitts and Stephen Dubners, the authors state that if suicide bombers want to go undetected, they should buy life insurance.[70,71] As the authors guide readers through terrorism profiling, they report that an absence of life insurance is a predictor of terrorism. Smart terrorists will therefore buy a policy to help avoid discovery. The British Intelligence Agency uses such criteria— some known and others unknown—to identify possible terrorists.[72] This kind of analysis of numerous dissimilar criteria across the entire population can only be done with Big Data technologies and algorithms. Thus, thanks to Big Data countries are more secure. In addition, the U.S. Government reportedly uses Big Data to analyze the online behavior of millions of Americans and non-Americans. According to officials, data from PRISM helped prevent 50 possible terrorist attacks.[73] In 2013, *The Guardian* revealed that the U.S. Government agency NSA collects data directly from servers belonging to American companies, such as Google, Apple, Microsoft, and Facebook.[74] According to the article, the PRISM program allows the government to collect emails, search histories, review file transfers, read live chats, and so on. Whether it is true or to what extent is beyond the scope of this book, but it show that Big Data technologies have the capability to help governments analyze what happens online in order to protect their countries. Of course, this is nothing new, as governments have been collecting data about citizens for many years.

There are two main areas that Big Data can affect to improve security. In the coming years, it will have a big impact on the way security is managed and handled worldwide. Some methods will be logical and others might be controversial, but Big Data will definitely affect the way we look at security.

Organizational Security

Organizations are swimming in security data. In 2012, at an RSA Conference panel discussion, Ramin Safai, Chief Information Security Officer at Jefferies & Co., said his investment bank has 5,000 employees and captures 25 GB of security-related data every day.[75–77] Buried in that data, they usually find 50 items that require closer examination, two of which eventually demand real attention. According to a whitepaper by EMC, 47 percent of enterprises collect, process, and analyze more than 6 TB of security data on a monthly basis.[78] Collecting the data is not the problem, and, as such, Big Data impacts organizational security in different ways.

It can be used to detect fraud or criminal activities and monitor risks among the employees of an organization. Within large corporations, it is especially difficult to monitor all employees' actions. However, with the right Big Data tools, organizations can watch employees without infringing on their privacy. Tools can analyze full text emails or scrape communication channels looking for anomalies or patterns that indicate fraudulent actions. Only when the tool indicates an issue needs real attention should managers become involved. After all, organizations do want to protect their (intellectual) property and prevent an aggrieved employee from making sensitive data public.

Big Data can also help prevent fraudulent actions by customers. Criminals always try to cheat and make money or receive services without paying for them. Examples include insurance, tax, and unemployment benefits frauds. Take insurance as an example. With Big Data, organizations can prevent, predict, identify, investigate, report, and monitor attempts at insurance fraud. Using massive amounts of historical data, organizations can determine what is normal activity and what is not, and then match that data with actions happening in real time. When combined with pattern analytics, it can help identify outliers who require (immediate) action. The fraud prevention industry is big business itself. The Insurance Information Institute estimated that insurance fraud accounts for $30 billion in annual losses in the United States.[79]

To prevent organizations from being hacked and to keep the collected data secure is the most important task of organizations. Unfortunately, there will always be criminals who are after sensitive data, such as credit card information, bank accounts, and passwords, or who want to steal digital money.[80] In 2013, a lot of attention was paid to the hacking of organizations, such as Facebook, Adobe, LinkedIn, and Evernote, where massive numbers of passwords were stolen. With the right Big Data tools, organizations can become much better at detecting abnormalities on the network or finding intruders.

Organizations should create an intelligence-driven security model that incorporates a 360-degree view of the organization and all risks that it faces. Together with the right Security Information and Event Management (SIEM) solutions, organizations can receive real-time analysis of security alerts generated by network hardware and applications.[81] Several security intelligence and analytics measurements can be used to ensure that all data within an organization is secure.

In order to stop a cyberattack, it first needs to be noticed. One of the benefits of Big Data security technology is that it allows organizations to monitor exactly which files, applications, documents, and users are traveling through the company network. It also allows organizations to monitor what data is going out and what is coming in, as well as from where and when. All this data can be used to find potential cyber threats active on the company network in real time. Technology can identify applications or users that access the network without having been approved by your organization. The right tools allow you to monitor abnormal and inconsistent communications from and to unknown sources for irregular periods of time that are transferring unusual amounts of data.

If the system detects any anomalies, it is important to take action immediately and determine the size of the attack. If necessary, shutdown systems to prevent further attacks. It is important to respond fast, as any additional second loss could result in more damage. When the attack is stopped, it is time to assess the damage. What security measures have been breached? What data was targeted? What data was lost?

Finally, inform your customers about what happened. It is important to be open and transparent, to explain in simple and clear language what transpired, what actions have been taken, and what plans are underway to prevent such attacks from recurring.

Being under cyberattack can be extremely harmful to an organization, especially because customers need to be able to trust companies to secure their data. Therefore, if a cyberattack is not dealt with correctly, it could result in a loss of customers. Train your employees how to deal with security threats, test them with fake attacks, and ensure that you have a crisis plan ready in case something does go wrong. If it does, try to document as much as possible and learn from it to prevent future attacks. Evaluate your actions and communicate that as well to your customers. If the organization deals with an attack correctly, trust might be restored afterward.

National Security and Public Safety

In 2012, the World Economic Forum identified Big Data as a very powerful tool for public safety and national security.[82,83] The hyperconnected world poses more and more risks that could have serious political, social, and economic implications.[84] The key is to address the ongoing arms race between cyber criminals on the one hand and the corporations, lawmakers, and governments that oppose them on the other, as stated by Rod A. Beckstrom, President and Chief Executive Officer of the Internet Corporation for Assigned Names and Numbers (ICANN) at the 2012 forum.[85,86]

Governments are responsible for ensuring that civilians are safe, especially during large events, and Big Data offers many possibilities for reaching this goal. Using different tools and with the cooperation of different organizations via a Big Data solution, it is easier to keep crowds under control and make events safer. Social media analysis is a great tool to do this. For example, governments use different Twitter analytic tools to scan and analyze tweets for security threats, and then take action accordingly. Big Data can also be used to monitor the movement of the crowd during an event and to prevent too many people from gathering at one place. In this way, they can prevent disasters such as the Love Parade in Germany in 2010.

Next to crowd control management systems, CCTV cameras are being used more and more. It is estimated that over 300 different cameras might record an individual throughout the course of a single day.[87] The United Kingdom is a big fan of security cameras. With more than 4.2 million CCTV cameras in place, it has more cameras than China.[88] There are approximately 100 million security cameras worldwide at the moment, and they are used to control important economic areas/buildings/highways/events.[89] Smart cameras can even be used to notify organizations in real time when a security breach is noticed.

Internet protocol (IP) cameras that are directly connected to the Internet will account for approximately 60 percent of all camera sales in 2016, and the percentage of HD security cameras will increase to 50 percent in 2014.[90,91] The percentage of HD CCTV smart cameras is still small, but it is anticipated that in 2016 the number of HD CCTV cameras will reach 3.7 million in the United Kingdom.[92] These are not ordinary cameras, but cameras that can hear and detect dangerous situations, isolate and follow movements, and identify who is recorded in a split second.[93] In The Netherlands, such cameras are protecting the border already.[94] These cameras register each and every vehicle that crosses the border and checks it in a database of wanted vehicles. Within a split second, a signal is given whether or not to stop the car. Big Data technologies enable simultaneous monitoring of all those cameras, only requiring a response when an incident is noticed.

CROWD CONTROL MANAGEMENT[95]

Big Data will have also a major impact on the way public services, such as police, health organizations, and fire departments operate. In The Netherlands, a remarkable, and for The Netherlands unique, initiative took place in December 2012. During the week before Christmas for the last nine years, a Dutch radio station called 3FM organizes Serious Request, an annual charity event. Every year the event is held in a different location. In 2012, the event took place in Enschede, in the Twente region. That year, the Twente police and the Safety Region Twente developed a Crowd Control Management tool to ensure the safety of all visitors. In six days, approximately 500,000 visitors came to the center of

Enschede, and thanks to the Crowd Control Management tool, no incidents occurred.

What Did They Do?

Three different tools monitored what was going on in real time in the center of Enschede.

Twitcident: Developed in conjunction with the Delft University of Technology, Twitcident is a tool that can sift through massive amounts of local tweets to find information about emergencies happening in real time.[96] The tool detects, filters, and analyzes tweets during massive public events and presents the data in a structured way so first emergency responders can use it. Twitcident provided fast and reliable information about the real-time situation in the center of Enschede, including the mood of the crowd and information about people in the crowd.

During Serious Request, Twitcident worked with a list of 533 search terms that resulted in 113,000 different combinations that were monitored by the system. In total, around 1.1 billion tweets were scanned. This resulted in 12,000 tweets that were marked suspicious and were checked manually in the Crowd Control Room.

UrbanShield System: This system provides a real-time situational overview of a complete area within a city.[97] This system is based on a Geographical Information System and uses GPS to show the real-time location of all first responders in an area. All police officers, firefighters, and city and private security guards who are part of the system are shown on a map. If a potentially threatening situation is noticed via the cameras on the street or via Twitcident, the closest first responder can be alerted to take immediate action.

Blue Mark: This tool can count the crowd. During large public events, it is important to know the size of the crowd in specific locations to ensure that not too many people stay at one square within the city.[98] Blue Mark uses sensors in people's smartphones to monitor the number of people and how they move through town. Each smartphone broadcasts a digital signature on a regular basis that can be counted using Bluetooth or Wi-Fi. No private information, such as account or phone identify was collected, so privacy was protected.

Crowd Control Room

Where used, these three tools achieved a multiangle, real-time, high-over picture of the situation in Enschede around the event and on the different city squares.[99] From the Crowd Control Room located in the city hall, officials managed the situation and, when necessary, moved into action. When messages came in via Twitter of active pickpockets, the cameras were able to locate the thieves and using the UrbanShield system, the nearest police officers were warned to take action. Within no time, the criminal was arrested and removed from the scene without anyone noticing. During this event, the tools were not automatically integrated, but that could change in the future.

TAKEAWAYS

Big Data has a big responsibility to guarantee the privacy of customers and the protection of their data. With the vast amount of data available to organizations and governments nowadays, anything and anyone can be monitored, traced, and analyzed, without the customers even knowing it. Consumers, however, are becoming more vocal, and organizations that do not respect their privacy and do not take data security seriously will be significantly affected. Switching costs between organizations have never been so low, so if consumers do not like how they are treated by an organization, they will move to a competitor.

For organizations, it is therefore important to comply with Big Data ethical guidelines. They should be transparent about what data is collected when and why, as well as what use they make of the data and how customers can delete data if they choose. Simplicity should become the standard when developing privacy policies, making it easy for everyone, even the digital immigrants, to understand, as well as making processes within the organization to change privacy settings easy to understand and available. They should ensure that the data is kept secure and anonymous, so that digital criminals do not get a chance to steal information. Data should be kept as secure as money in banks. Finally, an organization's Big Data strategy should specifically mention that the privacy of customers will be protected at all times. Everyone within the organization should breathe privacy and do what it takes to protect the privacy of the customers. Privacy should become part of the DNA of the company culture.

Although Big Data has the potential to become Big Brother, it can be averted if regulations are in place, organizations stick to ethical guidelines, and governments do not spy full-time on all citizens. It does not have to become like George Orwell's *1984*. However, it is not guaranteed, and governments, organizations, and consumers will have to always pay attention and work hard to ensure Big Data privacy, ethics, and security.

Big Data in
Your Organization

6

Big Data study from 2013 by Tata Consulting Services showed that 47 percent of the 1217 firms surveyed had not yet undertaken a Big Data initiative.[1] A similar research project by the SAS Institute in 2013 revealed that 21 percent of the 339 companies questioned did not know enough about Big Data and 15 percent of the organizations did not understand the benefits of Big Data.[2] Several other surveys show more or less the same picture. Many organizations have no idea what Big Data is, even though all those brontobytes heading our way will change the way organizations operate and are managed. Big Data offers a lot of opportunities for organizations. An IBM 2010 Global CFO Study indicated that companies leveraging Big Data financially outperform their competitors by 20 percent or more, and McKinsey reported a potential increase of 60 percent in operating margins with Big Data.[3,4]

Although many organizations do not yet understand Big Data, it is pouring into all organizations from almost every angle imaginable. Every day, small and medium-sized enterprises can easily collect terabytes of data, while startups can effortlessly reach gigabytes and large multinationals can even generate petabytes without any problem. However, simply having massive amounts of data is not enough to become an information-centric organization that stays ahead of its competition.

Note that I deliberately do not call these organizations data-driven organizations, but rather information-centric. The difference might seem subtle, but in fact the two terms are very different. Data, after all, is useless without the right tools at hand and the right culture in place. Only when data is transformed into information can it become valuable for an organization. Information-centric companies have a culture that relies on data that is stored, analyzed, and visualized, and in which the results form an integral part of the company's strategic decision making.

According to Paul Kent, Global vice president of Big Data at SAS, 37 percent of managers surveyed still base their decision on gut feelings, instead of data analytics.[5] A precondition for an information-centric company is therefore a cultural shift that allows data and the tools required to analyze and visualize it to be accessible to large groups within the organization, so that the decision will not be based on gut feelings or raw estimates.

Moving from a culture in which gut-feeling decisions or raw estimates are acceptable to a culture that truly incorporates Big Data is challenging. So, what is required to move from a product-centric organization to an information-centric organization, one in which decisions are based on hard data and extensive analyses? Where do you start? How do you convince your CEO, and which questions do you need to ask?

Many organizations have already successfully adjusted to the new Big Data reality. At Walmart, local stores are allowed to adjust their product assortment to match what local people are saying on social networks.[6] The Dutch SatNav company TomTom takes Big Data to the extreme by capturing 5.5 billion new global position measurements daily to improve its products.

TOMTOM AND BIG DATA

TomTom is a Dutch manufacturer of automotive navigation systems that was founded in 1991.[7] Apart from stand-alone units for cars, the company also develops mobile navigation apps and business solutions. On June 11, 2012, at a product launch of iOS 6, it was announced that TomTom would be the main mapping provider for Apple's new Maps app.[8,9] In 2012, TomTom's revenue was over $ 1 billion, and the company is massively into Big Data.[10]

On an average day, TomTom receives approximately 5.5 billion anonymous global positioning measurements from all its products. These include TomTom Home, the mobile app, In-Dash Navigation, Business Solutions, and Connected PND, which are used by over 60 million customers worldwide.[11–15]

In addition, TomTom has developed the community MapShare, which makes it possible for users of TomTom products to report changes on the roads as they are driving. These can be different speed limits, new street names, blocked roads, and new and altered traffic directions.[16] The collection of this crowd sourced data began in 2005.

TomTom does not only ask users to report traffic information, it also collects trip information from TomTom SatNav. Every time users docked their SatNav, their anonymized information was sent to TomTom. This allowed the company to collect 5,000 billion (5,000,000,000,000) items of trip data. Big Data at TomTom is seriously big business.

Map Speeds Versus Actual Speeds

All the data that TomTom collects is used to provide an actual up-to-date picture of local traffic. First, because of the massive amounts of data points received each day, TomTom can show the differences between map speed and actual speed, that is, the maximum speed allowed on a certain road versus the actual speed of people driving on that road. Quite often, the two are different.

This same information is used to determine how long it will take to drive from point A to point B. This information is very relevant, especially in The Netherlands where traffic jams are also monitored by the duration of a delay in addition to the length of a traffic jam. TomTom can measure the duration of a traffic jam by monitoring the GPS speed of drivers on the road. Of course, this also requires massive amounts of data.

Selling Location Data

The collected data was not always used in favor of drivers. In The Netherlands, TomTom sold the speed data captured by its SatNav's to the local police for a short period of time.[17] The police used this information to determine the location and frequency of speed traps, but the policy ended after complaints by Dutch citizens.

Open Map Data

In 2012, TomTom announced its latest endeavor in using crowd data to improve its products.[18] The company made its vast mapping data available to app developers, thereby providing an alternative to companies that now use maps from, for example, Google. The software is free for a trail period, but then a fee will be charged.

Taking Big Data to the Extreme

TomTom has been capturing incredibly vast amounts of data for a long time now. All this data is used to improve in real-time the driving experiences of its customers.

KEY CHARACTERISTICS OF INFORMATION-CENTRIC ORGANIZATIONS

Information-centric organizations know that data alone is useless. It becomes valuable through careful analysis by the right algorithms to retrieve the information necessary to make the correct business decisions. Companies with a successful Big Data strategy have an information-centric culture, in which all employees are fully aware that well-analyzed and visualized information results in better decisions. They have made the information available to anyone (of course, which data is made accessible depends on the job title of the employee), everywhere and at any moment. A good example is US Xpress, where all truckers have all information needed at their fingertips via iPads while on the road. The entire organization revolves around the use of information to make the correct (business) decisions.

Information-centric organizations also stay ahead of the pack through innovation, which allows them to constantly reinvent themself. These organizations are doing everything to lead the market. Because they are innovators and early adopters of new technologies, they have already implemented a Big Data strategy. Big Data timing is important, as in 5 to 10 years, it will be a commodity. It will no longer be called Big Data; it will just be data again.

Another strong characteristic of Big Data organizations is that they collect information about absolutely everything: social media data, log data, sensor data, and so on. So, store it now, and decide later if you need it. You can always decide to leave data out of your analysis, but you cannot analyze data you don't have. The price of storage should not be a barrier, as with Hadoop you can use commodity hardware to store unstructured and semistructured data in a raw format. Compressing data can even save a lot of storage. Store the data in a centralized location to prevent a balkanized IT infrastructure. Data that resides in silos across the organization is useless, as it cannot be combined easily in real time with other datasets. It is difficult to access and does not give the organization a helicopter overview of what sort of data is available.

Obviously, information-centric organizations collect a lot of data —and many different types. Apart from common data streams, such as social media, CRM, websites, and logs, these organizations ensure that many of the products they offer can also collect data. For online products, this is easier to achieve, but more and more offline products can collect massive amounts of data as well. Automotive companies, for example, can include hundreds of sensors in their cars to monitor how they are doing and plan maintenance checks before the car breaks down. And, then there is John Deere, which equips its tractors with intelligent sensors to monitor the machine's operations, as well as ground and crop constituents.[19] The more data that is collected, the better your Big Data strategy works. It does require out-of-the box thinking to find data in new products. As discussed in Chapter 2, theoretically it is possible to even turn a cup of coffee into data. So, think out of the box when finding data within your organization.

Analyzing data can be a difficult task when you have terabytes of different types of data. Although many Big Data startups claim that their products do not require an expensive IT department (Big Data Scientists are scarce and, thus, expensive), organizations implementing a Big Data strategy should at least train their IT staff to be able to deal with Big Data and perform at minimum basic analysis. Larger organization, of course, should focus on hiring Big Data employees. LinkedIn for example, has over 100 data scientists on its payroll.

Similarly, many of the 10,000 in-sourced IT staff at General Motors are capable of performing Big Data analyses. A well-trained data scientist can help you figure out the right questions you need to ask to get the right answers to take advantage of all the data available. Be sure to treat them well, because they are scarce and in high demand.

SOME GENERIC BIG DATA USES

Big Data has the potential to benefit organizations in any industry in any location across the globe. Big Data is much more than just a lot of data, and combining different data sets will provide organizations with real insights that can be used in decision-making and to improve the financial position of the company. Of course, for each industry and each individual type of organization, the possible uses will differ. There are however, a few generic Big Data uses that show the possibilities it has for your organization. In Chapter 7, I will discuss different industries in more detail, including some examples.

1. **Truly get to know your customers, all of them in real time.**

    In the past, we used focus groups and questionnaires to identify customers. This information was outdated the moment the results came in. With Big Data, this is no longer true. Big Data allows companies to completely map the DNA of their customers. Knowing your customer well is the key to selling to them effectively, but implement these strategies carefully so as not to cause privacy issues. A famous example of this is when Target found out about a teenager's pregnancy before her father even knew. The daughter received advertising for pregnancy products, which outraged the father. Later, they learned that Target knew this private information by analyzing which products the 16-year-old teenager bought at the local Target store.[20]

    If companies ensure that the privacy of customers is not threatened, Big Data can deliver personalized insights. Using interconnected social media data, mobile data, web and other Big Data analytics, it is possible to identify each customer, as well as what he or she wants and when, all in real time. Big Data enables a complete 360-degree view of all your customers, even if you have millions of them.

The benefits of such knowledge are that you can tailor recommendations or advertising to individual needs. Amazon has mastered this to perfection, as its recommendation engine determines what products a user has bought in the past, which items users have in their virtual shopping carts, which items they've rated and how, and what other customers with similar profiles have viewed and purchased.[21] Amazon's algorithm gives each customer a different webpage. And, this strategy pays off. The company reported a 27 percent sales growth to $13.18 billion during its third fiscal quarter in 2012, up from $9.6 billion during the same time in 2011.[22]

2. Co-create, improve, and innovate your products in real time.

In the past, consumer panels discussed what they thought, what they wanted, and why they wanted it. Companies also used panels to show consumers new products and find out what they thought of them. If they did not like a product, companies could potentially have to start all over again. With Big Data, such panels belong to the past.

Big Data analytics can help organizations gain a better understanding of what customers think of their products or services. What people say about a product on social media and blogs can give more information than a traditional questionnaire. If it is measured in real time, companies can act immediately. Not only can the reaction to products be measured, but also how that reaction differs among different demographic groups or people in different geographical locations or people expressing views at different times.

Big Data also allows companies to run thousands of real-time simulations to test a new or improved product virtually. By combining scalable computing power with simulation algorithms, thousands of different variations can run and be tested simultaneously. The simulation program can combine all the minor improvement tweaks into one product.

3. Determine how much risk your organization faces.

Determining risk is an important aspect of today's business. To define the potential risk of a customer or supplier, a detailed profile is created and placed in specific categories, each with its own risk levels. Currently, this process is often too broad and vague to be helpful. Often, a customer or supplier is placed in a wrong category and thereby receives an incorrect risk profile. A risk profile that is too high may not be that harmful, although income will be lost, but a risk profile that is too low could seriously damage an organization. With Big Data, it is possible to determine the proper risk category for each individual customer or supplier based on all of their data from the past and present in real time.

Especially in the insurance business, predictive analyses are used to determine how much money a customer will cost a company in the future. Insurers want to identify the right customer for the right product at the right price and lowest risk in order to ensure reducing claim costs and fraud. Using Big Data techniques, such as pattern recognition, regression analysis, text analysis, social data aggregation, and sentiment analysis (via natural language processing or monitoring social media), a 360-degree view of a potential customer is formed. This complete and up-to-date representation of a customer can lower risk significantly. Such an analysis can, of course, also be used to determine the potential risk of a new or existing supplier. For many financial institutions, this is a top priority in the coming years.[23]

4. **Personalize your website and pricing in real time toward individual customers.**

Companies have used split tests and A/B tests for some years now to define the best layout for their customers in real time. With Big Data, this process will change forever. Many different web metrics can be analyzed constantly and in real time, as well as combined for additional results. This will allow companies to have a fluid system, in which the look, feel, and layout changes reflect multiple influencing factors. It will be possible to give each visitor a website especially tailored to his or her wishes and needs at that exact moment. A returning customer might see a different webpage a week or month later if his or her personal needs changed.

Big Data can also affect prices. Yield management in ecommerce could potentially take on a whole new meaning. Orbitz experimented with this by showing Apple users more expensive hotels than PC users.[24] Orbitz had learned that Mac users spend $20 to $30 more a night on hotels on average than PC users.

Algorithms make it possible to react to events in the market or actions of competitors in real time and adjust prices accordingly. Companies that started using Big Data to personalize online offering toward individual needs are enjoying an increase in sales and profits.

5. **Improve your service support for your customers.**

With Big Data it is possible to monitor machines from a (great) distance and check on how they are performing. Using telematics, each part of a machine can be monitored in real time. Data will be sent to the manufacturer and stored for real-time analysis. Each vibration, noise, or error is detected automatically and, when the algorithm detects a deviation from the normal operation, service support can be alerted. The machine can even automatically schedule maintenance for a time when the machine is not in use. When the engineer comes to fix the machine, he or she will know exactly what to do because all the information is available. A good example is the construction company Nick Savko & Sons, Inc., a Columbus, Ohio, site-development company, that already uses telematics to improve the efficiency of its operations.[25] It uses GPS devices to monitor data, such as idle time, cycle times, productivity, and more. These devices were installed on the equipment required to complete work on the SX Railroad's $175-million transshipping terminal. All information could be monitored from a distance; it allowed the company to complete the project a month ahead of schedule.

6. **Find new markets and new business opportunities by combining your own with public data.**

Governments around the world are making their datasets public in an effort to stimulate innovation. In 2011, the European Union organized the Open Data Challenge,[26] which was Europe's biggest open data competition to stimulate startups to devise innovative solutions using the massive amounts of open data generated by governments. For example, the Dutch government focuses actively on stimulating the reuse of open cultural datasets and organizes hackathons to come up with new solutions.[27,28] By combining various datasets, companies can give new meanings to existing data and find new markets, target groups, or business opportunities.

Companies can also discover unmet customer desires. By doing pattern and/or regression analysis on your data, you might find needs and wishes of customers of which you were previously unaware. Big Data can also show companies where to market a product first or where to place a product. Vestas Wind Systems, a Danish energy company, used Big Data and analytics to select the best locations for wind turbines.[29] With that information, the company was able to harvest the most energy at the lowest costs.

7. **Better understand your competitors and, more importantly, stay ahead of them.**

What you can do for your own organization can also be done, more or less, for your competitors. Big Data will help organizations better understand their competition and where they stand relative to each other. It can provide a valuable head start. Using Big Data analytics, algorithms can determine if, for example, your competitor changes its pricing. You can then automatically adjust your prices as well. Organizations can also monitor the actions of the competition, such as following new products or promotions (and how the market responds to them). It can also track how the response changes over time. Remember that much that is done by you or your competitors is available as open data.

8. **Organize your company more effectively, and save money.**

By analyzing all the data in your organization, you may find areas that can be improved and better organized. For example, the logistics industry in particular can become more efficient by using the new Big Data source available in the supply chain or during transportation. Electronic on-board recorders in trucks can tell how fast they are driving, where they are driving, and so on. Sensors and RFID tags in trailers and distribution help on-load and off-load trucks more efficiently. In addition, combining information about road, traffic, and weather with the locations of clients can save substantial time and money.

Of course, these generic uses are just a small indication of the massive possibilities of Big Data, but it shows that Big Data provides endless opportunities to add business value and help you stand out from your competition. Each organization has different needs and will require a specific Big Data approach.

NIKE'S OPTIMIZED SUPPLY CHAIN

Nike wanted to understand the footprint of all materials used in its products. The company had no information about the 57,000 different materials used because the materials came from vendors two-to-three steps removed.

To gain insights, the company collected and performed a life-cycle analysis on all data related to those materials. This information was placed into a central database that has helped its 600 designers make much smarter decisions. As a result, business, sustainability, quality, and cost were affected.

Then, Nike took a remarkable step. It decided to share that data with the rest of the industry, so that all companies could populate the database and use it to make better decisions. The objective is to build a "vendor index" that contains details concerning every supplier, including ratings and trustworthiness.[30] The key is to turn Big Data into smart data at the point where the people in the supply chain who need to use it can actually have access to it. This is a great example of how opening up datasets can bring additional value to the entire supply chain.

For a company as large as Nike, it is, of course, difficult to move to an information-centric organization at once. As with any company that starts to build a Big Data strategy, Nike had to deal with different silos across the organization that contained valuable information. However, to use the data effectively, it had to be identified and aggregated. According to Hannah Jones, VP of Sustainable Business and Insights at Nike, "Innovation lurks in the shadows of silos."[31] Therefore, Nike started to remove the silos between the data and then identified the key performance indicator and key data needed from across the entire company. From that point forward, the company was able to create a platform that was truly valuable to Nike and its related companies.

BIG DATA AND RETURN ON INVESTMENT (ROI)

Understanding that Big Data offers a lot of value is an important starting point. However, as is common in almost any organization around the world, Big Data, like every new technology, needs to be sold to (senior) management in order to be executed. As with every other technology, management needs to understand what the return on the investment will be. Many organizations believe that a Big Data strategy requires a big investment with no guarantee on the usefulness of the results. As discussed in Chapter 4, this is not the case Although McKinsey reported that companies using Big Data can increase their operating margin by 60 percent and reduce expenditures by 8 percent, a lot of executives are reluctant to go ahead with Big Data because of the uncertainties.[32]

On the other hand, a 2013 study by Wikibon Consulting Group showed that an unfortunate 2 percent of the companies researched declared their Big Data deployments total failures, with no value achieved. The reasons for failure were, according to the research, a lack of skilled Big Data practitioners, immature technology, and a lack of a compelling business use. In order to ensure that this does not happen to your Big Data project, I will discuss a roadmap for a successful implementation of a Big Data strategy later in this chapter.[33]

As with any other new strategy; Big Data will affect the organization in unpredictable ways, and it will cost money to implement. How can an organization know what the return will be and how much budget should be allocated to developing Big Data? A 2012 research by the Columbia Business School and the New York American Marketing Association showed that a staggering 57 percent of marketing budgets are based on past budgets and not on the ROI of marketing efforts.[34] Results from the past are no guarantee of success for the future, so why would you use previous budgets to determine the investment for next year? Further, past budgets do not exist for Big Data in most companies.

The main cost involved in establishing a Big Data strategy is the operation and overall management (or integration) of Big Data into the organization. Good Big Data Scientists are as expensive as they are rare, and managing thousands of nodes within a data grid requires great skill. Luckily, there are Big Data startups that have developed efficient algorithms and/or data-as-a-platform solutions that provide all that is necessary to start with Big Data. Most have a transparent pricing plan that gives some insights into the expected costs.

However, determining the ROI will remain difficult, especially since no existing IT ROI models can be used. Traditional IT ROI models are based on elements, such as speed per transaction, energy saving from data centers, or minimizing data center equipment.[35] Big Data does not work on a speed-per-transaction basis. Often, what can be expected from the analysis remains completely unknown until it is done, thereby making traditional models useless. To develop a Big Data ROI, companies will have to start with the following steps.

1. Understand why you want to use Big Data and for what reason. Then, set your desired Big Data objective. For example, your objective might be a better understanding of your customers that will allow you to give them a better experience. In fact, 86 percent of people are willing to pay more for a great customer experience with a brand.[36] Selecting the right objective can therefore help determine the ROI.
2. Select the tools needed to meet your objectives. Different Big Data startups offer different solutions at different prices. Open source tools are free, but most of the time they offer a commercial support plan to help you implement the tool. Depending on the tool selected, commodity hardware or a cloud date storage solution may need to be bought. This gives some insight into the costs involved.
3. Start with a pilot project that will achieve your objectives on a smaller scale. The investments needed are quite often less problematic for CFOs to make available. The costs and returns will give far more valuable insight into the ROI than benchmarks or pre-Big-Data-era figures.

If implemented correctly, for sure, Big Data will bring value to your organization. Value can be in the form of faster time bringing a product to market because you know exactly what customers want and what their buying patterns are (perhaps before they even know). Big Data can also help you learn what your competition is doing or provide a better understanding of where the market is heading. Big Data can also offer efficient resource utilization. The amount of the ROI depends on the objectives set, the size of the organization, the (open source) tools selected, the hardware chosen, and the processes implemented. Many variables affect Big Data ROI. If chosen wisely, Big Data will result in a positive ROI and setting up a pilot project can give you the valuable insights needed.

BIG DATA ON THE BALANCE SHEET

At one time, IT was about saving money. In contrast, Big Data is about making money and creating value. As such, it could be placed on the company's balance sheet. A 2012 study by SAS showed that approximately 20 percent of large companies in the United Kingdom are already assigning financial value to their data on their balance sheets, so it is clear that more companies are beginning to understand and appreciate the value of data.[37] So, how should organizations proceed with Big Data and how should they account for it on their balance sheets?

A balance sheet shows the financial status of an enterprise at a given point in time, that is, its assets and liabilities. Assets can be tangible (e.g., machines and hardware) or intangible (e.g., trademarks, copyrights, and algorithms). Liabilities are all legal debts or obligations that arise during the course of business operations, such as loans and accounts payable.

Intangible assets can include data as well. In fact, AT&T valued data such as customer lists and relationships in 2011 at $2.7 billion on its balance sheet.[38] If such data can be included, why not the derived value of data, Big Data, or information as an asset?

However, data can become a liability if poorly managed or secured. A good example is the Dutch data security firm Diginotar, which went bankrupt because its data was not correctly secured.[39] As a result, the company was hacked. It is an extreme example, but it shows that the security of Big Data is of major importance and one that can be a liability if not properly protected.

Let's assume Big Data is an asset for a company. In fact, often people say "information is our greatest asset." David Rajan, Director of Technology for Oracle, found that 77 per cent of CIOs thought data should appear on the balance sheet as a key metric to define the value of a business.[40]

If that's the case, how do you value Big Data within an organization? Determining the cost of Big Data is at least easier: "simply" total how much it costs to create, update, store, retrieve, archive, and dispose of data. However, determining the ROI on Big Data projects is a lot more difficult, because of the many uncertainties.

The term Return on Data is a metric that defines the value of Big Data within an organization. Better usage of data could lead to more knowledge about your customer, which could lead to better products delivered in a shorter time span, which could lead to an increase in customer lifetime value (CLV). The difference between predicted CLV and current CLV could be the value of Big Data. When the purpose is to reduce fuel consumption within transport organizations, the return on data can be the amount of fuel saved annually less the costs required to install all the Big Data technology.

Formally putting Big Data on a company's balance sheet is a big decision that should be well founded. An advantage of placing Big Data on your balance sheet is that it would drive better control and governance of that data. Putting it on the balance sheet would therefore make people aware of the presence and value of data within an organization. This could lead to better use of it and could spur acceptance of Big Data as a strategy within organizations.

INTERNAL BIG DATA OPPORTUNITIES

Big Data affects all industries, but how does it affect different departments within an organization? Obviously, it has a positive affect on marketing, particularly in developing PR campaigns and Customer Relationship Management (CRM). But, Big Data also affects how the Human Resources department is managed. In addition, many organizations have legacy systems that contain a lot of usable and needed data. Not using that data would be like solving a puzzle with a few pieces missing; the picture is not complete.

Big Data and Its Impact on Customer Relationship Management

CRM is defined as a company's interaction with existing and future customers. It consists of all customer contact moments combined and is analyzed to provide better service. CRM has always involved collecting data, but most of it used to be structured data, such as contact information, most recent point of contact, products bought, and so on. With Big Data techniques, it is feasible to process, store, and analyze massive amounts of unstructured data not supplied directly by the customer and to use this to gain additional insights into customer behavior. With Big Data technologies, CRM can become a true revenue driver.

Previously, CRM systems usually failed to meet expectations, because they only managed the customer relationship.[41] Big Data CRM goes a lot further; it is all about serving the customer. By using Big Data, companies should be able to successfully resolve the problems with most standard CRM programs. Note that:

- A CRM system in place is only one part of the deal. The second is that employees need to be encouraged to use it effectively. As Big Data should be part of a complete cultural change within the organization, this problem should be solved.
- The lack of clear (technical) objectives leads to a poor system and incorrect collection and storing of data. Big Data requires strict guidelines and processes for storing and using data to guarantee that it is all compatible.

A few steps are necessary when implementing a Big Data CRM program. Let's look at what serving the customer from a Big Data viewpoint actually means. Serving the customer effectively will yield better results, but it requires a lot more than just managing the relationship. Four important phases of Big Data CRM create a complete circle of customer service: managing the relationship, interacting with the customer, analyzing customer touch points, and truly getting to know the customer (see Figure 6-1).

- **Managing** the customer with structured data, such as contact information, address, and latest contacts is one part. This is mainly

Figure 6-1 Big Data CRM Phases

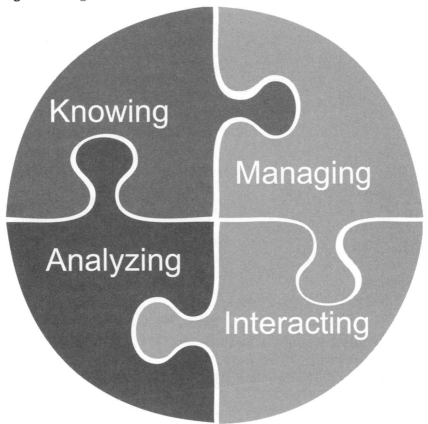

an inside-out approach, in which the company "manages" the customer by sending messages and storing rudimentary information. This is done with predefined channels at set business hours. It is a company-defined process performed by designated departments without a lot of flexibility. Nonetheless, it is an important starting point.

• **Interacting** with the customer using unstructured data, such as emails, tweets, Facebook posts, comments, and so on, is customer driven or an outside-in approach. This is a two-way communication process. The customer determines when to establish contact with the organization and expects to receive a quick response, even outside of traditional business hours. Everyone in the company should be included in such interactions.

- **Analyzing** the customers' activities with structured data, such as online visits, clicks, bounce rates, and so on, is a company-driven process, performed primarily by web analysts who complete an action when asked for an insight or deliver standardized reports to marketers on a regular basis. Big Data techniques will significantly change the role of the analyst, as he or she will be required to deliver results more proactively on a regular, preferably real-time, basis about more topics.

- **Knowing** the customer is where it really becomes fascinating. Big Data Scientists use unstructured and structured data to build algorithms that can perform extensive analyses on the data, allowing the organization to know each customer individually on a real-time basis. They can deliver predictive models to develop/deliver products truly needed by the customer, resulting in an increased conversion rate and more satisfied customers.

BIG DATA ENABLES THE INTERCONTINENTAL HOTEL GROUP TO BECOME A SERVICE-ORIENTED AND DATA-DRIVEN ORGANIZATION

With 4,602 hotels containing 675,982 rooms around the world in 2013, the InterContinental Hotel Group (IHG) is collecting massive amounts of data across its brands.[42,43] For the last few years, IHG has embraced the use of advanced analytics. The company moved from a structured dataset with approximately 50 variables to a Big Data solution that analyzes both unstructured and structured data in real time. Today, the company uses up to 650 variables from different sources to gather information about its hotels, competitors, and guests, as well as other internal and external data.

IHG has become a truly data-driven organization. As a result, employees make better decisions. Not surprisingly, reservations reach 150 million room nights each year. Each reservation requires and creates a lot of data, including the channel of the reservation, time of booking, location, and information about the guests. Further, IHG uses the data from its loyalty program, Priority Club Rewards, to create a better experience for guests.[44] Thus, the 71 million customers who are part of the world's largest hotel loyalty program, including alliances with 45 airlines, drive a lot of data.[45]

To streamline all data from the reservation system and the loyalty program, IHG decided to rebuild its reservation system a few years back.[46] The new system operates in multiple languages and provides real-time access to the loyalty program. It uses a service-oriented architecture based on open standards to ensure easy integration with existing business processes and make it scalable for future needs. Today, IHG can personalize each web experience for each guest, ensuring high conversion rates and driving growth in its own booking channel.

To ensure satisfaction, IHG also surveys guests on a wide range of topics and combines the answers with industry performance and economic data to help benchmark how well the company is doing. This helps IHG understand all external factors that influence performance. The chain also collects a lot of general metadata about its hotels and staff, such as the number of hotel rooms, the age of a property, available amenities, location, and tenure and experience of the staff, but the company also amasses less expected data, such as local demand drivers and the density of nearby competition.

All data is analyzed in real time and used to evaluate execution of marketing plans on a daily basis. Because of all this available data, IHG is able to make better decisions, especially in times of economic downturn. As Manish Shah, Director of Marketing Strategy and Analytics for IHG in the Americas, explains "[we] have re-evaluated the marketing mix and adjusted spending to better suit the business' needs in the current economy."[47,48] IHG uses several types of analyses to evaluate and sift through the massive amounts of datasets:

- Operational analytics are used to provide clear reporting to stakeholders within the organization on a tactical and operational level so they can make better decisions.

- Regression and correlation analyses discover patterns in the data, show where trends are going, and indicate which trends should be followed.
- Predictive analytics are used to predict guests' purchasing and stay behaviors in the different online and mobile channels.

IHG's main goal is to use Big Data to create a company-wide view of data that can be analyzed using robust analytics so that key insights are identified and can be used to make better decisions. Using all this data, IHG can take a deep dive into the analytics of its particular brand in any one country to see what really drives the top-line performance for that hotel. It can go even further and use the insights to segment hotels across the group into clusters with common interests, regardless of the brand. Within these clusters, predictive analytics can help determine what drives each cluster.

David Schmitt, Director of Performance Strategy and Planning, offers three lessons he has learned over the years, as IHG moved to a data-driven organization.[49,50] They are:

1. Create demand from the bottom-up with a small test case. Success stories will spread and make the entire organization smarter. Starting big is very difficult.
2. Perfection is unachievable, so don't wait for the next best tool to arrive. It is impossible to create the perfect dataset or the perfect model. New models and tools constantly appear on the market that can result in improvements, but waiting for such models will result in inertia. Start with the data you have, and move on from there.
3. You need to tell a story, as most managers do not care about technical details and the math behind the models; they just want it to work. Visualizing the story is very important, and IHG uses visualizations to tell a story rather than dive into the technical details.

Service-oriented, data-driven organizations, such as IHG, are great examples of how Big Data is helping industries become better and more efficient, while improving customer experiences. All organizations can learn from these examples and should work toward an information-centric organization as well.

When combined, all aspects of Big Data bring real value to an organization and take traditional CRM to a higher level. Organizations can use Big Data tools and techniques to process massive data streams that will flow into the organization. With the right algorithms, it is possible to perform the following analyses to deliver better service to the customers:

- **Pattern analysis** uncovers new patterns within a dataset or a combination of datasets. These can be structured data (rows of sequential demographic data) or unstructured data (tweets about products).
- **Sentiment analysis** discovers what customers are saying about your products/service. It can help address issues before they become too widespread and can help to improve service.
- **Marketing analysis** analyzes customer interactions not only with your organization but with each other to optimize marketing decisions and messages.
- **Recommendation analysis** gives the best recommendation to your customers to increase the conversion rate. The better the recommendation fits with the needs of the customer, the higher the conversion rate.
- **Influence analysis** determines which of your customers has the most influence over other customers. Knowing who influences whom will give organizations a big advantage and help better serve your customers.

Collecting, processing, and storing the correct data are only part of a truly valuable Big Data CRM program. Analyzing with the right tools to achieve valuable insights is another. To really have a CRM program that increases customer satisfaction, the organization must become information-centric.

It is no longer acceptable not to know your customer. Consumers who contact organizations through whatever channel want to be recognized and served appropriately. Using Big Data technologies to collect, store, and analyze the necessary data will truly make your CRM manageable and valuable, thereby giving your organization a competitive advantage.

Big Data and Its Impact on Public Relations Campaigns

Public Relations (PR) entails managing the spread of information between an organization and the public. As all of that information is data, it can be analyzed and used to improve PR activities. Enter the world of Big Data and that information can be turned into valuable insights. PR is all about getting the stakeholders to maintain a certain point of view about the organization. With Big Data, it is possible to understand what that point of view is, how it changes over time, what it takes to improve it, and what the effects are of PR activities.

Big Data can affect PR in several ways. Big Data delivers insights about the stakeholders, including who they are, what their beliefs are, and where they are from. This information can be used to develop a message tailored to the characteristics of individual stakeholders. One of the stakeholders should be the influencer. Companies need to identify the influencers: Who are they, where are they from, and how can they be influenced positively? However, in the world of social media, any customer can ultimately become an influencer. Big Data determines the sentiment among customers and how it changes over time in relation to activities done. Companies that have a 360-degree overview of its customers will be able to profile customers correctly and reach them with the right message to influence their sentiments. In addition, Big Data can provide the information and numbers needed to develop a PR story that resonates with the stakeholders. Finally, Big Data can save your organization in times of crisis. Let's discuss each of these groups one by one.

The Influencers

Influencers are people who have a large network and are therefore able to spread a message widely and quickly. Influencers can help the organization if you know where to find them and how to approach them. As Michael Wu, Lithium's Principal Scientist of Analytics, described, six types of data can be used to find the influencers:[51]

1. **Involvement velocity data:** How often someone shares information via the social networks, or the number of tweets or blog posts

on a certain topic. This tells you how involved the customer is in your company.

2. **Social equity data:** The number of followers someone has on a social network or the number of unique visitors to a blog.

3. **Citation data:** How often do others cite someone in tweets, comments, or posts. The more someone is cited, the higher his or her credibility.

4. **Status data:** Says something, but not everything, about someone's credibility.

5. **Self-proclaimed data:** The data someone posts about himself or herself, for example, on LinkedIn. However, as the influencer posts the information, it is less reliable.

6. **Social graph data:** The relationships of the influencers and how the network of the influencer is constructed.

With Big Data technologies, the above information can be aggregated, stored, analyzed, and visualized to find the list of top influencers for the organization. Once the influencers are identified, it is important to understand what they are saying and how they can be influenced positively.[52]

Customers

The top influencers can help spread your message. Knowledge about your customers will help you construct the right message for the right target group at the right moment. With Big Data, it is possible to understand who your customers are and how each customer group should be approached. When different sources of data, such as loyalty programs, CRM systems, reviews, and social media are connected with each other, a true 360-degree customer overview will be become apparent. This valuable information can help create a message that charms customers.

Tailored Stories with High Stickiness Factor

Understanding what information is best suited for which (potential) customers or influencers is only one aspect of the PR story. Great PR campaigns have two things in common: a high likeability and stickiness factor and the ability to go viral on the Internet. Although many people or companies claim to have the recipe for the perfect PR campaign, developing a viral PR campaign is difficult. Big Data however can make that process slightly easier. Combining public and social data of people who see the campaign can turn a PR campaign in a very personal, and potentially fun, message that is likely to be shared across social networks. Data technologies enable you to find the right persons —the persons whose public and social data in real time will help you to create a tailored message that sticks.

Visualize the Message

Visualizing datasets or combinations of datasets into rich graphs or infographics can help explain a story clearly and spread information about a product or service. Infographics, in particular, are great narrative tools that include data that impacts your organization.

Fine Tune the Communication over Time

Successful PR campaigns should be continuously observed and tweaked. Tracking how campaigns develop is important if your organization is to learn what does and what does not work, as well as for whom it works. Big Data can assist in providing real-time insights from around the world about how the PR campaign is perceived, what the online sentiment is, and what people are saying about it. A company that receives the analyzed data in real time has the opportunity to adjust quickly if necessary.

Save Your Organization in Times of Crisis

With Big Data tools, it will be feasible to know instantly when a crisis is about to hit the company. With the right predictive algorithms, it will even be possible to anticipate a crisis before it happens. Algorithms can analyze all the data that flows in and out of the company. It can also analyze all relevant internal and external data and determine when negative messages are being spread, where they are being spread, and about what topic. Your objective is to find these negative messages before they reach the mass public and have the potential to go viral.

If a crisis hits your organization, Big Data can help your PR department by providing valuable insights that can limit the effects of the crisis. This is true not only for businesses, but also for disaster relief. Big Data came in handy after Hurricane Sandy in New York, as it was able to identify citizens most in need of food packages and other supplies. Jim Delaney, COO of Marketwire, gives the example how the app Waze, the community-driven app that learns from users' driving mannerisms to provide routing and real-time traffic updates, helped during that disaster: "The Federal Emergency Management Association (FEMA) and the White House called upon Waze to determine where to send gasoline trucks in New Jersey."[53] And, "Based upon the data they found on Waze, FEMA and the White House informed the public which gas stations had fuel during the gas shortages and power outages."

Measuring the Big Data Results

Defining KPIs in the Big Data era is possible, but it depends on what you want to achieve. Do you want to improve sentiment? Do you want to involve your customers, or do you want to increase customer satisfaction? PR in the world of Big Data is about (online) reach and sentiment and bringing the right message to the right person at the right time. With the right Big Data technologies, it is possible to analyze your actions in real time, adjust if necessary, and then improve the results before the PR campaign is over.

Big Data and Its Impact on Human Resources

Big Data impacts how we live, how we work, and consequently how we work together. Therefore, Big Data should be on the agenda of the Human Resources (HR) Manager. When HR applies Big Data properly, it can improve employee productivity, decrease costs, and increase incomes. With Big Data, organizations can create better and happier employees.

Analyze Workplace Behavior

First of all, Big Data can help companies better understand workplace behavior. Sensors installed on office furniture can give insights into how meeting rooms are used by how many employees for how long and when.[54] It can provide information about how often employees are away from their desks, how long meetings take, and who meets with whom. Collecting this data and combining it with other data sources, such as who works with whom, who emails whom, and who has what knowledge, can spur collaboration and increase efficiency. The data can help design offices and place employees who deal with each other frequently closer together.

Research at a tech company has revealed that large lunch tables that can seat up to 12 people result in increased productivity because of the greater social interaction.[55] Another company, Cubist Pharmaceuticals, used data to reveal it had too many coffee machines. By reducing the number of coffee machines and creating centralized coffee spots, the company increased serendipitous interactions among employees.[56,57] When employees feel they are more efficient and have more interactions with others, they are likely to be happier at work. Happier employees work harder and, therefore, it is wise to use Big Data to design the office in the best way possible.

The Available Information

Big Data can also reveal the type of information available within the organization. There are tools available in the market that can scan and analyze all documents, emails, phone calls, chat messages, intranet data, and other communications to understand who possesses what information. These tools can reveal which employee is an expert on what topic and which information is lacking. Even more, it can provide insights into what information is about to be lost—if, for example, the one employee with specific knowledge about a certain topic is about to retire.

The data can also reveal which people within an organization do not have that much knowledge but can be regarded as networkers. These "connectors," as Malcolm Gladwell called them in *Tipping Point,* are very important within an organization, as they bring people together.[58] Losing a connector to a competitor can do serious harm to an organization, so it is wise to know who these employees are within the organization.

In addition, if employees can simply question the Intranet when they need information about a certain topic, Big Data can bring them in contact faster with the right person across your organization, anywhere in the world. The available knowledge becomes visible to everyone rather than remaining in silos.

Hiring New Employees

Knowing what knowledge is present also reveals what knowledge is missing. Such information can help HR find the right employees for the right job.[59] Even more, Big Data can also help evaluate job applicants. Tools can automatically scan résumés and social public data of applicants and score how well each applicant matches the job requirements. In addition, Big Data provides even more information during online assessments. The way an applicant answers questions, how long he or she takes per question, how many resources he or she uses, in which order the questions are answered, and so on, can provide more information about the applicant's behavior than the answers to the questions themselves. Test scores and college grade-point averages only say a little bit about the potential of an applicant. How he or she works is more important.

CATALYST IT SERVICES HIRES BIG DATA TO DO THE JOB

Catalyst IT Services is a technology outsourcing company in Baltimore that has screened more than 10,000 candidates.[60] Screening by hand would have been a daunting process requiring many employees and costing a lot of money. The founder of Catalyst IT Services, Michael Rosenbaum, came up with a major plan to change the traditionally slow process of recruiting.[61] Using technology and algorithms, the company built a program that screens applicant based on how an obligatory survey is completed. By successfully implementing a Big Data hiring strategy, the company managed to reduce employee turnover to 15 percent, compared to 30 percent for its U.S. competitors.[62]

Using Big Data, the process of hiring the right candidate for the right job has been much improved. Previously, the subjective opinions of hiring managers could result in the right person ending up in the wrong job. The data-crunching process now in place was developed around an online assessment that candidates need to complete. During the process of completing the assessment, the software gathers thousands of bits of job applicant data. This data about how a candidate completes the assessment is often more important than what the candidate actually said.

For example, someone who comes across a difficult question can immediately skip it or he/she can ponder it for a long time, going back and forth. This information tells a lot about how someone deals with challenges. One candidate might be better at assignments requiring a methodical approach, while another candidate might be better in another setting.[63] Catalyst IT Services likes to call it the "Moneyball-like model."[64] By using analytics based on data rather than personal perceptions, the company manages to recruit talent and assemble highly skilled teams that are custom tailored to its clients.

Analyzing these different attributes and matching them to specific situations can be done much better by a computer than a human, particularly because the method looks at many more variables than a human could ever do. Typically, the method looks at a couple of thousand data points,[65] such as time on a page in the assessment, keystrokes, public domain data, social network data, interaction data during the application, and résumé data. Subsequently, the algorithms will calculate a probability score of how a candidate will perform over a certain period on a certain project. Candidates who reach the threshold are interviewed. A majority of those interviewed are brought on board.

Using Big Data in the recruitment process is definitely an interesting approach, as recruitment has long been perceived as a task that could not be done by computers. Of course, Catalyst IT Services also still uses hiring managers to interview those candidates who reach above the threshold, but they have much more information at hand. Consequently, they can make a more informed decision that eventually will save money as the right person ends up in the right job.

Big Brother

There are also downsides to using Big Data within HR. One of the most important is that employees can get the feeling that their boss is watching their every move. A "Big Brother is watching feeling" among personnel can seriously upset productivity and employee happiness.

As always with Big Data, employers have to be transparent to employees about why specific data is used, analyzed, and made available internally. Employees need to shift their thinking so they understand that Big Data can help them and is not spying on them. Then again, for years, employees have needed ID badges with sensors to gain access to offices. As employees should be aware, the same technology can already be used to monitor employee behavior.

Legacy Systems and Big Data

Although 90 percent of the available data in the world was created in the last two years, there is still a lot of "old data."[66] In 2010 and 2011, we created a total of 3 zettabytes of data.[67] By using a very simple calculation, we can see that the amount of "old data'" is still approximately 0.3 zettabytes or 300 exabytes. If we compare that to the 2.5 exabytes of data that we currently create every day, it looks like it is nothing to worry about. Unfortunately, that is wrong. Those 300 exabytes of data can give us headaches and sleepless nights, while costing a lot of energy and money.

Why? Because a large proportion of those 300 exabytes reside in legacy systems that are incompatible with modern technology. Switching those systems off or simply importing the data into modern Big Data platforms is difficult. In particular, insurance companies and banks have legacy systems, some of which have been in place for decades. As a result of the many mergers and acquisitions in the finance world, banks sometimes have dozens of different legacy systems.[68] One bank even had 40 different legacy systems.[69] These aging cobbled-together legacy systems can often be found in payment and credit card systems, ATMs, and branch or channel solutions.[70] Such legacy systems cause a lot of headaches to organizations. For example, the Deutsche Bank had to postpone its Big Data plans due to its legacy systems.[71]

Not only banks have to deal with legacy systems. The car industry faces similar problems. Ford Motor Company has data centers that are running on software that is 30 or 40 years old.[72] The pharmaceutical and travel industries, as well as the public sector, also have to deal with legacy systems.[73,74] Replacing these legacy systems is almost impossible. Karl Flinders, an editor at *Computer Weekly* refers to it as "changing the engines on a Boeing 747 while in flight."[75]

Legacy systems consist of traditional, relational database management systems often on old and slow machines that are not capable of handling too much data at once. Hence, most of these systems process data at night, and it can take a lot of time to query the data required. Real-time processing and analyzing of data in legacy systems is impossible.

One of the solutions for this problem is to replace the entire legacy system of a company. Apart from the massive risks involved in such an operation, there are also significant costs involved, so it is not very likely that many organizations will adopt this strategy. However, as hard as it may seem, it is not impossible, as the Commonwealth Bank of Australia has shown. In the past five years, it has replaced the entire bank's core system, moved most of the services into the cloud, and developed many apps and innovations that brought the bank to the forefront of innovation.[76]

As such, it is imperative that a way should be found to have new innovative technologies that allow real-time analysis of various datasets coexist with legacy systems. Systems from the gigabyte or even megabyte era still contain valuable (historical) information. There are several ways to keep and use the historical data in the data warehouses.

1. Data can be macrobatched into the new Big Data solutions on a periodic timescale, for example every night. This data can then be used together with the "new" data.
2. One can send periodic summaries of the data from the legacy systems to the Big Data warehouse in order to use the data in those warehouses while preventing continuous querying of the legacy data.

Such solutions will enable the analysis of both new data and structured legacy data within a single integrated architectural framework. A platform like this will allow legacy data to remain within the existing data warehouses and, at the same time, enable near real-time analyses.

Using middleware to enhance systems and replace the hardware that supports them is, however, not ideal.[77] Another problem for the legacy systems is that a larger percentage of the IT budget will go to support Big Data projects. This will leave less money available for the legacy systems. In addition, the employees who are able to work with the legacy systems will become scarce and expensive.

If such a trend continues for a too long, there is a danger that the legacy system will fail one day, placing the company in a lot of trouble. The later organizations start to replace legacy systems—or at least try to make them compatible with Big Data technologies—the more expensive and difficult it will become.

Real transformative insights can only come when all data is used, including the data from legacy systems with incompatible data formats.[78] Therefore, eventually the data in legacy systems will need to be transferred to massively scalable storage systems, thereby replacing the critical search, calculation, and reporting functions of those legacy systems.[79]

In the end, the goal for any organization with legacy systems should be to truly retire these systems, as companies will not be able to support them forever. If, in the mean time, they simultaneously integrate legacy data in one platform to produce data aggregation, they can already reap the benefits from historical data to create valuable insights.

BIG DATA ROADMAP

The first step is knowing what Big Data is; the second is knowing how a Big Data strategy can benefit your organization; the third—and most difficult—is knowing how to implement that Big Data strategy. A lot of organizations perceive the third step as the hardest. And, in large process-directed organizations, that can be true. Therefore, convincing the board to proceed and defining where to start can be unnerving. In truth, however, the steps that need to be taken are clear and straightforward (see Figure 6-2).

First, organizations need to understand what Big Data is. Otherwise, defining a strategy is impossible. Understanding what Big Data is can help you get management buy-in within the organization. Quite often, Big Data is seen as an IT matter because, after all, you need hardware and software to implement the strategy. The hardware and software need to be developed by highly skilled technical Big Data employees.[80] These experts, especially in the beginning and when developing a solution on-premises, will form a large part of the Big Data

Figure 6-2 The Big Data Road Map

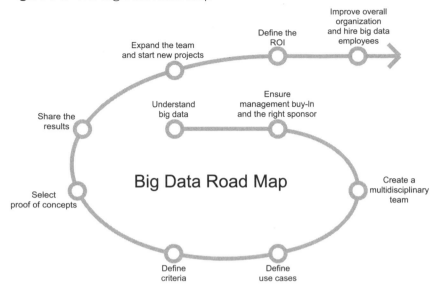

team, particularly when implementing proof of concepts and/or a Big Data strategy. There are also many blogs and events around the world targeted to the technical IT point of view that focus on Big Data engineering, architecture, and analytics. This is nothing strange, as Big Data has different IT requirements than earlier strategies. Therefore, sharing information is important and valuable.

However, we should not forget that IT is merely a means to an end to achieve a strategy defined by the organization. This strategy could be "to increase customer satisfaction" or "to increase revenue" or "to improve the operational efficiency." The route to achieve that strategy could be Big Data or any other solution. If the strategy is "to increase customer satisfaction," it would be strange to define it as an IT matter or have the IT Director be the sponsor. IT is simply too operational and supportive for it to lead or sponsor Big Data projects.

Finding a sponsor for a Big Data project is, however, vital for its success. The sponsor can be senior management or someone on the board, and he or she should be involved in and support the decision to move forward with Big Data. The reason is that starting a Big Data project is difficult and, in the beginning, the results can be uncertain.

Management buy-in ensures that the project is not stopped before any real results can be shown. The person in charge should be someone within the organization who understands all the different departments, has a helicopter view of the project, and is high enough in the company to direct and align the entire company.

Other critical requirements for a potential sponsor of Big Data projects are given below. The more of these requirements the sponsor meets, the more likely it is that the Big Data project will succeed.

- He or she must have a large network within the organization to get all different divisions aligned for the Big Data strategy.
- He or she must have some technical expertise to understand how Big Data works and how it will drive change.
- He or she must be able to identify new business opportunities based on the available data spread out in silos.
- He or she must be able to lead the team in the right direction, especially in uncertain situations.
- He or she must be able to get the necessary financial funds to start a Big Data strategy, but they also need to realize that failures in the beginning are part of the deal.

With the above list in mind, a C-level executive sponsor would be the best choice to spur the acceptance of the Big Data strategy. He or she can speed up necessary cultural change and can ensure that the four ethical guidelines are enforced. A board that is involved in a Big Data strategy can guarantee that the project will not be stopped before any real results can be shown.

Once senior management or the board approves the decision to move forward and a C-level executive sponsors the project, it is important to assemble a multidisciplinary team from all different departments within the organization that have links with the Big Data project. Data tends to be kept in silos throughout an organization. Focusing only on one part of the company could result in the omission of valuable data sources. Therefore, many departments should be included: marketing needs to be involved because of the customer point of view; product management to know how data is gathered by the products or services offered; human resources to comprehend the effect of data gathering on employees; compliance and risk to guarantee that the organization sticks to the four ethical guidelines discussed in Chapter 5; finance to keep the budget under control; and IT to build the required hardware and software.

Including all departments has a major advantage when defining the possible business use cases of Big Data. Brainstorming sessions will be more successful when people from different disciplines are involved. Each member of the multidisciplinary Big Data team should be able to offer a distinct point of view. Together, a large pool of possible uses can be defined. It is important during this phase to accept all possible ideas brought up during the sessions (as in normal brainstorming sessions, "no" and "that's not possible" do not exist). It is essential to let creativity flow, as this will allow you to find new data sources previously not considered.

Once a few dozen possible uses have been defined, it is time to develop criteria to rank them. It will help to divide the uses into different categories, such as those that fix bottlenecks within the operation or those that improve efficiency. Use criteria to rank all business use cases in the different categories. Criteria can be the impact on IT, the effect on implementing the solution, and/or a possible value proposition. It is not necessary to develop a scenario for each business use case, as there are too many unknowns at this moment.

Based on the criteria and the selected categories, it is possible to select the Proof of Concepts that will be realized. The multidisciplinary Big Data team should be able to realize the Proof of Concepts with minimal efforts. It is better to fail fast and fail often than to develop a complete solution and notice in the end that something was wrong. While Big Data has the potential to bring a lot of positive results, this may not be evident from the start. Don't be afraid to fail and restart, as it is part of the learning curve in how to deal with Big Data and to better understand how your organization can best benefit from it. For each organization, after all, the benefits will differ.

The moment the first results come in from the Proof of Concept, it is important to share them immediately with the entire organization. It will help get everyone involved in the Big Data effort, as for organizations to truly succeed with Big Data, an information-centric culture should be present. If the results of the Proof of Concepts are positive, it is time to expand the multidisciplinary Big Data team throughout the organization and to start more and larger projects. Extrapolate the lessons learned from the first projects and apply them to the new projects by better defining a possible ROI, IT impact, process implications, and other important criteria.

From there on, the entire process starts all over. Future projects should have a higher success rate and be implemented faster. In the end, Big Data projects should affect the net results of the organization positively, as long as they are implemented wisely and correctly. As an organization becomes more involved with Big Data, it is wise to train or hire Big Data Scientists. Some organizations train with their own personnel, while other companies hire consultants during the pilot project and then use them to train in-house staff. Both options are valid, and selection depends on the amount of time and money the company is willing to spend. When the right staff (trained or hired) is in place, building the right Big Data infrastructure and extrapolating the Big Data uses throughout the organization will happen faster. However, do not overspend during this phase; if the datasets only require, for example, a mere 1 to 10 TB of data, you do not need to build a complete Hadoop system. A 2012 Microsoft study revealed an overenthusiastic use of Hadoop, which is a waste of resources.[81]

BIG DATA COMPETENCIES REQUIRED

The Big Data era will require employees with different skills doing jobs that until recently did not exist. Developing and implementing a winning Big Data strategy also involves hiring the right employees. What type of jobs should be present within an organization and what are the competencies of the different employees? The following are the seven most important Big Data employees an organization should have if it has moved thoroughly into Big Data. Of course, if a company starts small, not all job types are required.

- Chief Data Officer
- Big Data Scientist
- Big Data Analyst
- Big Data Visualizer
- Big Data Manager

- Big Data Engineer
- Big Data Consultant

Chief Data Officer

The Chief Data Officer (CDO) should be responsible for the overall Big Data strategy within an organization. If Big Data is realized throughout the organization, at all different levels and departments, the CDO will have the responsibility to ensure the strategy is implemented correctly, the data is accurate and secure, and the customers' privacy protected. As data-driven decision making is an important aspect of information-centric organizations, the CDO should be a member of the executive board, reporting directly to the CEO.

Data in itself does not bring any value. It only becomes valuable when analyzed and turned into information. Therefore, the role could also be titled Chief Information Officer. However, to stress the importance of data and the enterprise-wide governance and utilization of data as an asset, Chief Data Officer is more appropriate. It emphasizes the connection between the officer and data that will lead to an information-centric organization.

The Chief Data Officer should supervise all the different Big Data initiatives. He or she should craft and/or manage standard data operating procedures, data accountability policies, data quality standards, data privacy, and ethical policies, as well as understand how to combine different data sources within the organization. The CDO should have the total overview of what is going on within the organization related to data and represent this as a strategic business asset at board level.

The Chief Data Office should also be responsible for defining the strategic Big Data priorities within the company. As the CDO has the best total overview, he or she can identify new business opportunities based on the available data and guide the different Big Data teams within the organization on which data to store, analyze, and use for what purposes. In the end, the CDO should be responsible for generating more revenue or decreasing costs through the use of data.

Another responsibility of the Chief Data Officer should be to adapt the four ethical guidelines discussed in Chapter 5. While driving the usage of data within the organization, the CDO should also be the data conscience of the company.

The Chief Data Officer should enforce radical transparency about what sort of data is collected and for what it is used. Consumers should be made aware of what data has been collected about them and allowed to delete it if the data is not stored anonymously. In addition, the CDO should enable users to easily adjust any privacy setting related to data collected. If this is done throughout the organization, it will build trust.

With all data collected and stored, security is crucial. Being hacked or having data stolen can seriously endanger the existence of a company. Therefore, this should be discussed at the highest level.

In the end, the CDO should be made accountable for whatever data is collected, as well as how it is stored, shared, sold, or analyzed. Big Data privacy and ethics are too important not to be discussed at the C-level.

The Chief Data Officer should also stipulate that all data within the organization be readily available to all departments (except, of course, sensitive data). Sharing data throughout the company can make the company more efficient and drive innovation. In organizations that store data and information in silos, the CDO should tackle the problem of separate data. So, the Chief Data Officer should share internal best practices and prevent the constant reinvention of the wheel.

Quite often, business and IT cannot agree on who owns what data within an organization. Therefore, the CDO should own all data because he or she also has the final responsibility for it. In the end, the Chief Data Officer should bridge the gap between IT and business. As Big Data should be a marketing and strategy matter, with support from IT, the CDO should be able to leverage and represent all different interests.

In addition to the above Chief Data Officer skill set, some other important qualifications should not be forgotten:

- Strong leadership and C-suite board communication skills.
- Experience in leading major information management programs in key business areas.

- Expertise or familiarity with Big Data solutions, such as Hadoop, MapReduce, and/or HBase.
- Experience in operationalizing data governance and data quality.
- Familiarity with the major Big Data solutions and products available on the market.
- Expertise in creating and deploying best practices and methodologies.
- Knowledge about managing and leading technical Big Data teams across multiple departments.
- Knowledge about building and supporting Big Data teams across the organization.
- Knowledge about developing business cases for technical projects with a lot of uncertainties.
- Familiarity with different modeling techniques, such as predictive modeling.

In the end, the Chief Data Officer should have a mix of technical and business backgrounds. He or she should not be too technical, as it could lead to excessive focusing on the bits and bytes instead of on the strategy. However, a CDO without technical background is not able to understand and talk to his or her Big Data team members. The balance between these skills is important so that the CDO will be able to smoothly navigate the technical and political hurdles.

The trend of Chief Data Officers is growing, and more and more organizations are making a seat available in the boardroom. With the increasing importance of Big Data, more organizations should do this, as it will drive innovation, lead to an information-centric culture, and eventually impact profits positively.

Big Data Scientist

The Big Data Scientist has been described as the sexiest job in the twenty-first century. Successful Big Data Scientists will be in high demand and will be able to earn lucrative salaries. But to be successful, Big Data Scientists need a wide range of skills that until recently did not even fit into one department.

They need to be familiar with statistical, mathematical, and predictive modeling techniques, as well as with business strategy. They need to have the skills to build the algorithms necessary to ask the right questions and find the right answers. They must be able to communicate their findings orally and visually. They should also understand how products are developed and, even more important, as Big Data affects the privacy of consumers, they need to have a set of ethical responsibilities.

Apart from the skills that Big Data Scientists can learn at a college or university, they also should possess the following special set of personality traits. They need to be:

- Curious. They should enjoy diving deep into material to find an answer to a yet unknown question, that is, a natural desire to go beneath the surface of a problem.
- Thinkers, who ask the right (business) questions.
- Confident and secure, as more often then not they will have to deal with situations with a lot of unknowns.
- Patient, as finding the unknown in massive datasets will take a lot of time and developing the algorithm to uncover new insights will often occur by trial and error.[82]
- See examples in totally different industries and be able to adapt that to their current problem. For example, the Los Angeles Police department uses an algorithm designed to predict earthquakes to anticipate where crimes are likely to happen.[83]

Big Data Scientists understand how to integrate multiple systems and datasets. They need to link and mash up distinctive datasets to discover new insights. This often requires connecting different types of datasets in different forms, as well as being able to work with potentially incomplete data sources and cleaning datasets.

Of course, Big Data Scientists need to be able to program, preferably in different programming languages, such as Python, R, Java, Ruby, Clojure, Matlab, Pig, or SQL. They need to have an understanding of Hadoop, Hive, and/or MapReduce. In addition, he or she needs to be familiar with many disciplines, such as:

- Natural Language Processing: the interactions between computers and humans.
- Machine learning: using computers to improve as well as develop algorithms.

- Conceptual modeling: the ability to share and articulate modeling.
- Statistical analysis: to understand and work around possible limitations in models.
- Predictive modeling: the ability to predict future outcomes of events.
- Hypothesis testing: the ability to develop hypotheses and test them with careful experiments.

The exact background of Big Data Scientists is of less importance. Great Big Data Scientists can have backgrounds in different fields, including econometrics, physics, biostatistics, computer science, applied mathematics, and engineering. Most of the time, their educational background is a Master's Degree or even a PhD. However, to be successful, they should have at least some of the following capabilities:

- Strong written and verbal communication skills.
- The ability to work in a fast-paced multidisciplinary environment, as in a competitive landscape new data keeps flowing in rapidly and the world is constantly changing.
- The ability to query databases and perform statistical analysis.
- The ability to develop or program databases.
- The ability to advise senior management in clear language about the implications of their work for the organization.
- At least a basic understanding of how a business strategy works.
- The ability to create examples, prototypes, and demonstrations to help management better understand the work.
- A good understanding of design and architecture principles.
- The ability to work autonomously.

In short, the Big Data Scientist needs an understanding of almost everything. Depending on the industry, the Big Data Scientist will need to specialize even further, as for example a marine Big Data Scientist requires a different set of skills than a historical Big Data Scientist.

Of course, the perfect Big Data Scientist who possesses all of the skills and capabilities described is extremely rare. Perhaps only a handful of Big Data Scientists have all the skills mentioned here. Organizations should chose and pick from this list what they deem most important in their Big Data Scientist and what the particular requirements are for the job.

Big Data Analyst

If the Big Data Scientist is king, the Big Data Analyst is the servant. A Big Data Scientist requires a wide range of skills and capabilities in order to, among other things, mash up and analyze different data sources. The Big Data Analyst primarily analyzes data in a given system and helps the Big Data Scientist perform the necessary jobs.

The Big Data Analyst requires specific set of skills and capabilities. In general, an analyst's next step may be that of a Big Data Scientist. An analyst needs to be able to provide business and management with clear analyses of the data at hand. This includes data mining skills (including data auditing, aggregation, validation, and reconciliation), advanced modeling techniques, testing, and creating and explaining results in clear and concise reports.

The analyst should have a broad understanding of and experience with real-time analytics and business intelligent platforms, such as Tableau Software. He or she should be able to work with structured query language (SQL) databases and several programming languages and statistical software packages, such as R, Java, MatLab, and SPSS. They also need knowledge of Hadoop and MapReduce. By using scripting languages, an analyst should be able to develop new insights from the available data.

The testing skills of a Big Data Analyst are particularly important. He or she should be able to perform A/B testing based on different hypotheses to directly and indirectly impact different KPIs. To perform such tests, as well as to build the reports that senior management needs, the analyst should have a certain business acumen, one that knows what drives an organization, what influences a strategy, and how the available data within an organization can contribute to the success of a strategy.

The personality traits needed for a Big Data Analyst are similar to those of a Big Data Scientist. He or she needs to have the curiosity to dive into the available data and enjoy searching for patterns that could indicate new insights. They should also be confident and independent enough to use very large datasets and come up with the questions that can help create management reports. Big Data Analysts generally have a Bachelor's Degree in subjects ranging from mathematics, statistics, and computer science to business administration, economics, and finance. In addition, a Big Data Analyst should have at least some of the following capabilities:

- Strong interpersonal, oral and written communication, and presentation skills.
- The ability to communicate complex findings and ideas in plain language.
- The ability to work in teams toward a shared goal.
- The ability to change direction quickly based on data analysis.
- Enjoyment in discovering and solving problems.
- The ability to proactively seek clarification of requirements and direction and taking responsibility.
- The ability to work in stressful situation when insights in (new) datasets are required quickly.

The Big Data Analyst supports the business and the Big Data Scientist in delivering valuable insights. The analyst should therefore enjoy working with others and be willing to learn more. For each organization, an analyst will, of course, need different specialized skills, but the above-mentioned skills are a good starting point for finding the right Big Data Analyst.

Big Data Visualizer

One of the most important aspects in working with Big Data is the ability to visualize the information in a way that it is understandable for (senior) management. Visualizing data helps them understand the data and find new patterns and insights. Some Big Data startups are developing a completely new way of visualizing data. One of them is Ayasdi[84]; another is Synerscope.[85] They take a new approach and do not use old-fashioned and not-very-insightful graphs and pie charts. If your organization can gain valuable insights with interactive visuals, you can be one step ahead of your competition. A Big Data Visualizer can help in creating these important insights.

A Big Data Visualizer should be a creative thinker who understands user interface design, as well as other visualizations skills, such as typography, user experience design, and visual art design. These give the visualizer the ability to turn abstract information into appealing and understandable visualizations that clearly explain the results of the analyses.

There is, however, a potential problem. Because the Big Data Scientist is the person who best understands the results of the data and the story that it tells, when turning the results over to the Big Data Visualizer, misinterpretation and biased presentation of results can occur. Therefore, a visualizer needs to understand how Big Data analyses are done, and he or she needs to have the necessary programming skills to actually build accurate visualizations. A background in computer science can help a visualizer better understand what the data means.

A Big Data Visualizer should have a solid background in using source control and testing frameworks, as well as agile development practices, to create and build compelling data visualizations and the ability to lead and advise management on how the visualizations work. He or she should be able to tell an understandable and comprehensible story, one that can be understood by the decision makers within an organization.

Mapping data is the difficult process of transforming structured and unstructured data into a graph. A Big Data Visualizer should be able to use metadata and metrics, as well as color, size, and position to highlight, group, and set up a hierarchy in the graphics. The visualizations should attract the user to play and interact with them.

As a Big Data Visualizer should be able to read the raw analyses, or even perform the analyses, as well as design, illustrate, and create the results, several skills are required:

- In-depth knowledge of JavaScript, HTML, and CSS and statistical programming languages.
- Familiarity with modern (JavaScript) visualization frameworks, such as Gephi, Processing, R, and/or d3js.
- Experience with common web libraries, such as JQuery, LESS, and Functional Javascript.
- Understanding of efficient and effective human–computer interaction.
- Sharp analytical abilities and proven design skills.
- A strong understanding of typography and how it can affect visualizations, principles of a good layout, a good use of space, and an inherent feel for motion.

- Proficiency in Photoshop, Illustrator, and InDesign, as well as other Adobe Creative Suite products.
- Excellent written and verbal communication skills, including the ability to explain the work in plain language to management people with no data experience.

In the end, the most important job of a Big Data Visualizer is to create compelling data visualizations out of abstract data that will help decision makers in their work. Exactly which skills are necessary depends, of course, on the type of job that needs to be done. A Big Data Visualizer, however, should always be able to select the best data visualization technique based on the characteristics of the underlying data to illustrate certainty, patterns, and other statistical concepts that will guide decision makers.

Big Data Manager

A team of Big Data Scientists, Big Data Analysts, and Big Data Visualizers, of course, need to be managed. The Big Data Manager is the middleman between the technical team members and the strategic management of an organization. Therefore, he or she needs to understand both sides of the coin. Ideally, the Big Data Manager has an IT background with strategic experience.

Big Data Scientists and Analysts are great at building the necessary tools for an organization, but in general they tend to be less effective in leading a team and dealing with changes from the top down. Therefore, a manager needs to lead the team.

The Big Data Manager has to coordinate team efforts, reward and/or stimulate certain behaviors, and ensure that the team keeps moving in the right direction. He or she must create a culture of innovation and creativity within the team and guarantee that the members are comfortable with the rapid changes likely to occur in this new field. In addition, the manager needs to keep the team focused on what needs to be done, as it is easy for Big Data Scientists and Analysts to become distracted and loose focus while building great algorithms. Sometimes, such distractions are good for the company, but others might do more harm. It is the manager's task to separate the good from the bad distractions.

As Big Data is most of all a marketing and strategic matter, the Big Data Manager needs to be able to explain the work done by the team members to the senior management of an organization. The manager coordinates the work of the stakeholders within the organization and ensures buy-in on time for the tasks at hand. As Big Data can affect any aspect or department within an organization, the manager needs good networking and strong communication skills. The manager should also be responsible for aligning the different data requests, as well as the different data sources within the organization.

As is always the case with new projects in a corporate environment, the expected ROI needs to be calculated. Although this is difficult in the beginning, it is the Big Data Manager's job to develop the business case, manage the planning and budget, decrease the risks involved, and ensure sufficient resource allocation. The team members should not be involved in project management. Rather, the manager should be a strong person, who is able to keep stand firm in complex and fast-changing environments.

A Big Data Manager should, of course, also have the following core management skills.

- The ability to communicate efficiently and effectively and be able to understand, interpret, and relate an organization's strategy and vision to the Big Data team.
- The ability to strive to build personal relationships with the team as well as to promote a true Big Data culture.
- The ability to be flexible in a changing environment and to explain changes correctly to the team members.
- The ability to instill trust in team members, as well as help them grow in their role.

Another important skill is to be able to work with Big Data Scientists, Analysts, and Visualizers. Big Data Scientists, in particular, are quite often highly educated, and this requires a different management approach. A good manager will provide the best working environment for all team members, removing them from all complexities and administrative work and ensuring timely progress. As the manager will supervise technical projects, he or she should have familiarity with several programming languages, including Python, R, Java, Ruby, Clojure,

Matlab, Pig, and SQL, and at least a basic, understanding of Hadoop, Hive, and/or MapReduce. In addition, the manager needs to have at least some knowledge of the following disciplines.

- Natural language processing
- Machine learning
- Conceptual modeling
- Statistical analysis
- Predictive modeling

The role of a Big Data Manager is a difficult one, so sufficient experience in management is advisable. If the manager is inexperienced, problems can develop because the tasks at hand are already complex and difficult.

Big Data Engineer

A Big Data Engineer builds what the Big Data solutions architect designs. Big Data Engineers develop, maintain, test, and evaluate Big Data solutions within organizations. Most of the time, they are also involved in the design of the solutions, because of their experience with Hadoop-based technologies, such as MapReduce, Hive MongoDB, and Cassandra. A Big Data Engineer builds large-scale data processing systems, is an expert in data warehousing solutions, and should be able to work with the latest (NoSQL) database technologies.

A Big Data Engineer should have experience with object-oriented design, coding, and testing patterns, as well as experience in engineering (commercial or open-source) software platforms and large-scale data infrastructures. Engineers should also have the ability to architect highly scalable distributed systems, using different open-source tools, and should have experience building high-performance algorithms.

A Big Data Engineer embraces the challenge of dealing with petabytes or even exabytes of data on a daily basis and understands how to apply technologies to solve Big Data problems and develop innovative solutions. To be able to do this, the engineer requires extensive knowledge of different programming or scripting languages, such as Java, Linux, C++, PHP, Ruby, Phyton, and R, and of different (NoSQL or RDBMS) databases, such as MongoDB, or Redis. Building data processing systems with Hadoop and Hive using Java or Python should be common knowledge to the engineer.

A Big Data Engineer generally works on implementing complex Big Data projects with a focus on collecting, parsing, managing, analyzing, and visualizing large sets of data to turn information into insights using multiple platforms. He or she should be able to decide on the required hardware and software design needs and develop prototypes and Proof of Concepts for the selected solutions.

Additional qualifications for the position include:

- Enjoyment at being challenged and in solving complex problems on a daily basis.
- Excellent oral and written communication skills.
- Proficiency in designing efficient and robust extract, transform, and load (ETL) workflows.
- The ability to work in cloud computing environments.
- A Bachelor's or Master's degree in computer science or software engineering.
- The ability to work in teams and collaborate with others to clarify requirements.
- The ability to assist in documenting requirements, as well as in resolving conflicts or ambiguities.
- The ability to fine tune Hadoop solutions to improve performance and the end-user experience.
- Strong coordination and project management skills to handle complex projects.

Big Data Engineer is a technical job requiring substantial expertise in a wide range of software development and programming fields. He or she should have sufficient knowledge of Big Data solutions to be able to implement those on the premises or in the cloud.

Big Data Consultant

The Big Data Consultant advises organizations about all aspects of Big Data, including how to formulate and implement a strategy and which technologies best fit the needs of the organization. A Big Data Consultant, therefore, should have business experience, as well as sound technical knowledge of a broad range of Big Data tools.

The Big Data Consultant designs strategies and programs to collect, store, analyze, and visualize data from various sources for specific projects. He or she should be able to lead a team and project, while ensuring quality and on-time delivery according to the specifications.

In addition, the consultant should produce accurate analyses of the datasets using smart algorithms and the latest Big Data technologies. He or she should be aware of the latest Big Data trends, as well as know which Big Data technologies are available on the market and would fit a chosen strategy. An understanding of the possibilities of public data is important as well. The consultant should be able to assess datasets and confirm the quality and correctness of the available data. Then, the consultant should be able to query the data, perform analyses, and present findings in a clear and understandable language.

The Big Data Consultant should have sufficient technical knowledge. He or she needs to be able to program, preferably in different programming/scripting languages, such as, for example, Python, R, Java, Ruby, Clojure, Matlab, Pig, and SQL, as well as to understand Hadoop, Hive, HBase, MongoDB, and/or MapReduce. In addition, he or she needs to be familiar with disciplines, such as text mining, clustering analysis, recommendation analysis, outlier detection, predictive analytics, and similarity searches, as well as different modeling techniques. The Big Data solution can be delivered on premises or in the cloud. Therefore, the consultant should also have experience with one of the large cloud-computing infrastructure solutions, such as Amazon Web Services, or Elastic MapReduce.

The Big Data Consultant should enjoy working in teams, as he or she will need to interact with Big Data Scientists and Big Data Engineers to produce powerful data processes with real-time analytics and reporting applications, as well as to build the necessary hardware and software for the chosen solution.

The consultant also needs to communicate effectively at the executive level, as quite often he or she deals with executive management when advising an organization. It is important for the consultant to ask the right questions to understand the problem at hand and propose the right solution.

The goal is to improve business results using Big Data technology. Therefore, he or she needs to translate business issues into Big Data solutions that will help (senior) managers in their decision-making. A Big Data Consultant should also have, apart from technical expertise, the "standard" strategy consultant skills, including:

- A Master's degree (or equivalent) from a leading university.
- Excellent oral, written communication, and interpersonal skills.
- Commercial awareness and a natural curiosity in solving complex problems.
- Enjoyment in working in a fast-changing and competitive environment.
- The ability to handle multiple tasks and responsibilities.
- The ability to work under pressure and meet regulatory deadlines.
- Self-reliance and the capability to work both independently and as a team member.
- The ability to deliver clear and concise presentations to (senior) management.
- The ability to develop and review project plans, identifying and solving issues and communicating the status of assigned projects to users and managers.

The role of a Big Data Consultant is important for organizations that require help in understanding Big Data and how to apply it. In addition, a consultant can give organizations that already have a Big Data solution new insights, thereby improving business results. It is a difficult, but highly respected, role, as so many technical and business skills are required.

SMALL AND MEDIUM ENTERPRISES (SMEs) CAN ACHIEVE REMARKABLE RESULTS WITH BIG DATA

Quite often, I hear that SMEs cannot join the Big Data movement or cannot develop a Big Data strategy because they have too little data. A 2012 survey by SAP, however, shows that 76 percent of the interviewed C-level executives of SMEs view Big Data as an opportunity.[86] Steve Lucas, EVP Business Analytics, Database & Technology at SAP, said: "Every company should be thinking about their Big Data strategy whether they are big or small."[87,88] Even companies with smaller amounts of data can develop a Big Data roadmap and become an information-centric organization. So, what are the Big Data opportunities for SMEs hereafter, and how can they leverage their "small data"?

By small data, I am not referring to IBM's definition of small data.[89] IBM defines small data as low volumes, batch velocities, and structured varieties. Small data, however, can be any form of data, structured and unstructured and in real time or in batch processed. Small data simply refers to smaller volumes, that is, gigabytes and a few terabytes instead of petabytes or more.

It is true that some SMEs might not have that much data. However, even SMEs have suppliers or distributors. When these companies start to work together and share their data, the amount of available data increases many times. We also see this process happening at large multinationals. Nike, for example, shares data from all its suppliers with the rest of the industry.[90] This allows other organizations in the supply chain to populate and use the database and make better decisions.

When SMEs start using and combining their data with that from suppliers and vendors, they suddenly have sufficient data to analyze, visualize, and use for improved decision making. They can also combine their existing "small data" with public datasets. These datasets are becoming increasingly available, and more and public platforms exist from which SMEs can download for free or buy additional datasets. Merging personal data with public data increases the data available for analyses. An additional benefit is that combining existing data with new public datasets can create completely new results, such as finding new markets or target groups.

SMEs should not look at the data they already have and collect, but should also be open to new ways to collect data. Creativity is key in this matter, as in the end, any product can be turned into data if sensors join the game. Sensors are becoming cheaper every day, and adding sensors to existing products can deliver completely new datasets that can deliver unexpected insights.

Big Data is not only about volume and velocity but also variety. The power of Big Data is the ability to combine unstructured and structured datasets to gain new insights. Unstructured data comes from a wide variety of sources, including social data, visuals, documents, emails, and even voice data. Combining several smaller datasets can deliver the same insights as combining large datasets. Gigabytes of data can therefore provide SMEs with the same insights as petabytes or exabytes do for large corporate multinationals.

As Jamie Turner from Real Business said: "with their limited resources [. . .] flexibility and agility are crucial for SMEs."[91] They indeed have to look for solutions that fit their available resources. Instead of developing a complete Big Data solution from IBM, SAS, or HP, they can use cloud-based solutions created by the smaller, and thus more flexible, Big Data startups. In addition, they can build their own Big Data solution with open-source tools. Although the latter still requires specialized personnel, it does not have to cost the world any more. Open-source tools are free of charge (of course without any service) and commodity hardware becomes cheaper every day, as discussed in Chapter 4.

Big Data is certainly not only for large organizations. There are plenty of chances for SMEs to gain valuable insights from their existing data or new datasets. The fact is that SMEs do have to be a bit more creative to solve the Big Data puzzle. They have to think out of the box to see the data opportunities within their companies as well as outside their organization. But, that is also true for large corporates in the end, if they want to take full advantage of Big Data.

So, small data can become Big Data by cleverly combining various datasets with different data formats. For example, combine weather data with your restaurant's sales data to discover the impact of rain on items sold and, as such, adjust your purchasing behavior. Combine your customer data with their sentiment online to surprise them and create long-lasting relationships. Track how your customers behave through your shop and combine it with your sales data to see how you can adjust and improve your floor plan. Or, combine online sales data with offline customer profiles to see how you can optimize your multichannel approach for your small retail shop. The opportunities are endless and also small data can provide big insights.

GOVERNANCE FOR THE ACCURACY OF BIG DATA

With large volumes of data that are used as an asset within your organization comes the responsibility to ensure that the data, as well as the analysis, are correct. Big Data governance should therefore be an important aspect of your strategy. The data governance structure within your organization should be capable of dealing with high volumes of a variety of data that needs to be checked and controlled whether correct or not. This requires extensive and smart algorithms that perform dazzling analyses within a fraction of a second and that deliver predictions and visualizations that are used to determine the course of an organization and that can affect many stakeholders.

It is vital that the data organizations collect, store, and analyze are 100 percent correct. With information-centric organizations that base decisions on algorithms, it is crucial that the algorithms and their (predictive) analyses are accurate. But who is capable of checking and controlling thousands of petabytes of data or extensive and extremely complex algorithms that improve over time? How do we ensure that consumer data is kept secure, private, and not mistreated? How do we guarantee that the predictions made are based on the right variables? How do we know that green is really green and not perhaps red?

The era of Big Data will require a new form of governance consisting of auditing and control, of checks and balances and, perhaps as well, of quality labels for organizations. An ISO for Big Data? This could lead to a completely new field within the global Big Data industry. When organizations start to place Big Data on the balance sheet, auditing and regulatory organizations will pay very close attention to how the data is stored, collected, analyzed, and visualized, as it can make or break an organization.

The Data

Responsibility for the reliability and accuracy of the data collected and stored begins with the user who provides the data using different applications to the organization that collects, stores, and analyzes it. Organizations will have to guarantee that users understand what data is collected when and for what purpose. They should inform users how the data will be used in the first instance, but also what secondary usage will be made of the data the moment this becomes clear. As discussed, this should be done through clear and understandable privacy policies and terms and conditions, which can also be understood by the digital immigrant. Users should also be kept up to date via email when usage of their data changes. Making these documents difficult to understand and/or changing them rapidly does not fit with an organization that wants to make the most of Big Data. Organizations should therefore make it extremely easy for users to adjust their privacy settings, as well as to delete or edit their data whenever they deem suitable. Organizations should not be allowed to push the responsibility on to the users.

Taking responsibility for how the data is used is only one aspect of data governance. Another is that organizations, as well as governments, should do everything to ensure that the data they collect is accurate. If this is not done correctly, it can go very wrong, as shown in the example of U.S. Senator Edward Kennedy being refused entrance in 2004 at several airports because his name somehow appeared on an terrorist watchlist.[92] Most of the time, users do not know what information is collected, but more importantly they do not always have access to their own data. Users should therefore be able to correct data if they discover it is incorrect or can be misread. This principle is incorporated into the Fair Credit Reporting Act (FCRA), which requires credit reporting agencies to provide consumers with access to their reports, so they can have inaccuracies corrected. But this is only for credit-reporting agencies and the law was originally passed in 1970, long before all other industries started collecting massive amounts of data. So, nowadays, the general public has no clue what entities are collecting what data and what they are or will be doing with it. Of course, giving consumers the ability to adjust incorrect data should require several security measures, so as to prevent misuse by criminals.

Organizations that collect and store data should take the necessary security steps to ensure that data is stored securely and cannot be stolen by criminals. Just as banks do everything to protect the money they have received from consumers and organizations and indemnify consumers and organizations when a bank is robbed, organizations should protect the data they have collected and indemnify users when their data is stolen.

The Algorithms

Algorithms are capable of amazing analyses and can turn massive amounts of raw data into information. The first step is to ensure that the data used by the algorithms is correct. The second is to guarantee that the algorithms themselves are correct. How do managers and consumers know that the algorithm works properly? How do they know that green is really green If major business decisions are based on an incorrect algorithm, it could have massive consequences for the organizations as well as for consumers. Consumers who apply for a loan have to trust organizations that use algorithms to determine their risk profile correctly and that they are not refused a loan or have to pay more because of inaccurate data.

Big Data technology vendors that have developed algorithms should receive a quality label that confirms their algorithms are working correctly and appropriately, serving the purposes for which they were designed. Organizations that use an algorithm developed by a Big Data technology vendor that already has such a quality label can be trusted more and are more likely to receive a positive assessment by the Big Data regulators.

Organizations that develop algorithms in-house should also have them checked to confirm that they meet local regulations. The authors of the book *Big Data*, Vicktor Mayer-Schönberger and Kenneth Cukier, therefore predict the rise of "algorithmists," who would be capable of and allowed to check any algorithm created by organizations.[93] These "algorithmists" would be knowledgeable about the different Big Data techniques that are available and would specialize in different sections to be able to read and assess algorithms. As algorithms are private company information, these "algorithmists" should sign nondisclosure agreements, just as conventional accountants.

Users will have more confidence in organizations that have had their algorithms checked and approved, as they know that their data is being analyzed correctly.

The Data Auditors

Data auditors, who can be internal or external, are responsible for ensuring:

1. The correctness of the data and confirming the fact that it is secured correctly.
2. The correctness of the algorithms performing the analyses on the data.
3. That the organization observes the four ethical guidelines.

Auditors can perform different levels of scrutiny. Organizations that deal with highly private personal information, such as health records or financial data, should undergo the strictest assessment, while organizations that use the data for innocent mobile applications can have less strict regulations. How these assessments or regulations look will differ by country but, in the end, a global set of data governance standards should be developed, similar to the International Financial Reporting Standards (IFRS) or the Generally Accepted Accounting Principles (GAAP).

TAKEAWAYS

Big Data will change how organizations are structured and managed. It will affect all departments, from those that deal with the core activities of an organization, such as operations or manufacturing of products, to supporting departments, such as human resources.

The challenge organizations will face in the coming years is how to become information-centric organizations that make decisions based on massive amounts of data that are collected in real time. Although the number of organizations currently taking full advantage of Big Data is still small, this will change in the future. The result will be that all companies, including the SMEs, will be able to take full advantage of the benefits of Big Data regardless of their industry.

The roadmap to an information-centric organization is a long and difficult, but one worth pursuing. Research has shown that organizations that have implemented a Big Data strategy successfully outperform their competitors by 20 percent.[94] The objective should be to eventually determine the return on data and put data on the balance sheet as an asset. As a result, organizations will be held accountable by data auditors, who will ensure that data is collected and stored correctly and securely and guarantee that the algorithms used are performing as intended.

In order to develop and implement a Big Data strategy, organizations will require several new types of employees with different competencies. The most important will be the Big Data Scientists, who have the ability to build to tools to give organizations the insights necessary to improve their bottom lines.

In the end, this roadmap can help your organization develop and implement a Big Data strategy that is good for the company, good for your customers, and good for society. Big Data is too important and has too many implications and advantages to be ignored.

Organizations will find many different uses for Big Data, including obtaining a 360-degree view of all its customers. Chapter 7 dives deeper into the different business use cases for different industries.

Big Data by Industry

By now, it should be clear that Big Data affects all organizations, small or big, in all industries. Let's dive deeper into 18 important industries and see what Big Data can do for them. The examples will help you understand the possibilities Big Data offers and perhaps will provide you with some out-of-the-box business use cases you can implement in your organization.

AGRICULTURE INDUSTRY

The agriculture industry has seen many changes in the past one hundred years. Since the birth of industrial agriculture in 1900, we have moved into the era of digitally enhanced agriculture, in which everything done before seeding and up to harvesting produces data that is used for analyses.[1] Big Data has already transformed the agriculture industry, but in the coming decade, this will become increasingly visible in all areas of agriculture throughout the world. Three factors will be most affected by the opportunities presented by Big Data:

1. Machines: Improved efficiency and reduced costs of operating.
2. Crops and animals: Improved productivity and efficiency.
3. Weather and pricing: Mitigation of the effect of weather conditions and optimized pricing.

The Machines

The Internet of Things, discussed in Chapter 3, will greatly change agricultural machines, including tractors, soil cultivating equipment, agricultural sprayers, harvesters, and cow-milking machines. The inclusion of sensors will provide the farmer with a lot of information in real time 24/7—without the farmer actually being present. These smart machines will talk to each other, and they will be able to anticipate problems and take appropriate action before actual damage is done. When a problem does occur, the farmer can immediately see the problem. If a problem is more serious, a service employee can visit the farmer before the equipment breaks down, thereby minimizing the downtime of machines. In addition, the effective use of sensors can increase productivity by streamlining many agricultural processes.

Apart from predicting failures and providing maintenance, sensors can also save farmers money spent on fuel. For example, computers can determine when and where conditions are best for driving when working the land, information that is especially useful for farmers with large acreages. When combined with machine-to-machine communication, this will help the farmer control the growing number of machines. Because machines communicate with each other, they know each other's positions and make necessary adjustments. With smart machines, one person can manage an entire fleet and still save time and money. In addition, diagnostics manage the machines in real time to ensure that the optimal settings are used to maximize productivity. All the data that is collected can be analyzed, so the farmer understands how the machines are operating and how operations can be improved even further.

The Crops and the Animals

Although optical, mechanical, electromagnetic, and radiometric sensors have been tested for almost a decade, Big Data technologies really make precision agriculture interesting. Precision agriculture means recognizing, understanding, and exploiting information that quantifies variations in the soil and crops.[2]

When ground sensors are combined with a smart irrigation system, farmers can optimize productivity. The irrigation system knows exactly which crops need what supplements, when, and how much. This means providing just the right amount of fertilizer, which saves money and increases output. To understand soil conditions and improve output even more, sensors can be implanted in the ground to better analyze soil conditions.[3] Algorithms will improve output by telling the farmer when to plant which crops where, as well as when is the best time to plough or harvest.

In addition to improving crops, farm animals will also benefit from Big Data technology. Sensors in the sheds will automatically weigh animals and adjust feeding. The sensors will then adjust feeding by evaluating the real-time condition. The animals will receive the right food in the right amount at the right moment. Chips in the animals will also monitor their health. Sick animals will automatically receive medication in their food. Conditions in the shed can automatically be adjusted. For example, if the animals are stressed, sensors will indicate the need for measures to ease the problem. Special collars will also help farmers with massive plots of land track their herds on their smartphones.[4] This might sound far fetched or scary, but if done correctly it will provide a lot of benefits for farmers.

The Weather and Pricing

Weather conditions can severely affect output. Although local weather conditions are difficult to predict, the right algorithms can warn farmers when to harvest or plough because of upcoming (extreme) weather. This can increase output.

If the data is combined with real-time market information, farmers can control price fluctuations better. The volatility in the agriculture market can be substantial. Speculation can increase or decrease profits on the sale of crops. With predictive analytics, the price of a certain crop can be determined upfront in each specific location. This will help the farmer get the right price for the right crop at the right moment in time at the right location.

Big Data turns the traditional agriculture industry upside down. Although investments for farmers can be substantial, the potential benefits of applying Big Data technologies in the field are enormous.

JOHN DEERE IS REVOLUTIONIZING FARMING WITH BIG DATA

John Deere is using Big Data to step into the future of farming. In 2012, the company released several products that connect John Deere's equipment to owners, operators, dealers, agricultural consultants—and other machines. This connectivity helps farmers improve productivity and increase efficiency.

John Deere added sensors to its machines to help farmers manage their fleets, decrease downtime of tractors, and save on fuel. Information from the sensors is combined with historical and real-time data regarding weather predictions, soil conditions, crop features, and other datasets. The data is then analyzed, and the farmer can retrieve the information on the MyJohnDeere.com platform, as well as on the iPad and iPhone app known as Mobile Farm Manager. This will help farmers figure out which crops to plant where and when, when and where to plough, where the best returns can be made from the crops, and even which path to follow when plowing. All this will lead to higher production and increased revenue.

Although John Deere claims that it does not yet use as many datasets as Walmart and Amazon, the company is collecting and processing massive amounts of data to truly revolutionize farming.[5] To cope with all this data, it decided to use the open-source programming language R, which can be programmed to forecast demand, predict crop yield, define land area and usage, and anticipate the demand for (spare) parts for combines. Employees use the Open Database Connectivity to import the multiple data sources and data types. R is then used to export this data to different channels.

One such channel is FarmSight, which was launched in March 2011.[6] FarmSight is designed to help farmers increase productivity in three ways.

1. Machine optimization monitors machine productivity and tries to figure out how to make them more efficient. It uses proactive diagnostics on service issues, such as filter changes and other maintenance items, to help reduce downtime and keep machines up and running.

2. Farming logistics data helps farmers control growing farms and the ever-expanding machine fleet. The objective is to improve machine-to-machine communications.
3. Decision support helps farmers make better decisions that prevent mistakes and increase efficiency.

Another channel is the MyJohnDeere.com platform, which is a portal through which users can manage their fleets, see weather forecasts, access any application (including third-party applications of third-party machines), and view financial information related to their farming.[7] Users have remote display access, so a consultant is able to see what is going on from a distance.

A third channel is the FarmSight Mobile Farm Manager, which provides farmers with all the information they need on the go.[8] The Mobile Farm Manager gives users access to historical, as well as real-time, field information, evaluates soil samples, and enables users to share information directly with trusted advisers for live remote advice while in the field. They can even view their operation maps and reports from any year on their iPads or iPhones.

John Deere has additional plans for improving technology further by using Big Data as much as possible. The company wants to help farmers plan, run, and analyze their entire farming operation as efficiently as possible.

AUTOMOTIVE INDUSTRY

Any industry that builds products using many different moving parts can be improved with sensors. Thus, the automotive industry is a natural. Sensors can be used in cars, motorcycles, and trucks. Together with information collected by satellite navigations, such as TomTom, and traffic conditions, cars are becoming smarter.[9] Before long, they will be able to drive independently.

Sensors provide a lot of possibilities. With them, cars have the potential to flag abnormal events in real time and proactively take corrective actions before performance problems arise. The car will inform the owner about an impending problem, and even make an appointment with the nearest car maintenance workshop, adding this to the owner's daily schedule.

Onboard sensors also give manufacturers information about how cars are used. How fast does someone drive or brake, and how did the car respond. The ability to monitor the performance of the car 24/7 will help manufacturers quickly identify the areas for improvement and adjustment. The time to bring new cars to market will be improved drastically.

The self-driving car from Google is already a true data creator. With sensors that enable the car to operate without a driver, it generates nearly 1 gigabyte of data every second.[10] All that data is analyzed to decide where to drive and how fast. It can even detect a new cigarette butt thrown on the ground or anticipate when a pedestrian might suddenly appear in the road. Imagine the amount of data that will be created every year. On average, Americans drive 600 hours per year in their cars.[11] That equals 2,160,000 seconds or approximately 2 petabytes of data per car per year. With the number of cars worldwide about to surpass one billion, it is almost unimaginable how much data will be created when Google's self-driving car becomes common on the streets.[12]

Improve the Supply Chain

Using public data, as well as data from the CRM database, car manufactures can predict which cars will be needed when and where. If sensors tell them when cars are about to break down and which parts are needed at what location, they can better predict their parts inventory. This will decrease inventory, optimize the supply chain for manufacturers and dealers, and improve customer satisfaction.

Dealer satisfaction can also be monitored and improved using the same data, as well as information from the blogosphere and social networks. When this happens in real time, complaints and possible crises can be avoided, thereby saving money and creating happy customers.

Improve the Customer Experience

Several data sources can be used to understand and monitor driving behavior[13] These (real-time) insights can then be applied to the (re)development of cars to optimize and improve the driving experience. Sensors within the seats can monitor how someone drives, including which radio channels he or she listens to and other information, such as air-conditioning usage. This data can be used to build a personal profile that is automatically loaded when a driver "registers" or "logs-in" on a (new) car.

Algorithms can improve driver behavior by providing driving performance improvement recommendations directly on the dashboard and/or the driver's smartphone app tailored to the situation at that moment.

All that data can be combined with social public data to better understand customers. Such public data, including geographic locations, housing, and other demographics, can give a 360-degree view of customers.

Save Money

When cars are connected to each other and the Internet, they can talk to each other. Cars can "see" where other vehicles are on the road and take action if needed. The cars know when a traffic jam is coming up, can suggest a different route, and optimize routing to prevent accidents and save fuel.

The same sensors can track when and where cars are stolen and can easily locate them. Algorithms can also detect car theft by notifying the police when the driving pattern unexpectedly changes.

The automotive industry can potentially benefit significantly by using Big Data technologies. Improvements include better driving behavior, improved cars, fewer accidents, and happier customers. Cars are becoming information-driven machines, and it is for good reason that General Motors insourced 10,000 IT staff members to create a completely information-centric organization.[14]

BIG DATA IS IN THE DRIVER'S SEAT AT HERTZ

How do you keep track of tens of thousands of customer touch points every day, divided over 8,300 locations in 146 countries? Hertz used to do this by manually registering customer satisfaction via local paper surveys that took weeks to analyze. Thousands of surveys were collected daily, including comments from the website, emails, and other messages. All of these valuable customer insights could not be used properly, as location managers had to process them manually, which was a labor-intensive task. Whenever action was required, it was usually discovered too late, and a customer was lost.

Since Hertz implemented a Big Data strategy, it has turned all customer touch points into unique moments. With the instant feedback Hertz receives from around the world, immediate action can be taken to improve service and thereby retain customers.

To really start using that valuable knowledge, Hertz brought in jShare (a team from IBM that leverages the latest technologies) and Mindshare to bring the process under control.[15] The plan was to enhance the collection of customer data and enable Hertz to perform all sorts of real-time analyses on the captured unstructured data. With this new software, Hertz can now make real-time adjustments in its operation to improve customer satisfaction levels, based on the real-time Net Promoter Score. In particular, Hertz used Mindshare's sentiment-based tagging solution to understand in real-time customer opinions in each of its 8,300 locations worldwide.[16]

Further, Hertz developed a "Voice of the Customer" program. This analytics system automatically captures customer experiences in real time, transforming the information into actionable intelligence. The system automatically categorizes comments that are received via email or online, as well as flags customers who mention #1 Club Gold or request a call back.

In the competitive market of rental cars, a company that understands customer feedback and can react to it in real time has a competitive advantage. The system allows Hertz to take instant action when signals start pouring in that service is low at a certain location. The Philadelphia location, for example, showed that delays for returns were occurring at specific times during the day on a regular basis. As soon as this was signaled, the company investigated the matter and solved the problems.

By applying advanced analytics solutions to its massive datasets, Hertz has cut the process time of information drastically, which has resulted in improved service at all its locations.

CONSUMER GOODS

The consumer goods industry is perfectly suited to the generation of unfathomable amounts of data in the coming years. Apart from the billions of 360-degree customer profiles that will be created by millions of companies, it could produce even more data if all those consumer goods were connected to the Internet of Things.

Improve Customer Satisfaction

For consumer organizations it is vital to know who the customer is.[17] Big Data can help create a 360-degree view of customers. By combining information from social networks (Facebook, Twitter, Tumblr, Instagram, LinkedIn, etc.), the blogosphere, (online) surveys, and online click behavior, as well as sales, product sensors, and public and open data, companies can develop detailed personas and microsegments to better target customers, improve conversion, and increase sales. It is important to understanding signals that reveal what consumers are seeing, doing, thinking, and sharing at any point in time. This is valuable to help drive relationships. When a customer gets in contact with an organization, the company knows who the customer is. This will improve customer service and, as such, customer satisfaction.

On the other hand, consumers need to feel that organizations are willing to listen to them when they have a question or comment. These observations are not always addressed directly to an organization via mail or a call center, but more often they are found on the blogosphere or a social network. By using Big Data tools, organizations can identify these questions and comments and respond to them accordingly in a timely manner.

Innovate Faster and Better

Developing a new product or updating an existing one generally takes a lot of time, because it is important to understand the market, to know what customers really want, and to test various possibilities. With Big Data, this information can be available in real time, 24 hours a day, thereby providing a company with insights from the moment a product is used for the first time. Feedback from sensors and analyses of public data streams enable companies to discover mistakes easily and to also identify requirements for future product updates.

Customer interactions with a company also provide valuable feedback that organizations can use to enhance innovation and product development. Whether this feedback is provided via the website or the call center (every conversation recorded by a call center can be turned into text, which could then be data mined for insights), it can be turned into market information for product improvements. This offers very useful information about what and how consumers feel about the brand and its products, as well as what they deem important. This lessens the need for expensive market research, while simultaneously significantly reducing the time to market of new and/or improved products.

In addition, prototyping can also be done virtually. Companies can test thousands of variations on a product within hours—or even minutes—instead of months and distill the best option for the largest target group, thereby reducing the time to market even more.

In highly competitive markets, it is of course also very important to understand what the competition is or will be doing. If a competitor introduces a new product, it is important to know how that product is perceived in real time. What is the sentiment? What are the complaints? What changes do consumers want to see in future updates? What is the price and how does the competition react to price fluctuations? All this information can be used to improve products and better react to what the competition is doing.

Optimize Sales and the Supply Chain

Real-time insights in point-of-sale (POS) data from all retailers can provide valuable insights to consumer goods manufacturers. In particular, they can learn how much of the product is sold at any time in any location around the world. Algorithms can automatically detect anomalies and warn the head office if action is required. The effect of price changes and the effects of marketing campaigns can also be evaluated in real time, giving the marketing team the opportunity to make changes instantly if the outcome is not as expected.

To anticipate expected demand for a product, a manufacturer can use different sales data, such as POS analysis, news reports, market information, competitor assessments, and weather conditions. These can provide valuable insights. By using predictive algorithms, the inventory can be optimized for just-in-time (JIT) inventory based on real-time demand forecasts. Cooperation with retailers can help shape demand at the store level to deliver an improved customer experience, which makes retailers happy.

Continuous monitoring of all equipment used in the operations can improve operational efficiencies.[18] Sensors added to equipment used in the production process give organizations a better understanding of how the machines are being used and where efficiencies can be achieved.

In addition, by using Big Data analyses, companies can predict upcoming price fluctuations and adjust purchases accordingly. These fluctuations can also be anticipated by following important parameters around the world that have an affect on the price. When these datasets are combined, predictive analytics can forecast price volatilities, demand, or shortages.

Make Knowledge Transparent

Consumer goods organizations tend to be large (international) businesses.[19] Most of the time in such large organizations, employees have difficulties knowing whom to ask for the right information. Algorithms can be used to make the knowledge within an organization accessible and searchable for everyone. Key influencers can be easily identified, along with specialists in specific areas. This would greatly improve the efficiency of the organization and reduce costs. Different departments within the same organization should not each reinvent the wheel. With all knowledge indexed, employees can simply perform a search query over the entire organization and find the best information and or colleague to consult.

Companies producing consumer goods should embrace Big Data, as the benefits are plentiful. This is especially true for large multinational consumer goods companies.

APPLE SWIMS IN MASSIVE AMOUNTS OF BIG DATA

It is no surprise that Apple deals with Big Data, but the specifics of how are not well known. However, with over 60 billion apps downloaded from its app store, Apple is swimming in massive amounts of data that can, and will be, analyzed for additional insights.[20]

Although Apple is a bit more secretive than other companies, such as Google, that are more willing to share some of their Big Data innovations, Apple does use some of the Big Data technologies, such as Hadoop or Large Scale Data Warehousing. One of the uses of Big Data is to understand how its own applications are used on the iPhone, iPads, or Macbooks, as mentioned by Jeff Kelly, Principal Research Contributor at Wikibon.[21,22] Using all the data that Apple has collected, it can test new features in their applications relatively easily and do A/B tests to improve the experience. The company uses data to understand how people are applying its applications. If it is a game application, the data can be used to understand where there is a bottleneck or where many people get stuck. That data will then be used to improve the gaming experience. In addition, feedback and reviews provided by users is also used in the App store to improve its products.

To store all that data, Apple uses Teradata equipment, and it now operates a multiple-petabyte Teradata system that is mostly driven by the launch of iCloud in 2011.[23]

Although Apple is gearing up for the Big Data era fast, it does not mean that the company has it all set out correctly. An article in *Forbes* in 2012 reported that one of the likely causes of Apple's failure to enter the Mobile Maps Application market was its struggle to catch up with Big Data.[24] While Google had already opened up its mapping functionality in 2005, Apple had to catch up in a much shorter timeframe, which turned out to be too short to develop a successful product.

It is obvious that Apple deals with massive amounts of data. Each of its products communicates back to the Apple data warehouse continuously.[25] Just think of the amount of data generated via Siri and stored for two years.[26] Then add the data collected via iTunes and iTunes Match, iCloud, and all other software and hardware. Although this is a lot of data, it is nothing spectacular or unexpected.

Clearly, Apple has been working with Big Data for some time. How much and how they do it exactly is difficult to find out. Whether Apple will reinvent Big Data with a new device, such as the iWatch, remains speculative. One thing, however, is for sure. Apple generates and collects vast amounts of data using several Big Data technologies and applies the results of data analyses in the development of products and services to improve the customer experience.

EDUCATION INDUSTRY

New technologies allow schools, colleges, and universities to analyze absolutely everything that happens with students, teachers, and employees, from student behavior to testing results to career development to educational needs based on changing societies. A lot of this data has already been collected and is used for statistical analysis by government agencies, such as the National Center for Educational Statistics.[27] With more and more online courses and the rise of Massive Open Online Courses (MOOCs), all that data acquires a completely new meaning. Big Data allows for very exciting changes in education that will revolutionize the way students learn and teachers teach. To fuel this trend, the U.S. Department of Education (DOE) was one of a host of agencies to share a $200 million initiative to begin applying Big Data analytics to their respective functions.[28,29]

Improve Student Results

The overall goal of Big Data within the educational system should be to improve student results. Better students are good for society, governments, and organizations, as well educational institutions. Currently, the answers to assignments and exams are the only measurements of student performance. During his or her student life, however, every student creates a unique data trail. This trail can be analyzed in real time to deliver an optimal learning environment for the student, as well to gain a better understanding of individual student behavior.

It is now possible to monitor all student actions. How long they need to answer a question? Which sources do they use? Which questions do they skip? How much research did they do? What is the relation between answers to questions? Which tips worked best for which student? Answers to questions can be checked instantaneously and automatically (except perhaps for essays), giving instant feedback to students.

In addition, Big Data can create more productive groups of students. Students often work in groups where the members do not complement each other. By using algorithms, it will be possible to determine the strengths and weaknesses of each student and create stronger groups that will allow students to have a steeper learning curve and deliver better results.

Create Mass-Customized Programs

All this data can help create customized programs for each student, even if a college or university has tens of thousands of enrollees. These will be created with blended learning, which combines online and offline courses. Students will have the opportunity to develop their own personalized program, following classes that interest them and working at their own pace, while having the possibility of (offline) guidance by professors. We already see this happening in the MOOCs that have been developed around the world. When Andrew Ng taught the Machine Learning class at Stanford University, 400 students generally participated.[30,31] When it was developed as an MOOC at Coursera in 2011, it attracted 100,000 students, who generated a lot of data.[32] It would take Andrew Ng 250 years to teach the same number of students. Being able to cater to 100,000 students at once also requires the right tools to process, store, analyze, and visualize all the data involved in the course. At the moment, these MOOCs are still mass produced, but in the future they can be mass customized.

With so many students participating in a MOOC, universities have the opportunity to find the best students from all over the world when making scholarship decisions. This will increase the overall ranking of a university.

Improve the Learning Experience in Real Time

When students start working independently in their customized blended learning program, students will teach themselves and be able to customize their courses. The professor can monitor students in real time and start more interesting and deeper discussions of topics of choice. This will give students an opportunity to gain a better understanding of the subjects.

When students are monitored in real time, digital textbooks and course outlines can be improved. Algorithms can monitor how the students read the texts, including which parts are difficult, which are easy, and which are unclear. Changes can be based on how often a text is read, how long it takes to read a text, how many questions are asked about a specific topic, how many links are clicked for more information, and how many and which sentences are underlined. If this information is provided in real time, authors can change their textbooks to meet the needs of students, thereby improving the overall results.

Even more, Big Data can give insights on how each student learns. This is important because it affects the student's final grade. Some students learn very efficiently, while others may be extremely inefficient. When course materials are available online, how a student learns can be monitored. This information can be used to provide a customized program for the student or provide real time feedback about how to become more efficient and thus improve their results.

Reduce Dropouts, Increase Results

All these analyses will improve student results and perhaps also reduce dropout rates. When students are closely monitored, receive instant feedback, and are coached based on their personal needs, it can help to reduce the number of dropouts.[33] which benefits educational institutions and society.

Educational institutions using predictive analytics on all the data that is collected can gain insights into future student outcomes. These predictions can be used to change a program if negative results are predicted or even run scenario analyses on a program before it starts. Universities and colleges will become more efficient in developing programs that will increase results, thereby minimizing trial and error.

After graduation, students can continue to be monitored to see how they perform in the job market. When this information is made public, it will help future students choose the right university. Big Data will revolutionize the learning industry in the coming years. More and more universities and colleges are already turning to Big Data to improve overall student results. Smarter students who study faster will have a positive effect on organizations and society.

PURDUE UNIVERSITY ACHIEVES REMARKABLE RESULTS WITH BIG DATA

Purdue University, located in West Lafayette, Indiana, has over 40,000 students and 6,600 staff members.[34] Founded in 1869, it was honored as having America's most innovative campus retention program in 2012.[35] Purdue University has prepared for the future by adopting Big Data, which has already achieved significant results.

Purdue University developed Course Signals, a system that helps predict academic and behavioral issues and notifies teachers as well as students when action is required.[36] The system ensures that each student achieves maximum potential, while decreasing the dropout rate and failing grades. The platform has been very successful and even won the Lee Noel and Randi Levitz Retention Excellence Award in 2012.[37] Course Signals is commonly viewed as the best example of how analytics can be applied to higher education to help improve student results so that they graduate in a timely manner.

Course Signals combines predictive modeling with data mining on Blackboard.[38] It uses various sources of data, such as course management and student information systems. As of week two in a semester, the data-mining tool Blackboard is able to interpret a student's academic preparation, engagement in, and effort within a course, and academic performance at a given point in time.[39] To achieve this, it uses student characteristics and academic preparation, the effort students put into the course (sessions, quizzes, and discussions, as well as time required to perform a task), and (past) performance (grades received so far and book data).

The algorithm predicts a risk profile for each student based on an easy-to-understand system: green (there is a high likelihood of success in a particular course), yellow (there are potential problems), and red (there is a risk for failure). The fact that this prediction can be provided in only the second week of a semester gives the students ample opportunity to improve results. The system immediately provides the students with various resources that can help them improve in the course. The risk profile can be adjusted per course.

Course Signals provides the teachers with feedback as well. When they run the software, teachers can follow up with the students instantly as problems arise. Teachers can run the software as often as they want, but the prediction is only updated when the program is accessed. The system has been in use since 2007, and the results are remarkable: improved grades for students and higher retention rates. As the website of Course Signals states, "As and Bs have increased by as much as 28 percent in some courses. In most cases, the greatest improvement is seen in students who were initially receiving Cs and Ds in early assignments, and pull up half a letter grade or more to a B or C."[40]

Purdue University has also partnered with EMC to solve its Big Data storage problems.[41,42] All 40,000 students will receive 100 gigabytes of space (that is four petabytes of storage), and they will work together to develop new ways to process, analyze, transfer, and manage the massive research datasets in the field of bioinformatics, among others.

It may be obvious that Purdue University has identified Big Data as very important for research and education. The institution is currently recruiting for several faculty positions to stimulate and further develop its Big Data agenda.[43] Purdue is far ahead of other educational institutions in adapting and implementing a Big Data strategy.

ENERGY INDUSTRY

Since the invention of the steam engine in the seventeenth century, we have come a long way in developing and supplying the world's energy. We have created networks that deliver electricity to 75 percent of the world.[44] As a result of Big Data, we can now take the next step in the evolution of energy. Big Data can turn the existing old energy network into smart networks that understand individual energy consumption.

This will increase efficiencies, lower prices and reduce our global carbon footprint.

The Smart Energy Grid

In the (near) future, more and more appliances will have sensors; they will become part of the Internet of Things. These sensors will enable bidirectional communication with energy companies, smart meters, and other in-home appliances.[45] As a result, the energy consumption of individual devices can be monitored and adjusted, if desired. Energy organizations are already developing smart meters that record consumption of electric energy in intervals and send that information back to the energy company, which can then understand and predict demand.

When more devices have sensors, products will be able to talk to each other, as well as to the different networks. This will help energy companies manage the utilization across the network. This is especially useful and important for the future of electric cars. Energy grids will not be able to cope with peak demand when consumers plug in their electric cars at the same time when they get home from work.[46] The more devices that have sensors and can talk to the energy network, the better energy companies can try to adjust to demand. A true smart grid, however, is still far away.

Such a smart grid will prevent energy losses and power outages across the network. Sensor systems called synchrophasors can monitor in real time the condition of power lines, collecting multiple data streams per second.[47] The sensors can also detect how the energy travels across the network and where and when energy is lost. This information can detect blackouts and provide energy companies with the possibility of responding faster when an outage occurs.[48]

Battelle's Pacific Northwest Smart Grid Demonstration Project is such a pilot smart grid, with 60,000 participants across five states.[49] This project aims to determine whether smart grids are as valuable as we think and whether they even make sense economically, as a smart grid requires substantial investments in hardware and software. Such a grid will also increase data tremendously, as meter reading will go from once a month to once every 15 minutes. This works out to 96 million reads per day for every million meters.[50] The result is a 3,000-fold increase in data that can be overwhelming if not properly managed.

Change Consumer Behavior

Consumers who can manage their own energy consumption based on real-time data and energy prices will probably change their behavior. A smart meter can advise consumers when to use a device to take advantage of times when energy costs are lower based on prediction of estimated demand. This will help energy companies better manage the energy demand. If appliances (for example, washing machines) can determine themselves when the best time is to start working based on set price ranges and energy demand in the network, better results can be achieved.

Forecast Demand and Prices

A smart grid that has connections with millions of appliances can estimate energy consumption for large regions. Monitoring how devices are using energy provides valuable data that can be analyzed to predict energy needs and possible shortages. This information can be used to deliver the right amount of energy to the right place at the right time. It can help flatten the peaks of energy across time and place. Energy distribution organizations can thereby improve both customer satisfaction and regulatory compliance by reducing the number and duration of power outages.[51] If energy companies can start making connections between network failures and events, they can also begin to understand the patterns that could indicate network problems, as well as isolate the locations and identify solutions in real time.[52]

When the smart grid flattens peaks in energy demand, the network will become more reliable. The problem with current networks is not so much capacity, but rather the ability to cope with peak demands. Smart grids can help minimize those extreme peaks that could cause power outages.

Big Data will also help optimize energy trading and thereby better anticipate price volatilities by performing almost real-time sophisticated analysis of the market based on thousands of different datasets.[53] Predicting energy supply and demand will help organizations sell energy profitably and hedge if needed. By understanding the market, they can protect themselves against the fluctuating pricing of energy. In the end, they will be able to deliver the energy cheaper and increase customer satisfaction.

Future Investment and Maintenance

Insights generated by analyzing the vast amounts of sensor data that come from the network can provide extra information about the quality of the network itself.[54] The data can help determine where future investments are necessary and where maintenance is needed. Instead of checking the network at regular intervals, Big Data tools can monitor equipment across the network in real time and take action only when it is required. This will save organizations money, as unnecessary investigations of possible problems will be prevented. The same information will inform companies which investments will yield the greatest returns.

Vattenfall, a Swedish power company, for example, has installed sensors in its wind turbines to predict when maintenance is needed.[55] This saves the company money on needless helicopter flights to the turbines, unnecessary maintenance checks, and costly consulting.

Big Data can be also be used to improve wind turbine placement for optimal energy output. The constantly changing weather data on micro and macro levels can help organizations forecast the best spots for their wind turbines or solar systems by informing them where, on an annual basis, the most wind or sun is foreseen. When combined with structured and unstructured data, such as tidal phases, geospatial and sensor data, satellite images, deforestation maps, and weather modeling, it can help pinpoint the best place for installation.[56]

The Danish energy company Vestas Wind Systems, for example, uses IBM Big Data analytics to analyze many different datasets to determine the best place for each wind turbine. Placing wind turbines at the wrong spot can result in insufficient electricity to justify wind energy investments, as well as an increase in electricity costs.[57]

Therefore, Big Data most important effect on the energy sector is to develop smart energy grids so that existing networks become more efficient. This will reduce energy consumption and prices. Smarter energy management can keep overloaded grids running and prevent the need for building new and expensive power plants.[58] Fewer power plants delivering more efficient energy at lower prices will affect our carbon footprint. So, in the end, it might turn out that Big Data is the most sustainable technology, reducing our impact on the environment even more than renewable energy sources.

FINANCIAL SERVICES INDUSTRY

If any industry can benefit from Big Data, it is the financial services industry. Of course, the first use that comes to mind is the ability to reduce risks, whether it be credit risk, default risk, or liquidity risk. But, many more possibilities exist. This industry, which has lost the trust of its customers since the crisis of 2008, can turn to Big Data to understand customers better and improve customer satisfaction. However, Big Data also offers other possibilities.

Reduce the Risk Companies Are Facing

Financial services firms have the ability to create an individual risk profile for each customer based on many variables such as past purchasing behavior, online and offline social networking, way of life, and information from public datasets. The more data that is used, the more accurate the risk profile, thereby decreasing credit default risks. The insurance company Insurethebox is a pioneer in using Big Data to reduce risk.[59] Customers install a device in their cars that measures exactly how, when, and where each insured vehicle is driven. Based on this information, an algorithm determines the driver's behavior (including acceleration and deceleration behavior, among other factors) and a corresponding risk profile results. Each customer then receives a tailor-made insurance offer. The better a customers drives, the better the offer.

Algorithms can also analyze trades and conduct high-volume transaction in nanoseconds to optimize returns and reduce trading risks, while taking into account different market conditions, such as the pricing of products or future demand.[60] Risky trades can be blocked automatically or the algorithm can flag high exposure in a changing market.

Big Data technologies also improve enterprise risk management. It is possible to add and use different data sets to determine the risk profile of a client who is requesting a loan. Factors such as claims, new business, investment management, or lifestyle of managers will provide a better picture regarding an organization's appetite for risk than a business plan based on many different and unknown future variables. The result will be more sophisticated and accurate predictive models that will reduce enterprise risks and help companies.

Fraud can also easily be detected with Big Data. For example, analyses could show when a customer suddenly deviates from a standard and long-standing pattern. Outlier detection is a powerful tool for discovering anomalies. Algorithms can easily detect instantly when a credit card is used in distant locations within a short time frame. This will indicate possible fraud detection. Even better is the ability to analyze a transaction based on different datasets while the transaction is taking place, allowing organizations to block a transaction before it has taken place rather than checking it afterward. Visa has implemented a system that can analyze 500 aspects of a transaction at once.[61] With an annual incremental fraud opportunity of $2 billion, Visa has every reason to pay a lot of attention to Big Data.[62]

Big Data can also stop criminals who use the "old-fashioned" technique of robbing a bank. Big Data enables banks to understand which ATMs are the most likely to be targeted by criminals and how often. This is based on geographic location and many other datasets. Banks can then take appropriate measures to reduce the risk of a robbery or install smart cameras that can detect criminal activities before they happen.

With a 360-degree customer view, it is possible to understand the individual behavior of the customers and how that will impact future demand. This can be based on historical data (for example, monitoring how someone drives to determine car insurance) and risk models (for example, based on where someone lives in relation to the online presence of that person). This will tell a great deal about the potential risk of an individual and, as such, determine an appropriate price.

Regain Trust of Customers and Improve Customer Satisfaction

As with any industry, financial services firms also want to develop 360-degree profiles and microsegmentations to better understand and approach their customers. These companies offer many different products from insurance to credit cards to regular banking accounts.

Analyzing the use of these products explains a lot about customer behavior. Although banks do not do this (or at least they say they do not), they have the capability to understand customers better than customers understand themselves based on payment information. For that reason, when Dutch payment provider Equens, which is the largest pan-European payment processor that takes care of all debit and credit transactions, decided to sell the transaction data, a lot of complaints appeared, and Equens had to withdraw the plan.[63] Customer satisfaction can be improved in many different ways. Online tools can be made faster, additional services can be offered (such as instant search results when entering a bank account number), and customer service can be improved by ensuring that representatives who answer phone calls have access to all necessary details because internal systems are aligned and connected.

Develop Products Customers Need

Social media algorithms make it possible to understand the sentiment of customers in real time, providing information regarding how they think about or use new products and services or react to commercials. In addition, algorithms can be used to identify the most important influencers and how they think about products or services. An analysis of how products are used can give insights into how they need to be improved. For example, a bank can analyze how a mobile banking application is used based on location, time of day, where people click, how they move through the app, and how long they use the app or search for items within the app. This can indicate areas that need improvement. Instead of asking customers for feedback using long and expensive surveys, the feedback here is instantaneous and the customer is not bothered. This will help optimize the product.

Increase Sales and Reduce Costs

Humans live pretty predicable lives. As so many products are bought with a debit or credit card, it is possible to find patterns in consumer behavior based on where the cards are used, how much money was involved, and the purpose. When this behavior is monitored, financial services organizations can take action based on future events, such as selling additional products at the right time to the right customer, thereby increasing the conversion rate. An example would be a consumer who suddenly buys more groceries because a significant other moved in.

The financial services industry is also known for large legacy systems that are expensive to maintain. With a Big Data platform, it is possible to migrate legacy data to new platforms, while, in turn, adding valuable data to the analysis. This data can deliver new insights, which could then lead to new revenue opportunities or a reduction in operation costs. Operational efficiencies can further be improved when transaction and unstructured data, such as that collected from voice recognition, social comments, and emails, are monitored and analyzed to anticipate future workloads and change staffing needs accordingly in call centers and branches. In addition, when all customer contact points are collected and shown via one platform, staff will be able to help customers faster and better.

Big Data makes it possible to monitor the activities of clients that could indicate churn. If a customer suddenly starts engaging in fewer bank activities, it could be the result of dissatisfaction and indicate a customer who is about to churn. In addition, if the financial services industry knows who the influencers are within market segments, it can ensure that those influencers do not churn, because if they do, it is possible that others will follow. If these activities can be identified, financial services companies can take preventive actions to ensure customer loyalty.

The possibilities for the financial services industry are almost endless, but they come with significant privacy issues. As the example of Equens in The Netherlands showed, consumers are very sensitive regarding personal financial information that banks use to make more money, particularly since consumers have lost so much trust in financial institutions in past years. Therefore, even more than for the other industries, the four ethical guidelines are extremely important when implementing Big Data strategy.

MORGAN STANLEY UNDERSTANDS HOW TO LEVERAGE ITS BIG DATA

Morgan Stanley is an American global financial services firm headquartered in New York City. Through its subsidiaries and affiliates, it offers its products and services in 42 countries with more than 1,300 offices. Customers include corporations, governments, financial institutions, and individuals. Morgan Stanley has over $300 billion in assets under its care and employs over 60,000 employees globally. With such a large company, traditional databases and grid computing are insufficient to deal with the vast amounts of data created. To deal with the vast amounts of data, the company started using Hadoop back in 2010.[64] In the past years, Morgan Stanley has have come a long way and is fully up-to-speed with Big Data.

In an article in Forbes, Gary Bhattacharjee, Executive Director of Enterprise Information Management at Morgan Stanley, describes the benefits for the firm by using Hadoop.[65,66] Although the nature of the company means that much cannot be revealed, he does share some insights into how Hadoop helped Morgan Stanley create a scalable and vast solution for its portfolio analysis. Information that used to take months to amass can now be collected in real time as events happen. An example Bhattacharjee shares is that Morgan Stanley uses Hadoop to look at its entire web and database logs to discover problems. For example, when a market event occurs now, the company is capable of understanding the impact in real time. Problems are discovered in real time, and events is completely traceable as to who did what, how, and when, and what caused the issue.

When Morgan Stanley started with Hadoop, the company used 15-year-old commodity servers, on which Hadoop was installed. Nowadays, Hadoop helps with its mission-critical investment projects.[67] With its Big Data projects, Morgan Stanley bets heavily on open-source tools.[68] According to Bhattacharjee, open-source tools allow Morgan Stanley's ecosystem to be extremely agile, with short product cycles and innovations happening a lot faster than when using products from HP or IBM, both of which have long product vendor life cycles.

But of course, that's not all of the ways in which Morgan Stanley uses Big Data. For Morgan Stanley Smith Barney (MSSB), a joint venture between Morgan Stanley and Citigroup formed in 2009 that manages $1.7 trillion in assets for four million clients, predictive analytics are used to make better recommendations for investments in stocks, municipal bonds, and fixed income.[69] For proper outcomes, predictive software requires vast amounts of data, and MSSB is not shy about data. Apart from the 450 reports the firm's equity analysts produce daily, employees use large amounts of public and social data to perform their analyses. All the information is used to make recommendations about whether to buy or sell stock based on real-time positions and market conditions. The system is constantly being improved and advisers can teach the program by deleting unnecessary or incorrect information.

In addition, Morgan Stanley decided to start using wire data to find errors within its applications.[70] Wire data is all the data flowing in systems between all physical and logical layers. Real-time wire data analytics can help detect and prioritize problems across their applications as they analyze how applications behave and then mine that data for useful information. To do this successfully, they use software from ExtraHop, a company that helps IT organizations harness the massive amounts of wire data flowing through their environments for real-time operational intelligence.[71]

Although Morgan Stanley is a global financial services firm, it understands that its data is one of its greatest assets and that it can be used to improve services and drive additional revenue across many different departments within the organization.

GAMING INDUSTRY

There are more than two billion videogame players worldwide. Electronic Arts (EA) has 275 million active users, who generate approximately 50 terabytes of data every day.[72] The gaming industry does $20 billion in annual revenue in the United States alone, of which $2 billion is in subcategory social games.[73] In the United States and Canada, the gaming industry is bigger than the movie industry, which sees annual ticket sales of $10.8 billion.[74] The world of gaming is big, growing rapidly, and taking full advantage of the Big Data technologies. Gaming companies can drive customer engagement, make more money on advertising, and optimize the gaming experience with Big Data.

An Improved Customer Experience

As with any organization, the 360-degree customer view is important for the gaming industry. Fortunately, gamers leave a massive data trail. Whether it is an online social game via Facebook, a game played on an offline PlayStation, or a multiplayer game via Xbox, gamers create a lot of data in different formats. They create massive datastreams with everything they do, including. how they interact, how long they play, when they play, with whom they play, how much they spend on virtual products, with whom they chat, and so on. If the gaming profile is linked to social networks or a gamer is asked to enter demographic data, the information can be enriched with an understanding of what the gamer likes in real life, and gaming companies can adapt the game to the profile of the gamer.

Based on all that data, targeted in-game products can be offered that have a high conversion rate. They can function just like on ecommerce websites, where products are recommended based on what other customers bought. Gaming companies can then recommend certain features that other players also bought or virtual products based on the gamer's level. This can result in an increased up-sell or cross-sell ratio and additional revenue.

Engagement can also be increased if analytics show that a player will abandon the game if the first levels are too difficult or if later levels are too easy. Data can be used to find bottlenecks within the game, where many players fail in performaing the tasks at hand. Or, it can be used to find the areas that are too easy and need to be improved. Analyzing millions of player data gives insight into which elements of the game are the most popular. It can show what elements are unpopular and require action to improve the game. Constant engagement is vital. With the right tools, the right reward can be provided at the right moment for the right person within the game to keep a player engaged.

Big data technologies also help optimize in-game performance and end-user experience. When for example the databases and servers of the games have to cope with a steep increase in online players, it is important to have sufficient capacity. With big data it is possible to predict the peaks in demand to anticipate on the required capacity and scale accordingly. This will improve the gaming experience (who likes a slow game) and thus the end-user experience.

Deliver a Tailored Gaming Experience

Games that are developed for different consoles or devices (tablets versus smartphones or Xbox versus PlayStations) result in different playing experiences. When all the data is analyzed, it can provide insights into how games are played on different devices and whether the differences among devices present any problems that need to be resolved. When gamers switch between devices, the game should automatically be optimized for the new device based on the player's history.

Big Data also allows the tailoring of advertisements to the player's needs and wishes of the player. With all the data created by gamers, a 360-degree in-game profile can be created that, when combined with open and social data, gives insights into the likes and dislikes of that gamer. This information can be used to show within the game only those advertisements that match the profile of the gamer, resulting in a higher stickiness factor, more value for the advertiser, and, subsequently, more revenue for the game developer.

Ample opportunities exist for game developers to improve the gaming experience with Big Data, drive more revenue, and make the game faster and better. Game developers should not miss out on Big Data, because the benefits are too big to ignore.

ZYNGA IS AN ANALYTICS COMPANY MASQUERADING AS A GAMING COMPANY

How much data would an online developer like Zynga create and use on a daily basis? The answer is, not surprisingly, a lot. In fact, the company operates on such a large scale that on a regular day Zynga delivers one petabyte of content.[75] To cope with the extreme high demands of data, Zynga has built a flexible cloud server center that can easily add up to 1,000 servers in just 24 hours. Its private and public cloud server park is one of the biggest hybrid clouds.[76]

Zynga is built on top of major platforms, such as Facebook, Google+, and Android/iOS, and offers its own Zynga API. Data at Zynga is divided into two types:

- Game data, which is Vertica driven and generates approximately 60 billion rows of data and 10 terabyte of semistructured data daily.
- Server data, which generates over 13 terabyte of raw log data from the server and app logs. This is stored in Vertica or Hadoop.

Interestingly, Zynga's database keeps growing, as it never deletes data because the process required is too complex.[77]

Metrics Driven Culture

At Zynga everything revolves around metrics, and for the management at Zynga, metrics are a discipline.[78] Management has a strong desire to track progress using metrics. To support this, reports are freely accessible by everyone and integrating external services is easy. Brian Reynolds, a game designer, explains that at Zynga, the designers are separated from those who analyze the metrics.[79] Analysts need to figure out what questions should be asked, and the designers develop/adjust the game to fit the answer.[80]

A great example of this data-driven decision-making is how the company pivoted the use of animals in Farmville 2.0. In the original version, animals were merely decorative.[81] However, data showed that more and more people started interacting with the animals and even used real money to buy additional virtual animals. So, in Farmville 2.0, animals became much more central, which subsequently drove more revenue.

Due to this metrics-driven culture, Zynga combines art with science.[82] Art is needed to create, develop, and implement an idea into a game. With the science behind it, the company listens to customers and determines whether the game is fun or not. Afterward, it can adjust and pivot games if necessary.

Zynga uses a large number of different databases for different tasks.[83] For example, it uses Splunk to store primary log analytics.[84] Seventy nodes and 650 million rows of data are stored daily in a streaming event database using a MySQL cluster. The company has sharded transactional databases and uses a Vertica Data Warehouse.[85]

The statistics that Zynga generates are gigantic as well. It generates over 6,000 different report types (3,000 every day) and receives 15,000 ad hoc queries from users on a daily basis. Analysts, product managers, engineers, and business intelligence teams use all these insights to optimize and improve operations and products.

HEALTHCARE INDUSTRY

Healthcare is rapidly becoming another digitized industry that will generate vast amounts of data that can be analyzed. If a fully sequenced human genome accounts for 100 gigabyte of raw data, it is clear that the healthcare industry will generate massive amounts of data in the coming years. All that data can be analyzed to create tailored medicines, improve treatments, and reduce fraudulent behaviors. According to Pricewaterhouse Coopers (PwC), fraudulent, wasteful, and abusive behaviors account for an estimated one-third of the $2.2 trillion spent on healthcare in the United States each year, so there is a lot to gain by using Big Data.[86,87] The potential of Big Data is enormous, but it will also require substantial investments, time, and energy in the coming decades.

Improve Patient Care

Many countries around the world are implementing Electronic Health Records (EHRs) programs that will optimize and centralize patient information. These EHRs will create a lot of data that, when deidentified, aggregated, and analyzed, will provide a lot of valuable information.[88] Such programs combine clinical data from labs and electronic medical records with patient data, historical background information, and social factors into one platform that can analyze and enhance predictive accuracy that will improve treatments. When the available data is centralized, it will enhance communication among all patient-care team members with the overall goal of improving the patient experience and quality of care.[89] Algorithms can analyze which treatment (or no treatment) will have the best outcome based on all the data, as well as the personal DNA of the patient.

Big Data technology can also be used to enhance the patient's experience. Hospitals that give doctors, nurses, and patients RFID-enabled chips embedded in the patient's or doctor's card will be able to effectively manage the healthcare experience.[90] These sensors can provide insights into the relationship between patient satisfaction and the amount of time a doctor or nurse spent with the patient. It can also show the distance nurses and doctors have to walk across the hospital to care for their patients and whether it is wise to relocate various departments to minimize travel time and optimize the use of expensive equipment.

Apart from monitoring the behavior of doctors or nurses, it is also possible to monitor patients all the time anywhere in real time. The data streams that are collected from bedside monitors when a patient is in a hospital can be analyzed in real time to detect subtle, but harmful, changes in vital signs and alert medical personnel when a change becomes dangerous. In the future, it will be possible to have sensors inside or attached to your body that will measure vital conditions and alert a doctor whenever necessary.[91] Such a telemedicine platform can be especially useful for patients in remote areas or for patients who have difficulties getting to a hospital.[92] By using predictive analytics in real time to analyze the data from these sensors, it will become possible to predict a stroke or heart attack before a patient notices anything is wrong.

Out-of-home healthcare can also be improved using quantified-self applications and medical applications on smartphones next to in-body sensors.[93] These applications can measure vital signs at regular intervals and help the patient determine the reason for a change. If required, the patient can be sent to a hospital in time, where on arrival the doctors will already know what is going on with the patient.

The objective for doctors and nurses is to eventually improve treatments and reduce hospital (re)admission rates. Algorithms can assist doctors in recommending and determining the best treatment for each situation faced by a patient by taking into account the EHRs, social factors, demographic information, and geographic data. With predictive analytics, the outcome of certain treatments can be analyzed before a patient receives treatment. As such, the best treatment is provided, thereby reducing the need for readmission. This will save hospitals, patients, and insurance companies a lot of money.

Personalized Medicines and Treatments

Sequencing human genomes and DNA has become inexpensive and fast. Between 2003 and 2013, the cost of sequencing a human genome, including analyzing and interpreting it, went from $2.7 billion to only $5,000.[94] A sequenced genome will provide doctors with a lot of information about a patient's health, including how the patient will react to certain medicines and the patient's risk for certain diseases. With Big Data, it is possible to improve the sequencing of DNA as well as lower the price to a point where it can be used in treatments regularly.[95] In the future, it can be used to tailor medicine to the human genome of a patient to obtain the best results. Combining all the patient's EHRs, diet information, and social factors with the sequenced DNA will enable doctors to recommend a tailored treatment as well as personalized medicine.

Algorithms can also analyze the effects certain drugs will have on different types of patients when combined with other medicines. During simulations, minor changes can be made to medicines and scenario analysis can be performed to determine what will happen when a certain medicine is adjusted. With Big Data and the right algorithms, this will replace the need to perform research on real patients, thereby saving valuable time and money and reducing the time to market for new medicines.

Prevent Fraudulent Behavior

Fraudulent actions can be detected using Big Data when the health insurance company's datasets are linked to public and social data.[96] This can determine if people are telling the truth if, for example, someone claims illness during a certain time but can be seen in holiday pictures during that same period on Facebook. In addition, doctors who submit insurance claims for treatments that were never performed can be more easily detected if aggregated claims over the entire population are analyzed, taking into account patient demographics, past procedures and treatments, diagnoses, and the ordering physician's utilization patterns.[97] With outlier detection analysis, doctors who claim too many treatments will easily be discovered and can be investigated more closely.

In addition, Big Data can determine overutilization of treatments, services, or medicines in a short timeframe by comparing historical data. Data about patients traveling great distances to obtain controlled medicine, the billing of "unlikely" services by doctors, or data about treatments related to their geographic area can provide a lot of insight into fraudulent behavior by doctors, hospitals, or patients.

By connecting various (open) datasets, insurance companies and hospitals will heave a wealth of information that can reduce the massive amounts of money lost because of fraudulent, wasteful, and abusive behaviors. The way Big Data can help prevent health insurance fraud can also be used to target health campaigns more specifically, particularly if certain conditions, treatments, or medicine are seen more often in certain geographic and demographic areas. This will lead to tailored and effective campaigns that will save organizations and society a lot of money.

The opportunities to use Big Data are enormous in the healthcare industry, although it will require a lot of investment. Many challenges still remain to be overcome.

BIG DATA ENSURES A HEALTHY FINANCIAL POSITION AT AURORA HEALTH CARE

Aurora Health Care has 1.2 million customers, 15 hospitals, 185 clinics, more than 80 community pharmacies, and over 30,000 employees, including over 6,300 registered nurses and nearly 1,500 physicians. This creates massive amounts of data. The not-for-profit Aurora Health Care system has decided to put that wealth of data to use to improve decision making and make the organization more information-centric.

In 2012, Aurora finalized Smart Chart, a $200 million records system that gathers all data collected in the past ten years into a single data warehouse. It began as an effort to "get nationally recognized measures of our clinical performance by scoring them against national standards" explains Phil Loftus, Chief Information Officer of the health group, in *Forbes*.[98] In other words, Aurora sought to combine nationwide data with its own data to benchmark results and create a national reputation for quality. The company used clinical data and data-mining tools to analyze the large amounts of data to achieve better insights.

Aurora created a hybrid Business Intelligence (BI) ecosystem blending a message-centric Exact-Transform-Load (ETL) approach, using a Relational Database Management System to do all dimension and fact table processing with a Big Data platform.[99] The SQL-MapReduce and nPath enabled analytics platform controls the traditional business intelligence reporting, as well as the next-generation Big Data analytics.

Aurora processes 18 different main streams of data in near real time. It includes financial, pharmacy, laboratory, and procedure data. The goal is to use all data in a highly secure and effective manner. The tasks are computed using a massive parallel processing system with multiple low-cost microprocessors, giving it 20 to 30 times more computing power than a traditional data warehouse.[100] This allows Aurora to look differently at the data, as well as to change the analytics from looking at individual patients to groups of patients who have the same diseases, such as diabetes or heart failure. This discloses new trends and insights and helps researchers more easily find the right patients for testing new medications. In addition, the Aurora system keeps thorough records of each patient's history. This data is available to doctors, nurses, and caregivers throughout the system, which ensures that the patients get accurate diagnoses and the best treatment based on their personal information.

Aurora also treats more patients at home. In 2013, nurses equipped with laptops visited approximately 2,300 patients at home. Secure wireless datacards enabled these nurses to access the computer system and review all relevant patient information.

Using all available data and near real-time data analytics, Aurora can predict and improve patient treatments and outcomes.[101] Using the different data streams, Aurora has decreased patient readmissions by 10 percent, which translates into a total saving of $6 million. Data helps doctors lower the cost of care by analyzing outcomes and recommending different procedures.

Aurora also decided to join and participate in the development of the Oracle Health Sciences Network, an information-sharing platform in the cloud that enables cooperation among life sciences institutes, researchers, and healthcare providers.[102,103] Aurora wanted to join this network as it will help improve the healthcare patients receive through participation in drug trials.

The results of the Big Data endeavor by Aurora Health Care are interesting. In addition to the savings achieved by reducing patient readmissions, the organization reduced query time, improved data insights, and saved 42 percent on treatment costs.

LEGAL PROFESSION
How Big Data Can Improve the Practice of Law

Many industries are starting to see the benefits that can be reaped from analyzing and visualizing the vast amounts of data created nowadays. The more conservative industries have been slower to adopt the new technology, but some are slowly waking up and looking in the direction of Big Data. One of these is the legal profession, including the judicial system and law firms.

However, many questions remain, such as: What are the benefits of Big Data for courts or law firms? How can Big Data help overcome common court procedural issues, such as overburdened dockets, delays, and rising costs? How should the legal system deal with sensitive data from trials? What are the implications of Big Data for legal practitioners? Clearly, many questions remain. Although Big Data is new to this industry, there are some great examples of its application. Let's dive deeper into this issue.

InformationWeek described the case of the boutique law firm Thomas Horstemeyer in Atlanta.[104,105] It has approximately 60 employees and specializes in the field of intellectual property. Instead of maintaining archives of the documentation about its different cases, the firm has moved everything to the private cloud. It has several storage area networks (over a dozen terabytes of data) in the office, and it performs several types of analyses on that data. The law firm created a pure virtual environment and, as such, it upgraded its firewalls and added load balancing, virtualized its servers, and replaced its phone system with VoIP.[106] In addition, it saved on capital expenses by no longer requiring vast amounts of storage space for old case files.

Although this does not seem to have much to do with Big Data, it is a beginning, as law firms traditionally tend to hold on to paper documents. However, digitization of paper documents allows for faster analysis of the available data and less time spent searching for information in old case files.

Other applications show how Big Data can contribute to the legal profession. First, it can greatly reduce costs and speed up court procedures, particularly when vast numbers of files and other relevant data can be analyzed instantly and correlated. To do this, law firms need to correctly collect, store, catalogue, and organize all their data. Computing power is now strong enough and cheap enough to store all that data. In the future, this could lead to completely new insights related to cases and could enable lawyers and public prosecutors to answer questions that are currently unanswerable.

For example, law firms could use algorithms that offer predictions on certain cases based on how similar cases fared in the same jurisdiction in the past. The small Californian law firm of Dummit, Buchholz & Trapp uses such technology, developed by LexisNexis, to determine in 20 minutes whether a case is worth taking on or not.[107] In the past, this took 20 days.

Second, Big Data will drive transparency into the legal profession, which will benefit both lawyers and corporate clients. The tool TyMetrix LegalView Analytics, for example, has collected vast numbers of invoices totaling tens of billions of dollars in legal spending on an ongoing basis.[108,109] This helps law firms benchmark themselves against the industry and determine the right price for certain cases. There are also tools like Sky Analytics that help law firms reduce and benchmark legal spending and control costs.[110] These tools give law firms an unparalled macroview into the costs of services, as well as provide advice for clients on how to cut the best deal on legal services in any given location.

Consumers can also take advantage of the democratization of data in the legal profession. The app RateDriver enables users to quickly determine the appropriate rate they should expect to pay for attorney's fees in 51 U.S. markets.[111,112]

Finally, Big Data can find new evidence that can be used in court. Several American case examples indicate that big data collected and analyzed from public datasets can be admitted as evidence.[113] In addition, the legal profession has always been data driven, but until recently all that data was on paper. Now that legal firms are slowly moving to the digital world, vast new opportunities are being created to improve research. Digital data at law firms can easily be connected to open and public datasets, thereby providing additional clarification and new insights. As LexisNexis Chief Architect Ian Koenig explains, "it is allowing us to find the right needle in the stack of needles."[114]

More and more big data startups are appearing in the market that focus specifically on the legal profession. One is Juristat, a St. Louis–based start-up that's doing the moneyball approach in court jurisdictions in America.[115] Juristat provides actionable analytics to lawyers and law firms, allowing them to optimize litigation strategies, marketing, and internal operations.[116] But the tool from Juristat can go even further; it can even predict how a flu outbreak might affect a jury verdict.

Big Data is still just beginning to affect the legal profession, and there is still a long way to go. Among others reasons, law forms are reluctant to digitize data because so much of its data consists of confidential information that might raise privacy and security issues. For many firms, Big Data therefore poses many risks and challenges, but, in the end, the only way forward is the digital way.

MANUFACTURING INDUSTRY

In 2013, General Electric (GE) announced the development of the "predictivity" platform in cooperation with Amazon Web Services.[117] The goal was to develop an Industrial Internet ready for the Big Data era. The Industrial Internet can be seen as the integration of complex physical machinery with networked sensors and software. It is a Hadoop-based software platform for high-volume, machine data management, and it will provide industrial companies with a collective architecture, merging intelligent machines, sensors, and advanced analytics. The development of such a platform shows the massive opportunities in the manufacturing and industrial industry for using Big Data.

The Industrial Internet will need to overcome some serious challenges before it is common in the manufacturing industry. First of all, turning a factory into a smart factory requires a large investment and a new way of working. It also requires Big Data standards and an ecosystem to ensure smooth operation between different companies, which has yet to be developed. Of course, the large number of sensors in the machinery will create a lot of data, probably driving us into the brontobytes era fairly soon. This will require powerful analytics that can handle vast amounts of data. In addition, providing security for all this data is a vital issue, as malware in the Industrial Internet could do more than "just" affect sensitive information; it could trigger direct physical destruction.[118] The Industrial Internet is just one of the benefits of applying Big Data in the manufacturing industry.

Optimize Operational Efficiencies

Using data during the production process and sensors attached to machines, the entire production process can be analyzed to understand how each section is performing. The moment a process deviates from the standard, an alert can inform the factory of the problem. Mistakes can be found much faster, and errors can be solved and bottlenecks eliminated. The sensors can identify the problem for the engineer, who will then know how to fix it expeditiously. With Big Data technologies, it is also possible to model the production of industrial products virtually, thereby optimizing the production process.

When all this information is visible in one central dashboard, the transparency created can help manufacturers improve their production processes. In addition, many organizations keep their data in silos across the company. In large multinational organizations, this information can be especially difficult to retrieve. Big Data can help organizations centralize all information on to one platform (in the cloud), giving all employees access to relevant information based on their role. Creating a product lifecycle management (PLM) platform that integrates datasets from multiple systems will significantly increase effective and consistent collaboration across the organization.

When information is accessible from a centralized platform in the cloud, it ensures that all departments throughout the organization will work with the same data. This will decrease the number of errors and, as such, increase operational efficiency. In addition, operational efficiency will be further increased when data sources from relevant suppliers are taken into consideration. As a result, suppliers will have more accurate information about when to deliver what materials.

Optimize the Supply Chain

Large Original Equipment Manufacturers (OEMs) can have thousands of suppliers delivering tens of thousands of different products to manufacturers. Each will trade at its own price, depending on market forecasts and other variables, such as sales data, market information, events happening in the world, competitor data, and weather conditions. Using sales data, product sensor data, and data from the supplier's database, industrial manufacturers will be able to predict demand accurately in different regions around the world.

The ability to track and predict inventory and prices and to buy when prices are low can significantly reduce costs for manufacturers. If they also know, using sensors in the products, when products are about to break and which part is needed where, they can forecast inventory needs and optimize the supply chain even more. Collaboration with different players within the supply chain can help shape demand at the manufactories to deliver a better B2B experience.

Save Money

Centralized monitoring of all processes during the manufacturing of the equipment can be accomplished using sensors. This can show anomalies or peaks in energy consumption, which can be used to optimize energy usage during the production process. For example, heat can be adjusted in buildings based on the number of people present.

The Industrial Internet enables manufacturing companies to use Big Data technologies to improve operational efficiencies, reduce costs, and create better products. It offers a lot of possibilities. In the coming years, more organizations within the manufacturing industry will see the need to optimize the supply chain and operational processes using

Big Data, helping the Industrial Internet as envisioned by GE to become reality.[119]

FORD DRIVES IN THE RIGHT DIRECTION WITH BIG DATA

Ford uses Big Data to learn what its customers want and to develop better cars in less time. To develop a product that requires 20,000 to 25,000 different parts, Ford is betting heavily on Big Data. Ford actually opened a lab in Silicon Valley just for this purpose.[120] To improve its cars in terms of quality, fuel consumption, safety, and emissions, Ford aggregates data from over four million cars that have in-car sensors and remote app management software. All data is analyzed in real time, thereby allowing engineers to notice issues immediately, understanding how the cars respond in different road and weather conditions and to any other forces that affect them.

Ford is already installing over 74 sensors in cars, including sonar, cameras, radar, accelerometers, temperature sensors, and rain sensors.[121] As a result, its Energi line of plug-in hybrid cars generates approximately 25 gigabytes of data every hour.[122] This data is processed in the factory in real time, and data is fed to the driver through a mobile application. The cars in Ford's testing facility generate up to 250 gigabytes of data per hour from high-resolution cameras and an array of sensors.[123]

Big Data at Ford is nothing new. As far back as the 1990s, the company began using in-car analytics. Then, in 2004, it developed a self-learning neural network system for its Aston Martin DB9.[124] This system was capable of keeping the engine functioning correctly, optimizing conditions to match the driver's behavior, and adjusting alerts and performance accordingly.[125] Since then, the culture of Ford has become data driven, although selling internal Big Data opportunities was more difficult than selling external Big Data opportunities.

Externally, for example, Ford used Big Data to find what improvements people wanted in their cars. Nowadays, Ford listens carefully to what customers are saying online, on social networks, or in the blogosphere. The company wants to learn whether, for example, the Ford Escape sport-utility vehicle should receive a standard liftgate or a powerliftgate.[126] In addition, Ford performs sentiment analysis on all sorts of content online and uses Google Trends to predict future sales.[127]

Internally, Ford uses Big Data to optimize its supply chain and to increase operational efficiency. From before parts even reach the factory to the car in the showroom, Big Data has infiltrated every part of the supply chain, thereby generating vast amounts of data.[128] With so many different parts coming from so many different suppliers, it is vital for Ford to get a complete and detailed overview of where all parts are located within the supply chain at any moment in time.

Information from websites, call centers, and the company's credit-processing arm, as well as sensors within cars, is used to improve products and services to better match customer demand and needs. In addition, Ford uses assembly sensors to optimize the production of its cars.

To collect and process all that data requires the right Big Data tools. Ford relies mainly on open-source tools, such as Hadoop, to manage the data and the programming language R to perform the statistical analysis. A range of other open-source applications related to text mining and data mining are also used.

The car manufacturer can no longer operate without understanding every aspect of its production. It also needs to know how cars are being used by drivers. Competition is fierce, and those companies that obtain valuable insights from Big Data will outperform their peers. Ford is driving in the right direction with its Big Data strategy to be ahead of it competitors.

NOT-FOR-PROFIT SECTOR
How Big Data Can Help the Developing World Beat Poverty

The amount of data created is not only growing in the developed world, but also in the developing world. However, a large part of the data created in the developing world has a different origin than elsewhere; the developing world is skipping the desktop and wired era and progressing rapidly to the mobile era. This requires a completely new approach, but it also offers a wide range of possibilities for overcoming poverty.

The United Nations also see the possibilities of Big Data. In 2009 U.N. Secretary-General Ban Ki-moon launched the Global Pulse initiative.[129] Global Pulse serves as an innovation lab created to raise awareness of the opportunities of Big Data and bring together different stakeholders, such as Big Data Scientists, data providers, governments, and development sector practitioners. The objective is to help catalyze the adoption of Big Data tools and technologies and to help policymakers understand human well-being and emerging vulnerabilities in real time to better protect populations from shocks.

In addition to the United Nations, the World Economic Forum (WEF) is discovering the possibilities of Big Data for the developing world. The WEF prepared a white paper discussing the possibilities of Big Data and the new possibilities it offers for international development.[130] The World Bank is researching Big Data and has developed a map that visualizes the locations of World Bank-financed projects to better monitor development impact, improve aid effectiveness and coordination, and enhance transparency and social accountability.[131,132] Finally, the International Aid Transparency Initiative makes information about aid spending easier to access, use and understand.[133] Of course, these are just a few of the many new initiatives.

Anoush Rima Tatevossian, who leads the global strategic partnerships and communications for the United Nations Global Pulse, notes that Big Data "offers a new tool in the development toolkit, and must be approached with a nuanced appreciation of its power, and also of its limitations."[134,135]

Mobile Data

For the vast numbers poor people, a simple or basic mobile phone is the only interactive interaction with the web. Although smartphones are the common device in the developed world, they still account for only 10.44 percent of global mobile website traffic.[136] On the other hand, traditional mobiles represent 78.98 percent of mobile worldwide website traffic (with tablets taking 10.58 percent of the traffic).

Luckily, vast opportunities exist for the developing world to use data created by basic mobile devices to identify needs, provide services, and predict and prevent crises to the benefit of the poor.

For example, Cignifi, a Brazilian startup, developed technology to recognize patterns in the usages of mobile devices.[137] The system recognizes phone calls, text messages, and data usage. Based on this information, it can recognize someone's lifestyle and his/her corresponding credit risk profile.

Cignifi uses Cell-phone Call Detail Records (CDRs) to determine a person's credit risk profile and thereby captures vast amounts of data that can be analyzed, such as time, location, recipient's location, duration of call, and so on. These all provide extremely valuable information when analyzed correctly. As Emmanuel Letouzé describes on his blog, CDRs from a city in Latin America could predict socioeconomic levels.[138]

But CDRs are not the only mobile data that can be used. What about data from the 100 million users who use the app Facebook for Every Phone?[139] Most of the Facebook users in the developed countries have probably never heard of this app, but every month it has 100 million active users who connect with each other via their mobile phones (not smartphones). All this valuable mobile data can be used. When combined with other datasets, it can help citizens in developing countries.

Business Use Cases

The Engineering Social Systems department (ESS) of Harvard has collected several inspiring use cases.[140] Big Data offers, for example, the possibility of predicting food shortages by combining variables such as drought, weather, migration, market prices, seasonal variations, and previous productions.

Or, what about the possibility to better understand the dynamics of residents in poor neighborhoods using mobile data to develop predictive models to better serve them. For example using CDR information to map changes in the neighbood's population and direct water pipe building efforts for the benefit of residents in poorer neighborhoods.[141] Time-series analyses performed on CDR combined with random surveys can lead to better insights about the dynamics of rural economies and provide insights on how governments should respond to economic shocks in rural and poor environments.

The World Bank offers an example in which Big Data is used to ensure the right distribution of the right medicines to the right location at the right moment in time.[142] A pilot programme called SMS for Life improved the distribution of malaria drugs at a health facility level in rural Tanzania, reducing facilities without stock from 78 percent to 26 percent.[143]

Big Data as a Catalyst

Big Data can be as a catalyst for long-lasting improvements, but we will have to look further ahead to see that. Mobile data alone is not sufficient to really create opportunities that could impact developing countries in the long run. Therefore, additional data sources are required, ranging from data from nongovernmental organizations (NGOs) to public and social data.

Many different NGOs are active in the developing world; they all do very valuable work to overcome poverty and reduce disease and hunger. What if all those NGOs used one standardized mobile app (smartphone or tablet) to collect data (a predefined set of metrics) in the same consistent manner across villages, countries, and continents? It would could create a fantastic high-level overview of what's going on in the developing countries.

When the data collected by the NGOs is combined with data from the mobile devices carried by citizens, social data from applications like Facebook for Every Phone, world food market data, and public data from (local) governments, Big Data can truly have a long-term impact on poverty by providing important insights.

The question, of course, remains: Why should NGOs cooperate in creating such a tool? Well, the answer to that is simple: If you share data, you can use the data. It will enable the NGOs to do a better job. Even more, the same data can also be shared with the private sector, such as, for example, FMCG companies or manufacturers that want to obtain a better view of emerging markets. Of course, this only occurs when private companies also share data. This is already happening; it is called "data philanthropy." The WEF refers to it as "corporations that are encouraged to share anonymized data for use by the public sector to protect vulnerable populations."[144] Nike is one of the pioneers of this approach, as it shares data from the 57,000 different materials it uses with the entire supply chain.[145]

Of course, governments should also open up their data to the public, private organizations, NGOs, journalists, and entrepreneurs. Kenya is one of the pioneers in Africa when it comes to opening up data. As the WEF report notes: "In 2009, Kenya opened the Open Data Portal where the government shares 12 years of detailed information regarding expenditures and household income surveys, as well as health facilities and school locations."[146,147] The portal can be accessed by anyone via the web or mobile devices.

As is the case in the developed world, governments in the developing countries should take the lead in creating the legal framework for sharing and using open data to protect privacy and ensure transparency, simplicity, compatibility, and security. In addition, the governments should stimulate the development of the required technical infrastructure and creation of an environment where smart individuals and organizations can use data to create new tools and applications. Governments can organize hackathons to develop, together with entrepreneurs, new solutions for poor people. This will ensure that data can be updated continuously through different organizations and becomes available and useful to citizens.

Big Data does, however, also requires a cultural and policy change, as a blog post by the World Bank shows.[148] Data in a study by Esther Duflo and Abhijit V Banerjee of 18 developing countries showed that the people in those countries were not literally starving of hunger (the study showed that they received enough food), but rather that their diets were not sufficiently nutritious.[149] This means that governments should not provide or subsidize more basic foods, such as rice or noodles, but they should provide or subsidize more nutritious food. This very important difference was made visible with Big Data.

Big Data offers many opportunities for the developing world to overcome poverty, but it requires that different organizations work together to achieve lasting results. In addition, the joining organizations should ensure the transparency and availability of the data. Transparency will stimulate awareness of the possibilities, ensure data governance, and reduce bureaucracy and corruption.[150] Availability of the data will ensure that multiple data sources can be fused, such as CDR, open, social, government, NGO, and corporate data, to create valuable and relevant new insights that will truly have a long-term impact.

MEDIA AND ENTERTAINMENT INDUSTRY
A Paradigm Shift Awaits the Media and Entertainment Industry

The media and entertainment industry is awaiting a paradigm shift. For many years, this industry focused on sending information and entertainment to viewers and users at a moment the industry thought appropriate (think TV channels). Broadcasting schedules were based on historical analyses and what the chief editor deemed best for the audience. With Big Data, this is all changing. Not only will advertising fundamentally change within this industry, but also what shows, series, or movies are developed, when they are developed, and for whom.

To achieve this, media and entertainment organizations should start building detailed 360-degrees profiles of their audiences. They can use a vast amount of different data sets to accomplish this goal. Behavioral analytics can help discover patterns in (un)structured data across consumer touch points, giving organizations better insights into the different types of customers they have. Consumer patterns derived from analyses of demographic, geographic, psychographic, and economic attributes will help organizations better understand and approach their customers. Accurate information about customers can be derived from sales and marketing data, including campaign information, point-of-sales data, and conversion data. All of this can be used to increase customer retention and acquisitions, grow upselling and cross-selling opportunities, increase online conversion, and improve the entertainment experience for the end user. When users also connect their social profile, the media and entertainment organization can obtain a true 360-degrees view of viewers and users.

These profiles can be used in several ways. First, organizations with such detailed customer profiles can increase advertising revenue by offering very targeted advertising that is more relevant and therefore more expensive for the advertiser. Advertising can become multiplatform (think second-screen advertising via tablets during television programs). When they start mining all the data, these organizations will gain valuable and nuanced insights into what the audience really wants.[151] This information can be used to create new products around existing shows or develop new programming or movies.

Big Data can also be used to predict whether a movie or a series will be a hit before shooting begins. Historical data about different shows, such as when a user pauses, forwards, rewinds, replays, or stops a television series, provides valuable information.

A combination of the detailed (social) profile of the person watching and the many different tags related to a series or movie created by viewers creates an extremely valuable data stream that provides insights into whether a series or movie will be successful. The best example here is Netflix's purchase of *House of Cards* based on a thorough data analysis of its 33 million users.[152] All that data even allowed Netflix to outbid other major players, including HBO and AMC.[153] In addition, the data showed Netflix that a significant number of its users were watching marathon style, so Netflix decided to go against tradition and release the entire season of *House of Cards* all at once.[154]

Finding the secret messages in the data that the audience is unknowingly broadcasting is key if companies in the media and entertainment industry are going to outperform their peers. They need to know: What phase of their lives are viewers in now, what do they think is important, what are they looking for, what do they recommend to whom and why, what motivates and inspires them, what are they watching, and how do they respond to it via social networks.[155] This kind of data, which is really generated at any point of contact through all channels, enables media and entertainment organizations to understand viewers' sentiment in real time. All the collected information can be used to deliver a personalized television experience via top boxes or smart televisions, where content is recommended based on the user's profile.

In addition, Big Data can be used to optimize multichannel advertising campaigns. Consumers are watching multiple devices at the same time. Optimizing advertising campaigns across multiple devices will strengthen the message of the commercial. With Big Data, it is possible to understand which consumers use a second screen, as well as where and when. The right message can then be delivered via the right channel.

The sports industry is, of course, a great example of how the entertainment industry leverages the experience for viewers using Big Data and second screens. During three tennis grand slams in 2013, IBM enabled viewers to access every available statistic about their favorite player, vote for players, and interact in other ways. IBM's program, SlamTracker, which was also used during the Australian Open, is a real-time statistics and data visualization platform that leverages predictive analytics technology.[156] The mobile application provided detailed statistics to the viewer while watching the game on television. This was a great step forward for the viewer, and it is only a matter of time such tools will also be available for television series or movies.

HOW TIME WARNER CABLE USES BIG DATA TO OPTIMIZE THE VIEWERS' EXPERIENCE

Time Warner Cable is an American cable telecommunications company that operates in 29 states. It was formed in 1989 after a merger between Time Inc.'s cable television company, American Television and Communications Corp., and Warner Cable. It has over 34,000 employees and over 14 million customers.[157] The company offers a vast range of services using the latest technology, including video-on-demand, HDTV, digital video recording, Internet access, and premium services such as HBO. In addition, consumers are now using many different streaming services, such as Netflix or Hulu (also called Over-the-Top content [OTT]), all running over the cable network.

As such, Time Warner Cable deals with a lot of data and uses Big Data tools to navigate through the changing media landscape to adjust its infrastructure to the changing needs of customers. The audience metrics received via customers provides a lot of insights into what customers want, as well helps create detailed customer profiles for personalized advertising. This can lead to a lot of new revenue streams, which can help cable companies like Time Warner Cable that are seeing customers move to the Internet.

Personalized Advertising

Time Warner Cable uses a vast array of datasets to create detailed customer profiles. In an interview with *Fast Company*, Joan Gillman, President of Time Warner Cable Media, explained that TWC combines public datasets, such as real estate records, demographics, and voter registration information with local viewing habits.[158] This enables Time Warner Cable Media, the company's advertising arm, to create and deliver advertising campaigns that are highly targeted.

But the company does do focus only on personalized advertising, but also on multichannel advertising. With millions of users downloading iPad apps and receiving data from their networks on different devices, a consistent experience is important.[159] In a pilot project in Texas, Time Warner allowed clients to create campaigns that simultaneously targeted the same customers via cable television, mobile apps, social media, the Internet, and other platforms. Then, the company used Big Data techniques to measure the engagement of the users on each platform and adjust the advertising campaign on each platform as necessary. For users, this means a consistent advertising experience across all platforms, which is extremely valuable to Time Warner Cable Media's clients.

Detailed Metrics Lead to Detailed Information

For cable companies like Time Warner Cable, aggregated user data is very important.[160] With this data, Time Warner can optimize its network and programming. Although it does not track what viewers are watching, it does know how often customers use which services (ranging, for example, from OTT services to interactive television to mobile television via iPads). This data provides the company with information regarding what customers are affected by bandwidth and how to deal with peaks in network demand.

To understand all this data, Time Warner Cable uses Alteryx.[161] It enables the company to understand how viewers watch programming, as well as how advertising clients performed. With interactive campaigns, Time Warner has been able to map the location of responding viewers to the locations of relevant stores. In addition, thanks to data analysis, it was able to perform cross-platform analysis to predict which homes would be interested in what movies via their Movie-on-Demand platform. This allowed the release of the right movies at the right time to the right homes, thereby increasing sales.

Growing Amount of Data

Time Warner Cable Media operates in 15 different markets and reaches over 7.9 million subscribing customers. All these customers provide a vast amount of data. To store all that data, Time Warner built its own warehouse. Currently, its database grows by 0.6 terabyte every day.[162] This might not seem like a lot in terms of Big Data, but it is sufficient for Time Warner Cable Media to create tailored advertising campaigns for its customers.

Running a cable company is an expensive business. With so many new services and Internet television initiatives, cable companies are not even guaranteed successes anymore. Therefore, they will have to innovate to create a tailored experience for viewers as well as for advertisers. Time Warner Cable understands that generating data is an inevitable part of the process and has already successfully used it to find new revenue streams, thereby improving marketing efforts and network infrastructure.

OIL AND GAS INDUSTRY

The multibillion dollar oil and gas industry uses Big Data technologies to optimize processes that enable the collection of data that will provide additional insights, better monitoring, and more revenue. Ample opportunities exist to also use Big Data to increase oil and gas production, as well as increase safety and mitigate environmental risks.

Exploration and Discovery

Seismic monitors with 2D, 3D, and 4D capabilities can generate vast amounts of data during oil and gas explorations.[163] This data can help find new oil and gas fields, as well as help identify potentially productive seismic trace signatures previously overlooked. With multiple parallel processing platforms, the data can be analyzed quickly and accurately, taking into account different data variables that affect the profitability of a new oil well, including production costs, transport of oil or employees, weather related uptime or downtime, and so on.

Massive amounts of drilling data can be analyzed and monitored in real time, alerting company employees to anomalies that might occur based on such different variables as weather, soil, and equipment sensor data. This will predict in real time the success of drilling operations.[164]

Seismic data can also be used to determine the amount of oil or gas in new or previously overlooked oil wells.[165] Combining various datasets, such as historical production and drilling data from local sites, can give additional insights into future production volumes. This is especially useful when environmental restrictions prevent new surveys. When added to public data about weather, ocean currents, and ice flows, an accurate prediction can be made regarding future production volumes.

An additional advantage of placing sensors within oil wells and across the earth's surface is that it provides even more information about how drilling affects seismic activities. The closer the sensors are to the activity, the earlier the seismic activity is detected. Warnings can then be sent to citizens who would be affected by a possible earthquake.

Optimization of Production

Data can be collected from various sources. These include sensor data from equipment about pressure, temperature, volume, shock, and vibration, geological data such as scientific models related to understanding the earth's subsurface, and weather data such as the impact of storms on rigs. This information can be used to detect errors or upcoming failures during drilling.

Sensors attached to drillheads and other equipment can be monitored to determine how the equipment is operating and to predict when a machine is about to fail or when maintenance is required. When combined with historical data about equipment failure, it becomes possible to monitor all equipment around the world in real time to minimize the impact of equipment failure.

All data can be collected and analyzed centrally to better understand what equipment works best in what environment. This will enable organizations to optimize how the equipment is used and reduce latency. Sensor data on equipment can predict failures and indicate required repairs before they affect operations. When this data is added to the ERP of the organization, new spare parts can be ordered before a machine fails and arrive on time for the engineer to use when the data indicates the need. Maintenance planning can be adjusted accordingly, thereby reducing downtime and inventory levels.

Mitigate Risk and Ensure Safety

Data from various sources can detect anomalies in drilling in real time so that decisions can be made faster to shut down, if necessary to prevent any major environment risks. In addition, videodata from smart cameras can show what is happening in real time. Algorithms can identify patterns or outliers that may indicate security breaches online and offline. Security can then be alerted to take action wherever security is compromised around the world.

Big Data and the oil and gas industry are a powerful combination. Apart from the massive benefits for the oil and gas companies, there are also side benefits for other industries due to the massive numbers of sensors used by this industry, as will be shown in the vignette about Shell.

SHELL DRILLS DEEP WITH BIG DATA

Increasingly, Shell uses Big Data to improve its operations and increase the output from its oil and gas wells. For the last two years, the company has been lowering optical fiber cables fitted with sensors into its wells. With this data, Shell can improve its analysis of wells and determine how much oil or gas is still left. These supersensitive sensors help Shell find additional oil in wells that were thought to have run dry. The sensors, which were developed by HP, generate massive amounts of data that is stored at a private section of Amazon Web Services.[166] In two years, Shell has already collected 46 petabytes of data; the first test in one oil well resulted in 1 petabyte of information. Knowing that Shell wants to deploy these sensors in approximately 10,000 oil wells, we are talking about 10 exabytes of data. This is the same amount of data that was created daily on the Internet in 2013. Because of these huge datasets, Shell started piloting with Hadoop in the Amazon Virtual Private Cloud.[167] All data that is received from the seismic sensors is analyzed by artificial intelligence developed by Shell and rendered in 3D and 4D maps of the oil reservoirs.[168] Although the analyses are done in the cloud, the visualizations are immediately available to the crew working at the local factory.

Currently, Shell has a large team of 70 people working full time in its data analysis department, plus hundreds more scattered over the world who participate on an ad hoc basis. The department consists of a mix of specialists in IT, oil and gas technology, mathematics, and physics. They are all working toward the same goal of getting more oil and gas out of the same or new wells.

Although Shell refuses to reveal how exactly it uses what data, it is doing something remarkable with the data that it does want to share. Shell and a few environmental organizations agreed to share data. As Gerald Schotman, Chief Technology Officer at Shell, explains, "during a brainstorm with environmental organizations we noticed that we can help migratory birds across the Sahara in their search for water. Or we share data with organizations concerning the migration of whales."[169]

PUBLIC SECTOR

The public sector creates massive amounts of data. It therefore offers ample opportunities for governments to save a lot of public money by using Big Data. According to the United Kingdom free-market think tank Policy Exchange, the government could save up to £33 billion a year by using public Big Data more effectively.[170] McKinsey has estimated that the potential annual value to Europe's public sector from Big Data is €250 billion.[171] There are many uses available to the public sector, from reducing tax fraud to improving services for citizens.

Improve Transparency and Decision Making While Reducing Costs

Governments can become more transparent and reduce the time officials and citizens require to comply with tax regulations.[172] A lot of government tax agencies store personal data, which is copied all over the public sector. Over and over again, citizens complete new forms with information most governments already possess. Prefiling forms reduces errors and speeds up process time. The Swedish Tax Agency offers services to help citizens complete prefilling of forms with personal data in a manner that reduces processing times.[173] The Dutch government also prefiles annual tax forms with information from employers, as well as bank accounts.

When all data is stored in one central location, it will be possible to give government officials access to all information. This will reduce errors and inefficiencies within the government and ensure that the correct information is used, while enabling all government officials to have access to the most up-to-date information on its citizens. Governments can make use of open-source tools like Accumulo, which was developed by the National Security Agency (NSA), to enable search queries and results based on the government employee's authorization.[174]

Governments that open up their massive Big Data sets and stimulate the free flowing of information contribute to transparency and build trust with citizens.[175] It will enable citizens to understand what data governments collect and what they do with the information. Sharing these data sets will also help governments develop new and innovative services, as citizens will help build solutions, and probably also make money out of it.[176] The transparency will enable citizens to monitor and understand how governments spend public money; this will encourage government officials to spend public money wisely or possibly not be reelected.[177]

A great example is provided by government officials who travel a lot to other countries. With an intelligent travel-and-expense management system powered by Big Data technologies, governments could gain a complete overview, including which officials have traveled where for what purpose and when.[178] Government officials who want to arrange a trip can use the system to understand whether travel is really required, so that only the required number of people are sent to the same place. This could save a lot of money.

Personalize Citizens' Experiences

By analyzing unstructured and structured social/public data, governments can respond to changing events and react quickly if citizens are not satisfied or are in need.[179] Segmentation and personalization could help identify citizens who need help because they have become unemployed or otherwise vulnerable. Algorithms can automatically define the help they require.

Governments can use the unstructured and structured online data as well as voice recognition data from citizen phone calls to understand (national) sentiment, learn what citizens are looking for (from the local neighborhood level to the national level), and help policymakers develop and prioritize new public services.[180] In addition, sentiment analysis can be used to discover potential areas of civil unrest so that preventive action can be taken, if required.

Such a personalized approach can also be used during elections to gain a complete understanding of what the voters are looking for and how they can best be targeted. The Obama campaign of 2012 is a great example of how Big Data can help politicians win elections.

Reduce Tax and Social Security Fraud

Taxes mean big numbers and a lot of data. With Big Data tools, governments can minimize tax and social security fraud. Algorithms can use pattern detection to find suspicious transactions occurring in real time. The combination of different local and national datasets will provide insights into the tax paying behavior of citizens.[181]

Abnormal behavior patterns can be spotted that indicate fraudulent actions.[182] Patterns can be used to create profiles and statistical parameters can identify suspicious transactions, which can then be monitored more closely.[183] Governments can also use demographic or social data to validate information and determine whether suspected outliers are really performing fraudulent actions, such as applying fraudulently for social security.

Keep a Country Safe and Healthy

Data can reveal trends in criminal prosecution and can create profiles of the prison population to determine whether the majority are low-level, nonviolent offenders or highly violent people. Officials in the justice system need to understand when and where violent crime is happening. The Las Vegas police use algorithms to detect the blocks in town where crime is likely to occur. These algorithms are based on historical datasets and a broad range of other datasets. By applying an information-centric approach based on many different datasets, the efficiency and effectiveness of a criminal justice system will improve.[184] Of course, Big Data tools enable governments to monitor what is happening within their country and to uncover malicious activities that could indicate an upcoming (digital) terrorist attack. Governments can collect, process, and analyze data from their own networks, as well as public data sources, to protect their countries from attack. This is exactly what PRISM (see Chapter 5) is doing, and it immediately raises the privacy issues involved in securing a nation against (digital) terrorist attacks.

Big Data can also protect the environment when there are risks of flooding or other weather-related disasters. Weather, water, and climate data can be combined with data from sensors in dikes, lakes, and rivers to gain a real-time understanding of the current environmental status. For example, these sensors could register when dikes are about to break and villages will be flooded, enabling governments to take preventive action. Instead of replacing or fixing protection barriers that do not yet require repair, sensors can help target maintenance protection efforts. This will increase safety levels and reduce costs.

The smart dike ("IJkdijk") in The Netherlands is full of sensors that help researchers understand complex information flows in water management systems.[185] The IJkdijk is a unique international testing facility that led in 2013 to the installation of four LiveDikes in The Netherlands.[186] These LiveDikes have sensors that are centrally monitored to provide a real-time picture of the condition of those dikes.

In addition, Big Data can help governments to predict epidemics. Google Flu Trends is better at predicting how many people have the flu in certain countries or regions than are government officials.[187] Certain search terms are very good indicators of flu activity. Google Flu trends combines and analyzes those search terms to estimate flu activity around the world in near real time. Like Google Flu Trends, governments can analyze EHRs, as well as social and search data, to understand and predict epidemics related to other diseases. This will enable governments to respond faster, thereby improving healthcare while reducing costs.[188]

When governments embrace the possibilities of Big Data, they can make a country more effective and efficient, decrease costs associated with bureaucracy, and improve citizen services.

BIG DATA DURING THE OBAMA CAMPAIGN

During the 18 months before Election Day in the United States in November 2012, the Obama campaign collected and spent more than $1.5 billion. In addition, over 1,000 paid staff worked on the campaign, along with tens of thousands of volunteers. More than 100 data analysts ran more than 66,000 computer simulations every day.[189] The objective of the campaign set out by Jim Messina was to "measure everything." The idea was to collect data on everything that happened during the campaign to ensure that organizers were being smart about everything. According to Chris Wegrzyn, the Director of Data Architecture of the Democratic National Committee (DNC), they had defined three major ways to influence the outcome of the campaign[190]:

- Registration: Increase the number of eligible voters.
- Persuasion: Convince voters to support Obama.
- Turnout: Increase the turnout on Election Day.

Each potential swing-state voter was assigned a number ranging from 0 to 100. There were four different scores based on the three different ways to influence voters:

- The likelihood that they would support Obama.
- The possibility that they would show up at the poll.
- The odds that an Obama supporter who was an inconsistent voter could be nudged to the polls.
- How much could someone be persuaded to vote for Obama by a conversation on a particular issue.

This metric was at the heart of the campaign and influenced the message sent to swing-state voters. To effectively manage this during the campaign, they divided the campaign team into different channels:

- Field channel (actively approach voters in the field).
- Digital channel (focus on recruitment of staff and volunteers and fundraising).
- Communication/press (focus on the persuasion aspect).

- Media (focus on persuasion by buying media time).
- Finance (focus on fundraising).

The problem with these different channels, however, was that data management was fragmented and an overview was difficult to achieve. That was when Big Data made its appearance. During the previous campaign, they had already learned a lot regarding new technologies and the use of social media. Now it was time to move forward. In 2008, the new technologies used and the analytics captured during the campaign allowed Obama workers to build an unprecedented massive and efficient program that evaluated data entered by field staff. They then progressed to data modeling and deep analytics. In 2012, they built an analyst-driven organization and an environment in which smart people freely pursued their (data-driven) ideas.

The DNC focused on three dimensions:

1. Volume: By Big Data standards, the amount of raw data collected was small. The committee had less than 10 TB to start with, but because they allowed their analysts to pursue data-driven ideas, this number increased tenfold in a short period of time.
2. Variety: Many sources of data were new to the DNC. Because of the short timespan, members did not have time to built ETL processes to bring it all together nicely.
3. Velocity: The data analysts, staffers, and volunteers created new data at high speed and that issue needed to be addressed.

To resolve all this, the DNC decided to use a SQL MPP database, a Massively Parallel Processing database.[191] It offered a high-speed performance, stability and scalability, which meant it could easily grow with the needs of the DNC.

In addition, the DNC built a positive feedback loop, so that the engineers could build on top of each other. This proved to be a powerful tool, and it led to unexpected innovations. For example, potential voters could receive tailored news on a topic they told a volunteer was of interest to them. This information was included in the database and resulted in personalized relevant emails that could be sent to these potential voters.

RETAIL INDUSTRY

Retailers that implement a Big Data strategy can achieve a 60 percent increase in their margins, as well as boost employee productivity by one percent, meaning there is every reason to move forward.[192] The retail industry collects vast amounts of data because any product purchased in a retail store or online generates data that can be analyzed for additional insights. The volume of that data will grow exponentially in the coming years, due in part to emerging new data sources such as RFID tags. Whether the purpose is to provide a smarter shopping experience that influences the purchasing decisions of customers to drive additional revenue or to deliver tailor-made relevant real-time offers to customers, Big Data offers opportunities for retailers to stay ahead of their competition.

Personalized Shopping Experiences

As with any industry, available data can be used to create detailed customer profiles that can be used for microsegmentation and offerings, such as a personalized shopping experience. A 360-degree customer view will inform retailers how to best contact customers to achieve the best results, while geographic location data (for example, using the geo tag in tweets, Facebook posts, or smartphones that are Bluetooth enabled) will allow retailers to know just the right moment to make a personalized and relevant real-time offer. Such optimized customer contact moments can also be used to recommend suitable and relevant products.

Retailers can recommend products by cross-analyzing in-store interactions with online behavior and then combining it with demographic, geographic, and transaction data collected online and offline (e.g., loyalty programs), In addition, the combination of different datasets will enable retailers to pinpoint the most likely purchasers for certain products. This is done using social media data, purchasing history, online and offline browsing patterns, the blogosphere or forums, customer loyalty, and demographic data.

Sentiment analysis will tell retailers how customers perceive their actions, commercials, and available products. What customers are saying online will provide retailers with additional insights into what they are really looking for, and it will enable retailers to optimize their assortments to suit local needs and wishes.

Accurate Demand Forecasts

Retailers can predict future demand using various datasets, such as web browsing patterns, industry advertising buying information, enterprise data, social media sentiment, and news and event information, to predict the next hot items.[193] Using such data as customer transactions, demographics, shopping patterns, research, and local buzz, the demand in local areas and different channels can be predicted. When combined, this information will enable retailers to stock and deliver the right products in the right amounts to the right channels and regions. In addition, retailers can improve shipments by evaluating top-selling products, making markdown decisions based on seasonal sell-through, stopping shipments for bottom-selling products, and communicating more effectively with their supply-chain partners to optimize inventory.[194] Such accurate demand forecasting will help retailers optimize inventory, improve just-in-time delivery, and reduce related costs.

Based on the forecasted demand, retailers can start using models that incorporate weather, seasonal, and news data to have the right number of staff present in stores.[195]

Innovative Optimization Possibilities

Customer demand, competitor activity, and shareholders value data can create models that automatically synchronize pricing with inventory levels, demand, and competition. In addition, market information about events or stories in the news and relevant supply chain information can be used to adjust pricing.

Big Data technology will also enable retailers to optimize floor plans. Using smart cameras within stores, retailers can gain insights into customer movements and behavior. In addition to cameras, retailers can also use passive information, such as Wi-Fi or Bluetooth data, to monitor movements throughout the stores and determine the most efficient traffic patterns. This can indicate which locations are more or less attractive and can be used to improve displays and product placement. Layouts can be adjusted accordingly to create a revenue-optimized floor plan.

Using financial, sales, and inventory data across all points of sale worldwide—department stores, specialty stores, and catalogs/Internet—retailers can also discover patterns that identify new revenue optimization opportunities or cost reduction possibilities.[196]

In this highly competitive market, retailers need to do what it takes to stay ahead of the competition. Big Data technology can help them outperform their peers financially while improving customer satisfaction.

WALMART IS MAKING BIG DATA PART OF ITS DNA

Walmart started using Big Data even before the term became known in the industry. In 2012, the company moved from an experiential 10-node to a 250-node Hadoop cluster.[197] At the same time, it developed new tools to migrate existing data on Oracle, Neteeza, and Greenplum hardware to its own Big Data systems. The goal was to consolidate ten different websites into one and store all incoming data in the new Hadoop cluster.

Many of the Big Data tools were developed at the Walmart Labs, which was created after Walmart took over Kosmix in 2011.[198] Some products developed at Walmart Labs are Social Genome, ShoppyCat, and Get on the Shelf.[199,200]

Walmart uses Social Genome to offer customers or their friends, who have mentioned a specific product online, a discount. To do this, the organization combines public data from the web, social networks, and proprietary data, such as customer purchasing data and contact information. This has resulted in a vast, constantly changing, up-to-date knowledge base with hundreds of millions of entities and relationships. It helps Walmart better understand the context of what customers are saying online. An example mentioned by Walmart Labs shows a woman tweeting regularly about movies. When she tweets "I love Salt," Walmart was able to understand that she was talking about the movie *Salt*, and not the condiment.

Walmart encountered several technical difficulties when developing the Social Genome, among others the quantity and velocity of data that pours into its Hadoop clusters. As the regular

Map-Reduce/Hadoop framework was not able to cope with the amount and velocity of the data, Walmart developed its own tool called Muppet.[201] This now open-source tool processes data in real time over all clusters and can perform parallel analysis.

The Shoppycat product developed by Walmart could recommend suitable products to Facebook users based on the hobbies and interests of their friends. It uses the Social Genome technology, among others, to help customers purchase gifts for their friends. An interesting aspect of this Facebook App is that Walmart will direct Facebook users to a different store if the desired product is sold out at a nearby Walmart store.

Get on the Shelf was a crowd-sourcing solution that gave everyone the chance to pitch his or her product in front of a large online audience.[202] The best products would be sold at Walmart with the potential to suddenly reach millions of consumers. More than a million votes were cast; in the end, three of the products are now carried at Walmart. In addition, Walmart is able to optimize the local assortment of its stores based on what the customers in the neighborhood are saying on social media networks.

Mobile Big Data Solutions

With over 200 million customers visiting one of its stores every week, Walmart obviously is focusing on mobile development. It has developed several iOS and Android Apps that use the latest technology to give customers the best shopping experience. The company created and subsequently open-sourced two tools: Thorax and Lumbar.[203,204] Thorax is a framework to build large-scale web applications; Lumbar is a Java-built tool that can generate modular platform specific applications.

Walmart's Big Data ecosystem processes multiterabytes of new data and petabytes of historical data on a daily basis, covering millions of products and hundreds of millions of users from internal and external sources. It analyzes over 100 million keywords to optimize the bidding of each keyword on a daily basis.

Walmart's use of Big Data impressively illustrates what can be accomplished if Big Data is truly incorporated into a company's DNA. To date, Walmart has been able to optimize the local assortments of merchandise available in Walmart stores based on what customers in the neighborhood are saying on social media. When Walmart combines all Big Data efforts with its mobile efforts, truly exciting solutions can be created. Walmart is also developing in-store mobile navigation using personal smartphones with which it can steer customers through aisles of products they have been talking about on social media and therefore are more willing to buy. Of course, this will result in increased revenue for the already largest retailer in the world.

TELECOM INDUSTRY

If they choose, telecom organizations can know everything about their customers, including where they were when, with whom they connect frequently, what their daily habits are, and so on. This is all thanks to the growing number of call detail records, location data, social media data, and network traffic data.[205] The global telecom industry has experienced a massive growth in data because of the invention of smartphones and tablets, the next generation mobile networks, and the world that is becoming connected to the mobile Internet. Those telecom companies that use this vast amount of data efficiently will outperform their peers, grow their market shares, and improve their bottom lines.

Improve the Customer Experience

Telecom organizations are collecting such vast amounts of data because the European government requires it. As a result, they can relatively easily generate a 360-degree view of their customers using their own data (call data, geo data, internet usage data, and so on) and public data from social networks. With such a detailed view of their customers, they can start to create highly customized experiences with targeted promotional offerings. These intelligent, mass-personalized, multichannel marketing campaigns can target the customer at the right moment at the right location with the right message. The integration of customer intelligence, behavior segmentation, and real-time promotion execution can increase sales, promotional effectiveness, and market share, while reducing costs.

When all the relevant data is centrally stored in a platform that is accessible by call center representatives, it will be possible to modify subscriber calling plans when necessary, thereby driving customer satisfaction and improving customer profitability.[206] New personalized products or services can be offered to customers based on real-time usage patterns, which will reduce costs for the customer and increase customer satisfaction.

Innovate and Build Smarter Networks

Network traffic is increasing to double digits because of better positioning and the rollout of 4G worldwide.[207] Understanding how, when, and where customers are using networks can lead to better networks that automatically adapt to high demands. Algorithms could monitor and analyze network traffic data in real time, thereby optimizing routing and quality of services while decreasing outages and increasing customer satisfaction. The analyses can also be used to optimize the average network quality, coverage, and deployment over time.

Data from tracking all connected devices in real time on the network can be combined with public datasets about events happening in real time. If an event drives up Internet or cell phone usage, a telecom organization could learn this in real time and take preventive action as needed. Moreover, sensors in the network, for example at antennas, can monitor the equipment and notify the office if an action or maintenance is necessary.

In additional, Big Data tools can be used to easily identify problems, perform real-time troubleshooting, and quickly fix network performance issues, which will improve network quality and lower operating costs. For example, when sensors in the network suddenly notice a high rate of dropped calls, immediate action can be taken to decrease downtime and optimize the network.

Although real-time, deep-packet inspection can be used to optimize traffic routing and drive network quality of service even more, in many countries, including The Netherlands, it is forbidden.[208] It even caused a stir when consumers found out that telecom organizations were monitoring what applications or which websites they were visiting from their mobile devices.

Decrease Churn and Reduce Risks

To decrease churn rates, telecom organizations can start to better understand which customers are influencers and what their (latent) needs are. This understanding can provide valuable information. For example, if one of these influencers switches companies, it could have a domino effect. The ability to combine billing, drop-call, and sentiment analysis can give telecom organizations the ability to reduce churn rates by knowing upfront what is going to happen. Predictive analytics can automatically inform when action is required to prevent a customer from going to a competitor. As a result, the telecom company can offer a tailor-made deal just in time.

Big Data tools can also be used to reduce losses from customer or dealer commission fraud. Calls from the same number from two different locations could indicate a cloned subscriber identity module (SIM) card, which means fraud. Preventive measures can be taken immediately and automatically, if needed. In addition, historical payment data or call data records can be used to detect and identify fraudulent behavior in real time.[209]

Telecom organizations generate vast amounts of customer data that can also be used to deliver relevant and timely location-based promotional offers and other services to third parties. Telecom organizations' ability to sell their data, with its anonymous customer insights, to third parties or local governments could be a welcome source of additional revenue. There are a lot of benefits for telecom organizations, so operators should start experimenting with the data to gain an understanding of its vast possibilities and opportunities.[210]

T-MOBILE USA REDUCES ITS CHURN RATE BY 50 PERCENT IN ONE QUARTER

Some of the metrics captured by telecom organizations includes when people call, how long they talk, direct messaging peaks, Internet usage, and so on. If you have 33 million customers, as T-Mobile USA does, we are talking serious Big Data.[211] Strangely enough, not many telecom organizations are putting all this Big Data to use. T-Mobile USA, however, does, and with its Big Data strategy, it reduced churn rates by 50 percent in just one quarter.

To fully use all of this data, T-Mobile USA combines a lot of subscriber and network data from multiple databases and source systems. It uses several tools to store, analyze, search, and visualize all its data. The hardware is based on the Informatica Power-Center.[212] The company uses Splunk to search through log files and Tableau Software to visualize all data.[213,214] Backed by these technologies, it started using six "data zones" that are connected to business objectives:

1. Customer data zone: Provides a 360-degree view of each customer used to minimize customer dissatisfaction.
2. Product and services zone: Determines which products and services are used by whom and when in order to drive innovation.
3. Customer experience zone: Identifies the channels that interact with the customer and when. Used to regain and optimize service levels.
4. Business operations zone: Contains all billing and accounting information, as well as the finance and risk management data. Used to define the best areas for optimization and performance.
5. Supply chain zone: Identifies how purchase orders, shipments, and logistics operate. Used to drive innovation within the supply chain and to cut costs.
6. Network zone: Stores all (raw) data that supports management. Used to drive innovation and grow quality customers.

These zones place physical data storages and networks in a virtualized environment. The virtualized data zones help T-Mobile USA identify complex systems, differences in data definitions, or incompatible data. It also prevents duplicate content or incorrect business rules and decentralizes rule management.

But how did T-Mobile USA tackle the churn rate? By using a "tribal" customer model. This is based on the fact that some people have greater influence over others because of their extensive social networks and connections to different (online) groups. If one of these customers switches telecom providers, it could cause a domino effect by leading others in his or her network to follow.

For each of these influential customers, an additional Customer Lifetime Value (CLV) is calculated. This new CLV allows T-Mobile USA to determine its most valuable customers.

Next, the churn expectancy of a customer is based on three different analyses:

1. Billing analysis: This includes customer product usage, such as how often and where and for how long a user calls whom, how many text messages are sent to whom, and internet usage. If more and more calls are going to a different provider, this could indicate that the network of the customer is switching, resulting in a higher chance that the customer will also switch.
2. Drop call analysis: If a user relocates to a different area and the data shows that the customer receives limited coverage in the new area, an alert is sounded and a customer representative can offer a new phone or a free femtocell to prevent the customer from switching.
3. Sentiment analysis: This includes predicting triggers and indicators of what customer actions are going to be and how they think of T-Mobile USA, allowing the company to respond proactively.

These different analyses are combined into an integrated single view for customer care. This system, called "Quick View," offers agents and retail store associates multiple key indicators, including the CLV in a split second on one screen. Additional information regarding high-value subscribers is sent automatically to agents along with customer-specific offers, such as a new service plan.

This tailor-made and customer-centric approach caused a drop in monthly leaving by T-Mobile USA customers. After losing almost 100,000 customers in the first quarter of 2011, the company reduced the churn rate to 50,000 in the second quarter. Since then, T-Mobile USA has focused on retaining its loyal, high CLV subscribers, as well as on upgrading its customers to higher quality products, thereby leading to higher customer satisfaction and increased revenue.

TRANSPORTATION INDUSTRY

The transportation sector is on the brink of a paradigm shift thanks to Big Data.[215] Smarter transportation will result in operational efficiency, improved end-to-end customer experiences, reduced fuel consumption, and increased flexibility. Logistics companies are already working hard to use sensor data in trucks to optimize routing and decrease fuel consumption. American logistics company US Xpress has installed almost 1,000 sensors in each truck to monitor where drivers are going, how fast they drive, how often they break, when maintenance is required, and the drivers' capabilities. But, many more opportunities exist for the transportation industry.

Optimize Freight Movements and Routing

Consolidating shipments and optimizing freight movement can enable same-day regional delivery. Knowing exactly which products are in which warehouses can help companies like Amazon deliver the right product at the right time to the right customer within 24 hours. Removing supply-chain waste and analyzing transaction-level product details will ensure efficient transportation of freight.[216]

Satellite navigation and sensors can track trucks, trains, airplanes, or ships in real time. Routing can be optimized using public data about road conditions, traffic jams, weather predictions, delivery addresses, location of gas stations (in the cases of trucks), and so on. Whenever a change of address comes in from the head office, it can be pushed to the driver or captain in real time. The system will automatically calculate and optimize the ideal and least expensive route to the new destination.

Sensors in trucks, trains, ships, and airplanes can also give real-time information about how the vehicle is performing, how fast it is going, how long it is on the go, how long it is standing still, and more. All this data, combined with sensors that monitor the health of the engine and equipment, can predict errors and arrange for necessary maintenance without losing too much time. It is even possible to automatically book maintenance at the most efficient location, while the engineer instantly knows what the problem is and how it can be solved.

Large logistic organizations can have hundreds or thousands of trucks, trains, airplanes, or ships. If their usage is not optimized, a company can lose a lot of money. With sensor data, companies can locate all their trucks at any moment, as well as know their inventory and destination. This information can help the transportation company optimize its fleet and increase efficiency.

Determine Inventory on Hand

In-transit stock is still part of an organization's inventory, even though it has physically left the warehouse. It is important to know the exact inventory at all times, especially if last-minute changes need to be made. When all products contain sensors, they can be tracked in real time and adjustments and/or inventory counting becomes very simple.

Inventory management analytics can be used to create a centralized platform that offers organizations a detailed overview of departure and arrival times, order cuts, and the ability to provide customers with detailed information on their freight.[217]

Improve the End-to-End Customer Experience

Customers want to know exactly where their freight is and when it will be delivered. With a smart transportation system, freight shippers and customers are given the information and tools to decide the best way to get their product from origin to destination across different modes of transport, considering cost, time, and convenience.[218] A package can use several modes of transport; with a smart transportation system, customers can determine how their freight goes from A to B. This will enable customers to better manage their supply chain, as well as costs.

Transportation organizations will be able to develop 360-degree profiles of their customers to create a single enterprise view.[219] Using various open, public, and social datastreams, as well as company information about customers, shippers will be able to improve their marketing effectiveness and increase customer loyalty and revenue.

Reduce Environmental Impact and Increase Safety

Fuel consumption can be reduced in several ways. First, sensors can monitor the engine and optimize fuel input. When combined with optimized routing, which is created by taking into account weather conditions, driving behavior, road conditions, and location, a lot of fuel can be saved.

Sensors can also monitor how fast a driver is going and whether the driver is sticking to the rules of the road. They can monitor if the driver is behind the wheel too long or if breaks are too long. It can keep the driver awake and thus prevent accidents, while keeping the driver accountable. More and more cities around the world are experimenting with smart transportation systems that will reduce pollution and increase road safety. The city of Brisbane, Australia, has developed a complete, real-time overview of the city's transportation network, which provides a platform to develop and test new strategies in a stable and real-time virtual environment.[220] This platform enables the city to predict and reduce traffic congestion, resulting in happier commuters and shippers, while reducing emissions. The city also uses variable speed limits and roadway queue management algorithms to improve highway safety. With increasing demands by customers to have their freight delivered as fast as possible and as inexpensively as possible, transportation companies face a challenge that luckily can be tackled with Big Data.

US XPRESS DRIVES EFFICIENCY WITH BIG DATA

US Xpress combines 900 different data elements from a vast number of trucking systems, such as sensors for petrol use, tires, brakes, engine operations, geospatial data, and driver comments across a fleet of 8,000 tractors and 22,000 trailers into one Hadoop database and analyzes it in real time to optimize what's happening. US Xpress in Chattanooga, Tennessee, uses hundreds of billions of data records to save over $6 million a year.[221]

When the company started in 2009, its IT environment was distributed over 130 different databases.[222] Employees managed to enter 178 different ways of writing Walmart. They had 90 mainframe screens to monitor and performing a query on data took weeks or even months. Data was a mess and, therefore, useless. It needed to be cleaned and combined before it could help improve efficiency and save money. The company developed a one-stop solution that could combine all different data streams into one interface, the DriverTech system.

The DriverTech system processes, analyzes, and reports back data from tens of thousands of sensors in real time. With real-time data, US Xpress can interpret how drivers are driving, why some trucks are standing still with engines running, how they could reduce fuel consumption, and even where all this happens. The geospatial analysis that US Xpress performs allows the company to monitor what is going on in real time and minimize any downtime. This happens because employees know when a truck arrives at a depot for maintenance or reloading.

US Xpress combines truck data with unstructured data gathered when drivers talk on trucker blogs about the DriverTech interface that is used inside the cabin. This allows US Xpress to quickly address issues with a new release, especially if it is combined with records about how the interface is used by the drivers. For example, when the new touchscreen buttons appeared to be too small, the company learned about it through social media and made the necessary adjustments quickly.[223]

An important aspect of managing the fleet is its mobility. All fleet managers control dozens of trucks. Each of them now has an iPad that provides real-time data they need to know about their trucks. Nowadays, US Xpress actually owns a private App store, where drivers can download different apps to meet their needs. The most important aspect is that managers and drivers all have the necessary information at their fingertips in real time.

To move from a data-poor to an information-centric organization, the company came-up with a 36-month information management strategy, including 13 strategic projects that were implemented one after another. Each new project is built on the success of its predecessor, so that development keeps flowing. It is clear that US Xpress developed and executed a Big Data strategy. Analyzing all the data collected and optimizing routing led to $20 million in fuel savings in the first year. In addition, US Xpress can now take corrective action when drivers are on idle for too long.[224]

As a result, they have won several technology awards, including the Ventana Leadership Award for "Overall IT Leadership."[225,226] Not a bad achievement for a trucking company.

TRAVEL AND LEISURE INDUSTRY

The global travel industry is expected to grow to 10 percent of global GDP by 2022; this means an annual revenue of around $10 trillion.[227] This massive industry will become a lot more efficient when Big Data is thoroughly implemented in every aspect. In the past years, large steps forward have been made. For many consumers, travel without Big Data would be impossible—or at least tedious and annoying.[228]

Travel companies are known for capturing and storing massive amounts of data. During every step of a traveler's journey, they collect data, including flight paths, transaction data, customer data, yielding, check-ins, and more. Almost every hotel has a Customer Relationship Management (CRM) program, and let's not forget that yield revenue management was invented in the travel industry years ago. Until recently, all the data was just stored and travel companies had difficulty actually putting it to use by combining various datasets. With Big Data tools, however, this information can be used to make customers feel more appreciated and better served, resulting in additional revenue and higher profits.

Exceed Customer Expectations

Particularly in the travel industry, a personal approach is vitally important, and the opportunities for Big Data are tremendous. If we look at the conversion rate on travel websites, 92 percent of customers do not convert and 60 percent never return after a first visit.[229] A 360-degree customer profile includes data collected from social networks (reviews via Yelp or TripAdvisor), the blogosphere, (online) surveys, click behavior, reservation systems, and CRM loyalty programs. Detailed purchasing history and timing, browsing history, service history, revealed price sensitivity, and known or inferred demographics, as well as other interests available online, can determine what drives a customer, whether booking a rental car, a hotel, or a flight.[230]

The ability to analyze all that data instantly and determine a customer profile will enable travel companies to deliver the right message at the right time to the right person via the right channel. With that, their conversion rate should increase.

Tailored messages during a booking process can help a consumer decide which channel to choose. When, for example, the data shows that a customer appreciates a hotel room overlooking the sea, that room is automatically suggested during the booking process.

It is also possible to predict and understand future demand patterns for hotels, conference centers, or holiday destinations, such as theme parks or casinos. By combining financial data, events data, and news information, room rates can be adjusted to reflect anticipated demand.

The challenge in the travel industry will therefore be to connect all these different platforms, websites, and products during the journey of a traveler. Would it not be great if a traveler would get a message if his plane is delayed, including the new gate, that would allow him or her to leave later from work and still plan a meeting? The hotel he booked would also receive a message that he is delayed, knows the new expected time of arrival, and can have refreshments ready to minimize the impact of the delay. That would truly be exceeding expectations.

Speed Is Key in Online Travel

Online, speed is everything in travel. Consumers generally move away within seconds if an online answer takes too long. After all, there are many other websites offering exactly the same service. Each website needs to sift through millions of records from various sources, such as airline agencies or global distribution companies, and deliver a result. The one that does this faster will see a positive impact on revenue. By building its own Big Data system, a German travel company is now able to process 1,000 queries per second while searching through 18 billion offers across 20 parameters and to deliver an answer within a second.[231]

Big Data is also increasingly applied at airports, where, for example, it is used to count the number of people present in real time, to develop heatmaps for expected noise pollution in the surrounding areas, or to visualize retail sales at departure gates to see how far travelers wander. The potential of Big Data in the passenger industry is tremendous.

Airlines can also better serve their customers using Big Data. British Airways used Big Data to develop a personalized service program called Know Me. It tracks as much information as possible during a customer journey and acts accordingly.[232] If a customer's bag is accidently lost, he or she might receive a free upgrade on the next flight.

With Big Data, such customized offers can be suggested in real time before, during, or after booking or checking in at a counter.

In the data intensive travel industry, Big Data offers a lot of opportunities, including developing new and innovative (online) products based on insights found after combining different datasets. Organizations in the travel industry should start investigating and experimenting with the massive possibilities of Big Data.

FOR CAESARS ENTERTAINMENT, BIG DATA IS MORE IMPORTANT THAN GAMBLING

Caesars Entertainment, known for its numerous luxury hotels and casinos in, among other places, Las Vegas, has become an information-centric organization, in which data drives decision making.[233] As a result of the collection of massive amounts of data, Caesars can cultivate customer loyalty and surprise guests with free gifts after, for example, a bad day at the casino.

Its data-driven strategy is based around the Total Rewards program, which has more than 45 million members.[234] All members are tracked throughout their entire travel journey, from the moment they book until the moment they leave the hotel or casino. The entire data trail is tracked and analyzed and used to provide superior services to guests.

Because of its data-driven strategy, Caesars has been able to recoup 85 percent of all costs spent on customers, up from 58 percent in 2004. It has also given Caesars valuable insights into guest behavior. As Joshua Kanter, Vice President of Total Rewards for Caesars Entertainment, Las Vegas, says, "Big Data is even more important than a gaming license."[235,236]

With all this data, Caesars gives loyal visitors very targeted benefits, while avoiding spending too much money without results. The goal is to define the right profile for each guest who arrives at a casino. Cameras record everyone's action. A player who is guessing is more likely to lose money than a disciplined player. Caesars combines this kind of data with data collected during the customer's trip. Such data includes where they book their stays or travel arrangements, dining choices, gambling preferences, and other activities at the company's properties. All this information is stored, analyzed, and used to provide personal benefits to guests. Consequently, a guest receives a free dinner or hotel room to keep him or her satisfied. On the other hand, the tracking software is also used to prevent any of the 75,000 employees being too big-hearted in giving away freebees.

Caesars Entertainment uses the same type of analytical program to analyze the insurance claims of all its employees and their family members. Managers of Caesars are able to track many different variables about how employees use medical services. This aggregated and anonymous data can help the organization identify differences. One property, for example, Harrah's in Philadelphia, showed a higher use of the emergency room compared to the overall organizations. Managers brought this to the attention of the employees and the rate dropped significantly.[237]

What will the future look like? Kanter expects that security cameras that are now everywhere in the casinos will be able to predict traffic flows in casinos and determine bottlenecks.[238] Subsequently, this information can be used to inform guests via their smartphones which restaurant or table is busy and what the waiting time will be.

TAKEAWAYS

This chapter examined 18 different industries to show the possibility of Big Data for your organization. Many more industries could benefit from Big Data, ranging from fishing to the publishing industry. Each will require its own data and tools and have its own applications. With Big Data, almost anything is possible. Organizations need to use their creativity to define the best use for their situation.

Although different industries and organizations may have varying uses for Big Data, looking beyond your own organization or industry will broaden your view and provide new insights and ideas. Best practices from other organizations and industries are valuable in providing a better understanding of the endless possibilities of Big Data and how you can achieve a winning strategy that will let you outperform your competitors.

The Future
of Big Data

8

The semantic web, or web 3.0, is often referred to as the next phase of the Internet. Led by the World Wide Web Consortium (W3C), the ambition is to transform the current web of unstructured and semistructured data into a "web of data." According to W3C, the semantic web will make it easier to share and reuse data across application, community, and enterprise boundaries.

In 1998, the inventor of the web, Tim Berners-Lee, already called the semantic web "a web of data, in some ways like a global database."[1] This database will be comprised of all unstructured, semistructured, and structured data currently online but still residing in silos. In that same white paper, Berners-Lee described the rationale for developing the semantic web as, "the Web was designed as an information space, with the goal that it should be useful not only for human–human communication, but also that machines would be able to participate and help. One of the major obstacles to this has been the fact that most information on the Web is designed for human consumption, and even if it was derived from a database with well-defined meanings (in at least some terms) for its columns, that the structure of the data is not evident to a robot browsing the web."

The semantic web will enable all people and Internet connected devices (think: the Internet of Things) to communicate with each other as well as share and reuse data in different forms across different applications and organizations in real time. Obviously this has everything to do with Big Data.

In Chapter 1, I discussed the 7 Vs of Big Data: volume, velocity, variety, veracity, value, visualization, and variability. Velocity is the speed at which data is created; volume is the sheer amount of it; variety is different forms of data; veracity is the accuracy of the data; value is the economic benefits the data brings to companies, organizations, and societies; visualization is the art of making the data easy and understandable; and variability is the changing meaning of data over time.

Together these 7Vs define Big Data, and they immediately show the challenges of the semantic web and the future of Big Data: How to connect, link, and make available all the data on the web that is created in large volumes at high speed in different formats with different variables, but still ensur the correctness, quality, and understandability of that data for people and machines. It also shows how Big Data can help create the semantic web. All the technologies currently being developed for Big Data, such as Hadoop, open-source tools, and the technology developed by startups, will enable the development of the semantic web. Its development requires that processing, linking, and analyzing data become better and less expensive.

In a blog post, Ramani Pandurangan, Vice President of Network Engineering at XO Communications, describes the semantic web as "essentially a framework to link metadata (data about data) of data stored in disparate databases on the Web so that it will allow machines to query these databases and yield enriched results."[2] When all databases that are currently still in silos are connected, it will become possible for machines to find, connect, and communicate with that information.

A great example of this and a glimpse on the future of Big Data is the Knowledge Graph of Google, which was introduced in May 2012.[3] Google calls it the future of search, indexing things and not strings. Knowledge Graph is very promising, but as mentioned by Larry Page, Cofounder of Google, they "are still at one percent of where Google wants to be."[4] In 2013 the semantic network created by Google contained 570 million objects and over 18 billion facts about relationships between different objects that are designed to understand the meaning of keywords entered for searching purposes. The objective is to develop a Star Trek experience, in which users can simply ask computers natural questions. Google is not the only organization working on semantic search. Big Data startups like Ontology also aim to connect things instead of strings, but Ontology focuses on enterprise applications rather than the web.

The semantic web as discussed by Tim Berners-Lee in 1998 focuses especially on machines connecting and communicating with the web. Nowadays, we call this the Internet of Things. Connecting 25 or 50 billion different devices that are interoperable can only happen when those devices can browse, connect, and communicate with the web as people do. It will become even more important when in about a decade a trillion sensors will be connected to the web in real time.[5]

Therefore, the technologies involved with Big Data do not only stimulate the development of the semantic web. They will also require that the semantic web works correctly and takes full advantage of the promises of Big Data. When a semantic web is operational, the future of Big Data can really unfold, and it promises to be a bright future.

Jason Hoffman, CTO of Joyent, predicts that the future of Big Data will be about the convergence of data, computing, and networks.[6] The personal computer represented the convergence of computing and networks; the convergence of computing and data will result in analyses on exabytes of raw data that enable ad hoc questions to be asked on very large datasets.

The future of Big Data will allow us to ask questions and find answers more easily by asking questions in natural language. At the moment, users still need to know what they want to know, but in the future, it will all be about the things that you don't know.[7]

The real advance will come when organizations no longer have to ask questions to obtain answers, but will simply find answers to questions never thought of. Advanced pattern discovery and categorization of patterns will enable algorithms to perform decision-making for organizations. Extensive and beautiful visualizations will become more important and will help organizations understand the brontobytes of data.

THE FUTURE OF BUSINESS ANALYTICS

The future of Big Data will also transform the way we analyze the vast amounts of new data. In the past, we tried to understand how the organizations or the world around us behaved by analyzing the available data using descriptive analytics. This answered the question: "What happened in the past with the business?" With the availability of Big Data, we entered the new area of predictive analytics, which focuses on answering the question: "What is probably going to happen in the future?" However, the real advantage of analytics comes with its final stage, which can be called the future of business analytics and is called prescriptive analytics. This type of analytics tries to answer the question: "Now what?" or "so what?" It tries to offer a recommendation for key decisions based on future outcomes. To understand what this will mean for your organization, let's look at what the difference is among these three different types of analytics and how they affect your organization?

First, these three types of analytics should coexist—business, predictive, and prescriptive. One is not better than the other; they are just different. All, however, are necessary to obtain a complete overview of your organization. In fact, they should be implemented consecutively. All of them contribute to the objective of improved decision making.

Descriptive Analytics Is About the Past

Descriptive analytics helps organizations understand the past. In this context, the past can be one minute ago or a few years back. Descriptive analytics helps to understand the relationship between customers and products; the objective is to learn what approach to take in the future. In other words, learn from past behavior to influence future outcomes.

Common examples of descriptive analytics are management reports that provide information regarding sales, customers, operations, and finance, and then look to find correlations among the variables. Netflix, for example, uses descriptive analytics to find correlations among different movies that subscribers rent. To improve its recommendation engine, Netflix uses historical sales and customer data.[8]

Descriptive analytics is therefore an important source for determining what to do next. With predictive analytics, such data can be turned into information regarding the likely future outcome of an event.

Predictive Analytics Is About the Future

As is clear from the examples in this book, predictive analytics provides organizations with actionable insights based on data. It offers an estimation regarding the likelihood of a future outcome. To do this, a variety of techniques are used, including machine learning, data mining, modeling, and game theory. Predictive analytics can, for example, help to identify future risks and opportunities.

Historical and transactional data are used to identify patterns, while statistical models and algorithms are used to capture relationships in various datasets. Predictive analytics has really taken of in the Big Data era, and there are many tools available for organizations to predict future outcomes. With predictive analytics, it is important to have as much data as possible. More data means better predictions.

Prescriptive Analytics Provides Advice Based on Predictions

Prescriptive analytics is the final stage in understanding your business, but it is still in its infancy. In the 2013 *Hype Cycle of Emerging Technologies* by Gartner, prescriptive analytics was mentioned as an "Innovation Trigger" that will take another five to ten years to reach its plateau of productivity.[9] Prescriptive analytics not only foresees what will happen and when, but also why it will happen. It provides recommendations for acting on this information to take advantage of the predictions.

It uses a combination of many different techniques and tools, such as mathematical sciences, business rule algorithms, machine learning, and computational modeling techniques, as well as many different datasets ranging from historical and transactional data to public and social datasets.[10] Prescriptive analytics tries to see what the effect of future decisions will be in order to adjust the decisions before they are actually made.[11] This will improve decision making a lot, as future outcomes are taken into consideration in predictions.

Prescriptive analytics is very new; it has only been around since 2003, and is so complex that there are very few best practices on the market. Only three percent of companies use this technique—and it still has lots of errors in it.[12] One of the best examples is Google's self-driving car that makes decisions based on various predictions of future outcomes. These cars need to anticipate what's coming and what the effect of a possible decision will be before they make that decision to prevent an accident.

Prescriptive analytics could have a very large impact on business and how decisions are made. It can impact any industry and any organization and help organizations become more effective and efficient.

With an understanding of descriptive, predictive, and prescriptive analytics, your business will find it easier to make better informed decisions that take into account future outcomes. Prescriptive analytics is the future, and IBM has already called it "the final phase" in business analytics.[13]

The Brontobytes Era

Big Data Scientists will be in very high demand in the coming decades, but the real winners in the startup field will be those companies that can make Big Data so easy to understand, implement, and use that Big Data Scientists are no longer necessary. Large corporations will always hire Big Data Scientists, but the much larger market of SMEs cannot afford to do this. Those startups that enable Big Data for SMEs without the need to hire experts will have a competitive advantage.

The algorithms developed by those Big Data startups will become ever smarter, smartphones will become better, and everyone will be able to have a supercomputer in a pocket that can perform daunting computing tasks in real time and visualize them on the small screen in your hand. And, with the Internet of Things and the Industrial Internet and trillions of sensors, the amount of data that needs to be processed by these devices will grow exponentially.

Big Data will only becomes bigger, and those brontobytes will become common language in the boardroom. Fortunately, data storage will also become more widely available and less expensive. Brontobytes will become so common that eventually the term Big Data will disappear. Big Data will become just data again.

However, before we have reached that stage, the growing amount of data that is processed by companies and governments will create privacy concerns. Those organizations that stick to ethical guidelines will survive; other organizations that take privacy lightly will disappear, as privacy will become self-regulating. The problem will remain, however, with governments, as citizens cannot choose not to deal with them. Important public debates about the effects of Big Data on consumer privacy are inevitable; together, we have to ensure that we do not end up in Minority Report 2.0.

The future of Big Data is still unsure, as the Big Data era is still unfolding. It is clear, however, that future changes will transform organizations and societies. Hopefully, this book made clear that Big Data is here to stay, and organizations will have to adapt to the new paradigm. Organizations might be able to postpone their Big Data strategy for a while, but we have seen that organizations that have already implemented a Big Data strategy outperform their competitors. Therefore, start developing your Big Data strategy, as there is no time to waste if your organization also wants to provide products and services in the upcoming Big Data era. Good luck!

Glossary

A

Aggregation   The process of searching, gathering, and presenting data.

Algorithms   Mathematical formulas that can perform certain analyses on data.

Analytics   Communication of the discovery of insights from data.

Anomaly detection   The search for items in a dataset that do not match a projected pattern or expected behavior. Anomalies are also called outliers, exceptions, surprises, or contaminants, and they often provide critical and actionable information.

Anonymization   Making data anonymous; removing all data points that could identify a person.

Application   Computer software that enables a device to perform a certain task.

Artificial Intelligence   The development of machines and software capable of perceiving the environment, taking corresponding action when required, and even learning from those actions.

B

Behavioral analytics   Analytics that inform about how, why, and what, instead of just the who and when. It looks at humanized patterns in the data.

Big Data Scientist   Someone able to develop the algorithms that make sense out of Big Data.

Big Data startup   A young company that has developed new Big Data technology.

Biometrics   The identification of humans by their characteristics.

Brontobytes   Approximately 1000 yottabytes; the size of the digital universe tomorrow. A brontobyte contains 27 zeros.

Business Intelligence   The theories, methodologies, and processes to make data understandable.

C

Classification analysis　A systematic process for obtaining important and relevant information about data, also called metadata; data about data.

Cloud computing　A distributed computing system over a network used for storing data off-premises.

Clustering analysis　The process of identifying similar objects and clustering them to understand the differences as well as the similarities within the data.

Cold data storage　Storing old data that is hardly used on low-power servers. Retrieving the data will take longer.

Comparative analysis　A step-by-step procedure for comparisons and calculations that detect patterns within very large datasets.

Complex structured data　Data that is composed of two or more complex, complicated, and interrelated parts that cannot be easily interpreted by structured query languages and tools.

Computer generated data　Data generated by computers, such as log files.

Concurrency　The performance and execution of multiple tasks and processes at the same time

Correlation analysis　The analysis of data to determine a relationship between-variables and whether that relationship is negative (–1.00) or positive (+1.00).

Customer Relationship Management　Managing sales and business processes. Big Data will affect CRM strategies

D

Dashboard　A graphical representation of the analyses performed by algorithms.

Data aggregation tools　The process of transforming scattered data from numerous sources into a single new source.

Data analyst　Someone who analyzes, models, cleans, or processes data

Database　A digital collection of data stored via a certain technique.

Database-as-a-Service　A database hosted in the cloud on a pay-per-use basis, as, for example, Amazon Web Services.

Database Management System　Collecting, storing, and providing access to data.

Data center　A physical location that houses the servers for storing data.

Data cleansing　The process of reviewing and revising data to delete duplicates, correct errors, and provide consistency.

Data custodian　Someone responsible for the technical environment necessary for data storage,

Data ethical guidelines　Guidelines that help organizations be transparent with their data, ensuring simplicity, security, and privacy

Data feed　A stream of data, such as a Twitter feed or RSS.

Data marketplace　An online environment to buy and sell datasets.

Data mining　The process of finding certain patterns or information from datasets.

Data modeling   The analysis of data objects using data modeling techniques to create insights.

Dataset   A collection of data.

Data virtualization   A data integration process to gain more insights. Usually it involves databases, applications, file systems, websites, and Big Data techniques).

Deidentification   The same as anonymization; ensuring a person cannot be identified through the data.

Descriptive analytics   A form of analysis that helps organizations understand what happened in the past.

Discriminant analysis   Cataloguing of the data. Distributing data into groups, classes, or categories. A statistical analysis used when certain groups or clusters in data are known upfront and that applies the information to derive the classification rule.

Distributed File System   A system that offers simplified, highly available access to storing, analyzing, and processing data

Document Store Database   A document-oriented database especially designed to store, manage, and retrieve documents that are also known as semistructured data.

E

Exploratory analysis   The finding of patterns within data without standard procedures or methods. It is a means of discovering the data and identifying the dataset's main characteristics.

Exabytes   Approximately 1000 petabytes or 1 billion gigabytes. Today, one exabyte of new information is created globally on a daily basis.

Extract, Transform, and Load (ETL)   A process in a database and data warehousing that extracts the data from various sources, transforms it to fit operational needs, and loads it into the database

F

Failover   Switching automatically to a different server or node should one fail.

Fault-tolerant design   A system designed to continue working even if certain parts fail.

G

Gamification   Using game elements in a nongame context; very useful to create data and therefore coined as the friendly scout of Big Data.

Graph Databases   Databases that use graph structures (a finite set of ordered pairs or certain entities) with edges, properties, and nodes for data storage. It provides index-free adjacency, meaning that every element is directly linked to its neighbouring element.

Grid computing A method of connecting different computer systems in various locations, often via the cloud, to reach a common goal.

H

Hadoop An open-source framework built to enable the process and storage of Big Data across a distributed file system.

HBase An open source, nonrelational, distributed database running in conjunction with Hadoop.

HDFS (Hadoop Distributed File System A distributed file system designed to run on commodity hardware.

High-Performance Computing (HPC) The use of supercomputers to solve highly complex and advanced computing problems.

I

Industrial Internet The integration of complex physical machinery with networked sensors and software.

In-memory A database management system that stores data on the main memory instead of the disk, resulting is very fast processing, storing, and loading of the data.

Internet of Things Ordinary devices that are connected to the Internet at any time and anywhere through sensors.

J

Juridical data compliance The need to observe the laws of the country in which data is stored. This is particularly relevant when you use cloud solutions.

K

Keyvalue databases Databases that use a primary key, a uniquely identifiable record, that makes it easy and fast to look up information. The data stored in a key value is usually some kind of primitive programming language.

L

Latency A measure of time delayed in a system.

Legacy system An old system, technology, or computer that is no longer supported.

Load balancing The distribution of the workload across multiple computers or servers to achieve optimal results and utilization of the system.

Location data GPS data describing a geographical location.

Log file a file automatically created by a computer to record events that occur while operational.

M

Machine2Machine data Two or more machines that communicate with each other.

Machine data   Data created by machines using sensors or algorithms.

Machine learning   Part of artificial intelligence in which machines learn from what they are doing and improve over time.

MapReduce   A software framework for processing vast amounts of data.

Massively Parallel Processing (MPP)   The use of many different processors (or computers) to perform certain computational tasks simultaneously.

Metadata   Data about data; it provides information about what the data is about.

MongoDB   An open-source NoSQL database.

Multidimensional databases   Databases optimized for online analytical processing (OLAP) applications and data warehousing.

MultiValue Databases   A type of NoSQL and multidimensional databases that understand three-dimensional data directly. They are primarily giant strings that are perfect for directly manipulating HTML and XML strings.

N

Natural language processing   A field of computer science that studies interactions between computers and human languages.

Network analysis   The viewing of relationships among nodes in terms of the network or graph theory. It means analyzing connections between nodes in a network and the strength of the ties.

NewSQL   An elegant, well-defined database system that is easier to learn and better than SQL. It is even newer than NoSQL.

NoSQL   sometimes referred to as "Not only SQL,'" as it is a database that does not adhere to traditional relational database structures. It is more consistent and can achieve higher availability and horizontal scaling.

O

Object databases   Databases that store information in the form of objects, as used by object-oriented programming. They are different from relational or graph databases, and most of them offer a query language that allows an object to be found with a declarative programming approach.

Object-based image analysis   Analyzing digital images using data from individual pixels, whereas object-based image analysis uses data from a selection of related pixels, called objects or image objects.

Operational databases   Databases that perform the regular operations of an organization and are generally very important to a business. They use online transaction processing that allows them to enter, collect, and retrieve specific information about the company.

Optimization analysis   The process of optimization during the design cycle of products performed by algorithms. It allows companies to virtually design many different variations of a product and test them against preset variables.

Ontology   The representation of knowledge as a set of concepts within a domain and the relationships between those concepts.

Outlier detection   An outlier is an object that deviates significantly from the general average within a dataset or a combination of data. It is numerically distant from the rest of the data and, therefore, indicates that something is going on and requires additional analysis.

P

Pattern recognition   The identification of patterns in data using algorithms to make predictions about new data coming from the same source.

Petabytes   Approximately 1000 terabytes or 1 million gigabytes. The CERN Large Hydron Collider generates approximately 1 petabyte per second

Platform-as-a-Service   Services providing all the necessary infrastructure for cloud computing solutions.

Predictive analysis   The most valuable analysis within Big Data, as it helps predict what someone is likely to buy, visit, and do or how someone will behave in the (near) future. It uses a variety of different datasets, such as historical, transactional, social, and customer profile, to identify risks and opportunities.

Prescriptive analytics   Analysis that foresees not only what will happen and when it will happen, but why it will happen, and provides recommendations about how to take advantage of the predictions.

Privacy   The seclusion of certain data/information about oneself that is deemed personal.

Public data   Public information or datasets created with public funding.

Q

Quantified self   A movement to use applications to track one's every move during the day in order to gain a better understanding about one's behavior.

Query   A request for information to answer a certain question.

R

Reidentification   The combination of several datasets to find a certain person within anonymized data.

Regression analysis   An analysis that defines the dependency between variables. It assumes a one-way causal effect from one variable to the response of another variable.

RFID (Radio Frequency Identification)   A type of sensor using wireless noncontact radiofrequency electromagnetic fields to transfer data.

Real-time Data   Data that is created, processed, stored, analyzed, and visualized within milliseconds.

Recommendation engine   An algorithm that suggests certain products based on previous buying behavior or the buying behavior of others.

Routing analysis   The way to find optimized routing using many different variables for a certain means of transport to decrease fuel costs and increase efficiency.

S

Semistructured data   A form of structured data that does not have a formal structure. It does however have tags or other markers to enforce a hierarchy of records.

Sentiment Analysis   The use of algorithms to learn how people feel about certain topics.

Signal analysis   The analysis of measurement of time varying or spatially varying physical quantities to analyze the performance of a product. Especially used with sensor data.

Similarity searches   Searches to find the closest object to a query in a database, where the data object can be any type of data.

Simulation analysis   The imitation of the operation of a real-world process or system. Simulation analysis helps ensure optimal product performance taking into account many different variables.

Smart grid   The use of sensors within an energy grid to monitor what is going on in real time, thereby helping to increase efficiency.

Software-as-a-Service   A software tool that is used on the web via a browser.

Spatial analysis   The analysis of spatial data, such geographic or topological data, to identify and understand patterns and regularities within data distributed in geographic space.

SQL   A programming language for retrieving data from a relational database.

Structured data   Data that is identifiable because it is organized in structurelike rows and columns. The data resides in fixed fields within a record or file or the data is tagged correctly and can be accurately identified.

T

Terabytes   Approximately 1,000 gigabytes. A terabyte can store up to 300 hours of high-definition video.

Time series analysis   The analysis of well-defined data obtained through repeated measurements of time. The data is measured at successive points spaced at identical time intervals.

Topological data analysis   This analysis focuses on the shape of complex data and identifies clusters and any statistical significance that is present.

Transactional data   Dynamic data that changes over time.

Transparency   The policy of keeping consumers informed about what happens with their data.

U

Unstructured data   Data that is in general text heavy, but may also contain dates, numbers, and facts.

V

Value   A benefit of Big Data for organizations, societies, and consumers. Big Data means big business, and every industry will reap the rewards.

Variability   The ability of the data to change (rapidly). In (almost) the same tweets, for example, a word can have a totally different meaning.

Variety   The presentation of data in many different formats: structured, semi-structured, unstructured, and even complex structured.

Velocity   The speed at which the data is created, stored, analyzed, and visualized.

Veracity   The correctness of the data. Organizations need to ensure that data and the analyses performed on it are correct.

Visualization   Complex graphs that can include many variables of data while still remaining understandable and readable. These are not ordinary graphs or pie charts. With the right visualizations, raw data can be put to use.

Volume   The amount of data, ranging from megabytes to brontobytes.

W

Weather data   An important open and public data source that can provide organizations with a lot of insights if combined with other sources.

X

XML Databases   Databases that allow data to be stored in XML format. XML databases are often linked to document-oriented databases. The data stored in an XML database can be queried, exported, and serialized into any format needed.

Y

Yottabytes   Approximately 1000 zettabytes, or the data stored on 250 trillion DVDs. The entire digital universe today is one Yottabyte, and this will double every 18 months.

Z

Zettabytes   Approximately 1000 exabytes or 1 billion terabytes. It is expected is that by 2016, more than one zettabyte will cross our networks globally on a daily basis.

Notes

CHAPTER 1 THE HISTORY OF BIG DATA

1. www.edstephan.org/Graunt/graunt.html
2. 1.usa.gov/13dyXly
3. www.wired.com/wiredenterprise/2012/06/how-social-security-saved-ibm/
4. www.codesandciphers.org.uk/virtualbp/fish/colossus.htm
5. www.gwu.edu/~nsarchiv/NSAEBB/NSAEBB260/nsa-3.pdf
6. news.google.com/newspapers?id=ZGogAAAAIBAJ&sjid=3GYFAAAAIBA J&pg=933,5465131&dq=data-center&hl=en
7. www.bbc.co.uk/history/historic_figures/berners_lee_tim.shtml
8. www.nytimes.com/1996/08/30/us/clinton-s-speech-accepting-the-demo cratic-nomination-for-president.html?pagewanted=all&src=pm
9. strata.oreilly.com/2010/01/roger-magoulas-on-big-data.html
10. www.forbes.com/sites/danwoods/2011/11/03/explaining-hadoop-to -your-ceo/
11. www.-0.1ibm.com/software/data/infosphere/hadoop/mapreduce
12. uidai.gov.in/about-uidai.html
13. www.youtube.com/watch?v=UAcCIsrAq70
14. www.mckinsey.com/insights/mgi/research/technology_and_innovation/ big_data_the_next_frontier_for_innovation
15. gigaom.com/cloud/big-data-adoption-issues-whats-the-big-deal/
16. www.emc.com/about/news/press/2011/20110628-01.htm

CHAPTER 2 WHAT IS BIG DATA?

1. www.theverge.com/2013/5/19/4345514/youtube-users-upload-100-hours -video-every-minute

2. scoop.intel.com/what-happens-in-an-internet-minute/
3. articles.washingtonpost.com/2013-03-21/business/37889387_1_tweets
   -jack-dorsey-twitter
4. news.cnet.com/8301-1023_3-57584305-93/google-search-scratches-its
   -brain-500-million-times-a-day/
5. youtu.be/e6K0VHz6FVc
6. www-01.ibm.com/software/data/bigdata/
7. www.emc.com/leadership/programs/digital-universe.htm
8. www.emc.com/collateral/analyst-reports/idc-extracting-value-from-chaos
   -ar.pdf
9. gigaom.com/2010/09/13/sensor-networks-top-social-networks-for-big
   -data-2/
10. www.computerworld.com/s/article/9225827/Shell_Oil_targets_hybrid
    _cloud_as_fix_for_energy_saving_agile_IT
11. arstechnica.com/science/2012/04/future-telescope-array-drives-development
    -of-exabyte-processing/
12. www-01.ibm.com/software/data/bigdata/
13. nosql.mypopescu.com/post/6361838342/bigdata-volume-velocity-variability
    -variety
14. blogs.forrester.com/mike_gualtieri/12-05-17-whats_your_big_data_score
15. www.mckinsey.com/insights/mgi/research/technology_and_innovation/
    big_data_the_next_frontier_for_innovation
16. www.bigdata-startups.com/internet-of-things-with-trillions-of-sensors-will
    -change-our-future/
17. www.mckinsey.com/insights/mgi/research/technology_and_innovation/
    big_data_the_next_frontier_for_innovation
18. www.coursera.org/
19. class.coursera.org/bigdata-002/class/index
20. www.pcworld.com/article/257045/6_5m_linkedin_passwords_posted
    _online_after_apparent_hack.html
21. edition.cnn.com/2013/03/04/tech/web/evernote-hacked
22. www.wired.com/wiredenterprise/2013/03/digital-thieves-pull-off-12000
    -bitcoin-heist/
23. www.wikihow.com/Protect-Data-from-Getting-Hacked
24. www.prweek.com/uk/news/1179319/
25. www.dutchnews.nl/news/archives/2013/05/direct_debit_processor_plans_t
    .php
26. www.telecompaper.com/news/dutch-govt-wants-to-scrap-paper-corre
    spondence—945636
27. www.informationweek.com/government/information-management/white
    -house-shares-200-million-big-data/232700522
28. youtu.be/44W0svJxCq8

29. beforeitsnews.com/international/2013/03/neelie-kroes-on-the-big-data
-revolution-2454490.html

30. money.cnn.com/magazines/fortune/most-admired/2013/list/

31. www.infoworld.com/t/big-data/disneys-big-data-dream-no-mickey-mouse
-effort-213713

32. www.nbcnews.com/travel/disney-world-track-visitors-wireless-wristbands
-1B7874882

33. disneyparks.disney.go.com/blog/2013/01/taking-the-disney-guest-experience
-to-the-next-level/

34. www.nbcnews.com/travel/disney-world-track-visitors-wireless-wristbands
-1B7874882

35. www.nytimes.com/2013/01/07/business/media/at-disney-parks-a-bracelet
-meant-to-build-loyalty-and-sales.html?_r=0

36. www.nytimes.com/2013/01/07/business/media/at-disney-parks-a-bracelet
-meant-to-build-loyalty-and-sales.html?pagewanted=2&_r=0

37. www.nytimes.com/2013/01/07/business/media/at-disney-parks-a-bracelet
-meant-to-build-loyalty-and-sales.html?pagewanted=1&_r=0

38. gigaom.com/2012/09/16/how-disney-built-a-big-data-platform-on-a
-startup-budget/

39. www.slideshare.net/cloudera/hadoop-world-2011-advancing-disneys-data
-infrastructure-with-hadoop-matt-estes-disney

40. gigaom.com/2012/09/16/how-disney-built-a-big-data-platform-on-a
-startup-budget/

41. www.mckinsey.com/insights/mgi/research/technology_and_innovation/
big_data_the_next_frontier_for_innovation

42. www.tcs.com/SiteCollectionDocuments/Trends_Study/TCS-Big-Data
-Global-Trend-Study-2013.pdf

43. www.sas.com/news/preleases/survey_big_data_disconnect.html

44. techcrunch.com/2012/10/17/big-data-to-drive-232-billion-in-it-spending
-through-2016/

45. news.cnet.com/8301-19882_3-57373474-250/path-ceo-we-are-sorry-and
-weve-deleted-your-address-book-data/

46. rt.com/news/twitter-sells-tweet-archive-529/

47. privacyinpractice.com/blog/2013/02/whatsapp-ened-privacy-lessons-app
-developers-world-over

48. www.cisco.com/en/US/solutions/ns340/ns517/ns224/big_data_wp.pdf

CHAPTER 3 BIG DATA TRENDS

1. www.telecomlead.com/smart-phone/apples-smartphone-market-share-to
-dip-to-14-1-in-2017-from-19-5-in-2012-canalys-72280/

2. www.smartinsights.com/mobile-marketing/mobile-marketing-analytics/ mobile-marketing-statistics/
3. venturebeat.com/2013/02/06/800-million-android-smartphones-300 -million-iphones-in-active-use-by-december-2013-study-says/
4. www.gartner.com/newsroom/id/2408515
5. venturebeat.com/2012/11/23/ericssons-massive-mobile-report-6-4b-global -cellular-plans-75-of-all-new-phones-in-asia-and-africa/
6. www.slideshare.net/MeasureWorks
7. www.gomez.com/wp-content/downloads/19986_WhatMobileUsersWant _Wp.pdf
8. www.gomez.com/wp-content/downloads/19986_WhatMobileUsersWant _Wp.pdf
9. www.worldtimezone.com/4g.html
10. gigaom.com/2013/02/26/eu-digital-chief-throws-e50m-in-5gs-direction-to -help-continent-regain-mobile-lead/
11. www.huffingtonpost.co.uk/2013/04/05/4g-is-still-too-expensive_n_3018818 .html
12. venturebeat.com/2012/11/23/ericssons-massive-mobile-report-6-4b-global -cellular-plans-75-of-all-new-phones-in-asia-and-africa/
13. www.forbes.com/sites/chuckjones/2013/05/02/tablet-market-forecast-to -grow-almost-5x-by-2017/
14. venturebeat.com/2013/02/07/mobile-enterprise-report-costs-up-control -down-byod-soaring-and-it-getting-frustrated/
15. www.microsoft.com/en-us/windows/windowsintune/explore/byod.aspx
16. www.informationweek.com/security/mobile/ibm-launches-bring-your-own -device-secur/231902875
17. www-03.ibm.com/press/us/en/pressrelease/39136.wss
18. www.zoomdata.com/
19. www.youtube.com/watch?v=e6K0VHz6FVc
20. pandodaily.com/2013/02/13/forget-mobile-vs-desktop-the-future-of -computing-will-be-a-question-of-head-vs-wrist/
21. pandodaily.com/author/nathanielmott/
22. storm-project.net/
23. www.cloudera.com/content/cloudera/en/home.html
24. www.gridgain.com/
25. www.spacecurve.com/
26. spacecurve.com/spacecurve-sets-real-time-big-data-performance-record/
27. www.ge.com/stories/industrial-internet
28. www.gereports.com/now-departing/
29. www.gereports.com/brains-for-planes/
30. www.slideshare.net/SITAOnline/atis-potential-ofcollaborationjameshogan
31. www.sita.aero/content/sita-signs-ten-year-partnership-with-etihad-airways
32. www.sita.aero/content/empower-your-crew

33. idcdocserv.com/1414
34. www.progressive.com/
35. www.progressive.com/auto/snapshot-how-it-works.aspx
36. www.glowcaps.com/
37. www.fastcompany.com/1548674/hp-invents-central-nervous-system-earth -and-joins-smarter-planet-sweepstakes
38. www.semsorgrid4env.eu/
39. www.ibmbigdatahub.com/blog/next-best-action-internet-things
40. www.gizmag.com/heineken-ignite-smart-beer-bottles/27020/
41. files.tribalddb.nl/spark/BLOG%20POSTS/hei_ignite_production_backstory SK%20(2).pdf
42. www.wwrf.ch/
43. analysis.telematicsupdate.com/infotainment/telematics-and-m2m-commu nications-creating-internet-things
44. www.fastcompany.com/1548674/hp-invents-central-nervous-system-earth -and-joins-smarter-planet-sweepstakes
45. www.v3.co.uk/v3-uk/the-frontline-blog/2129028/hp-predicts-zettabytes -created-2020
46. www.computerworld.com/s/article/9234563/By_2020_there_will_be_5_200 _GB_of_data_for_every_person_on_Earth
47. www.esquire.com/blogs/politics/hybrid-age-9715111
48. www.electroiq.com/articles/sst/2013/03/-14-trillion-opportunity-in-internet -of-things—predicts-cisco.html
49. www.gartner.com/technology/research/it-spending-forecast/
50. www.ibm.com/smarterplanet/us/en/ibm_predictions_for_future/ideas/
51. www.emerce.nl/nieuws/ik-bouw-tricorder-ja-ja-hij-werkt-al
52. www.songdo.com/
53. newsroom.cisco.com/songdo
54. www.wired.com/culture/lifestyle/commentary/imomus/2007/01/72368
55. www.forbes.com/sites/csr/2012/08/06/choice-at-the-supermarket-is-our -food-system-the-perfect-oligopoly/
56. www.future-store.org/
57. wiki.answers.com/Q/How_many_supermarkets_are_there_in_each_state _in_the_U.S.
58. foodzy.com/
59. www.myzeo.com/sleep/
60. runkeeper.com/
61. www.lifelapse.com/
62. www.fitbit.com/premium/about
63. www.economist.com/node/21548493
64. jawbone.com/up
65. foodzy.com/
66. www.moves-app.com/

67. www.moves-app.com/press
68. venturebeat.com/tag/quantified-self/
69. www.patientslikeme.com/
70. www.23andme.com/
71. blog.23andme.com/news/announcements/understanding-sharing-at-23 andme/
72. delphi.com/news/pressReleases/pr_2013_01_06_001/
73. www.jeffbullas.com/2012/04/23/48-significant-social-media-facts-figures -and-statistics-plus-7-infographics/%23e5fZgwTPL4wacMHt.99
74. www.statisticbrain.com/twitter-statistics/
75. investors.linkedin.com/releasedetail.cfm?ReleaseID=761589
76. techcrunch.com/2012/02/11/pinterest-stats/
77. wallblog.co.uk/2012/11/05/social-media-statistics-2012-from-facebook -and-twitter-to-instagram-and-pinterest-infographic/
78. www.techinasia.com/2013-china-top-10-social-sites-infographic/
79. blog.vint.sogeti.com/wp-content/uploads/2012/10/Big-Social-Predicting -Behavior-with-Big-Data.pdf
80. www.bigdata-startups.com/BigData-startup/bluefin-labs
81. thenextweb.com/twitter/2013/02/06/twitter-confirms-it-has-bought-bluefin -labs-to-develop-its-tv-analytics-and-advertising-business/?fromcat=all
82. edition.cnn.com/2012/08/02/tech/social-media/facebook-fake-accounts/ index.html
83. www.bigdata-startups.com/big-social-data/bluefinlabs.com
84. www.guardian.co.uk/technology/2012/mar/17/facebook-dark-side-study -aggressive-narcissism
85. blog.vint.sogeti.com/wp-content/uploads/2012/10/Big-Social-Predicting -Behavior-with-Big-Data.pdf
86. readwrite.com/2010/09/29/the_short_lifespan_of_a_tweet_retweets_only _happen
87. www.youtube.com/watch?v=VaJjPRwExO8
88. uk.reuters.com/article/2012/10/26/uk-nestle-online-water-idUKBRE89 P07Q20121026
89. www.reputationinstitute.com/thought-leadership/global-reptrak-100
90. www.zdnet.com/ten-examples-of-extracting-value-from-social-media-using -big-data_p7-7000007192/#photo
91. uk.reuters.com/article/2012/10/26/uk-nestle-online-water-idUKBRE89 P07Q20121026
92. www.holmesreport.com/people-info/13662/Smart-Router.aspx
93. www.youtube.com/watch?v=HD_W3EMuC1U
94. cxo-advisor.co.za/content/nestl%C3%A9-collaborating-salesforcecom -drive-digital-transformation
95. ec.europa.eu/commission_2010-2014/kroes/index_en.htm
96. ec.europa.eu/information_society/policy/psi/index_en.htm

97. blogs.ec.europa.eu/neelie-kroes/opendata/

98. open-data.europa.eu/open-data/

99. data.overheid.nl/

100. data.overheid.nl/handreiking/Wat-levert-het-op-voor-de-overheid

101. www.whitehouse.gov/sites/default/files/microsites/ostp/big_data_press _release.pdf

102. www.logica.com/we-do/business-consulting/

103. www.forumstandaardisatie.nl/fileadmin/os/documenten/Internationale _benchmark_v1_03_final.pdf

104. www.foia.gov/

105. agimo.gov.au/files/2013/03/Big-Data-Strategy-Issues-Paper1.pdf

106. www.google.com/publicdata/directory

107. aws.amazon.com/publicdatasets/

108. bigdata-startups.com/big-data-startup/infochimps

109. www.bigdata-startups.com/BigData-startup/datamarket

110. www.google.com/publicdata/directory

111. aws.amazon.com/datasets?_encoding=UTF8&jiveRedirect=1

112. www.enigma.io/

113. www.quandl.com/

114. www.figshare.com/

115. www.datahub.io/

116. www.opensciencedatacloud.org/

117. www.datamob.org/

118. www.freebase.com/

119. opendata.socrata.com/

120. flatworldbusiness.wordpress.com/2013/03/09/why-gamification-is-like -chocolate-and-big-data-is-like-bacon-sxsw/

121. www.gartner.com/newsroom/id/2251015

122. gamifyforthewin.com/2013/01/big-data-to-save-gamification/

123. www.slideshare.net/romrack/gamification-meets-big-data

124. www.smh.com.au/it-pro/business-it/just-do-it-nike-opens-access-to -customer-data-20130122-2d3tt.html

125. nikeaccelerator.com/

126. www.linkedin.com/pub/stefan-olander/4/78/133

127. gigaom.com/2012/11/05/nikes-olander-democratizing-sports-data-is-a -tremendous-opportunity/

128. nikeinc.com/news/nikeplus-experience

CHAPTER 4 BIG DATA TECHNOLOGIES

1. www.abiresearch.com/press/big-data-spending-to-reach-114-billion-in -2018-loo

2. www.forbes.com/sites/danwoods/2011/11/03/explaining-hadoop-to-your -ceo/
3. news.cnet.com/8301-1001_3-57451565-92/vmware-works-to-make-hadoop -virtualization-aware/
4. www.greenplum.com/news/press-releases/emc-goes-social-open-and-agile -with-big-data
5. www.cioinsight.com/it-strategy/linux-open-source/slideshows/five-pros-and -five-cons-of-open-source-software/
6. www.informationweek.com/big-data/news/big-data-analytics/why-recom mendation-engines-are-about-to/240161676
7. blog.linkedin.com/2011/03/02/linkedin-products-you-may-like/
8. www.casertaconcepts.com/blog-2/webinar-recording-slides-building-a-big -data-recommendation-engine/
9. www.amazon.com/Inside-Careers-Homepage/b?ie=UTF8&node =239367011
10. www.marketingpilgrim.com/2012/01/amazon-retains-top-spot-in-customer -service-poll-zappos-third.html
11. www.fastcodesign.com/1669551/how-companies-like-amazon-use-big -data-to-make-you-love-them
12. aws.amazon.com/elasticmapreduce/
13. gigaom.com/2011/10/18/amazon-aws-elastic-map-reduce-hadoop/
14. gigaom.com/2011/10/18/amazon-aws-elastic-map-reduce-hadoop/
15. aws.amazon.com/s3/
16. aws.amazon.com/publicdatasets/
17. www.technologyreview.com/news/509471/amazon-woos-advertisers-with -what-it-knows-about-consumers/
18. www.cnbc.com/id/100638376

CHAPTER 5 BIG DATA PRIVACY, ETHICS, AND SECURITY

1. www.ted.com/talks/malte_spitz_your_phone_company_is_watching.html
2. www.guardian.co.uk/uk/2013/jun/21/gchq-cables-secret-world-communi cations-nsa
3. www.scmp.com/news/hong-kong/article/1266777/exclusive-snowden-safe -hong-kong-more-us-cyberspying-details-revealed
4. www.theguardian.com/world/2013/jun/16/g20-surveillance-turkey -targeted-gchq?guni=Article:in%20body%20link
5. www.guardian.co.uk/uk/2013/jun/23/mi5-feared-gchq-went-too-far
6. www.foxnews.com/politics/2013/06/18/nsa-chief-defends-surveillance-says -helped-prevent-terror-more-than-50-times/

7. eur-lex.europa.eu/LexUriServ/LexUriServ.do?uri=OJ:L:2006:105:0054:0063 :EN:PDF

8. www.huffingtonpost.com/2009/12/07/google-ceo-on-privacy-if_n_383105 .html

9. www.youtube.com/watch?v=NP5okzCjrj0

10. join.app.net/

11. www.theatlanticwire.com/technology/2013/03/facebook-new-news-feed/ 62816/

12. www.facebook.com/about/graphsearch

13. www.nytimes.com/2013/03/26/technology/facebook-expands-targeted -advertising-through-outside-data-sources.html?_r=0

14. www.pcworld.com/article/2027694/get-ready-for-facebook-graph-search .html

15. www.nbcnews.com/technology/technolog/3-privacy-settings-tweak-facebook -graph-search-rolls-out-1B7988034

16. mashable.com/wp-content/uploads/2011/01/privacy-lg.jpg

17. www.techdirt.com/articles/20040203/191241.shtml

18. mashable.com/2013/05/24/app-net-invites/

19. wi.mit.edu/

20. www.1000genomes.org/

21. wi.mit.edu/news/archive/2013/scientists-expose-new-vulnerabilities-security -personal-genetic-information

22. www.cephb.fr/en/cephdb/

23. healthaffairs.org/blog/2012/08/10/the-debate-over-re-identification-of -health-information-what-do-we-risk/

24. dataprivacylab.org/people/sweeney/

25. papers.ssrn.com/sol3/papers.cfm?abstract_id=1450006

26. www.hhs.gov/ocr/privacy/hipaa/understanding/summary/index.html

27. randomwalker.info/

28. www.cs.utexas.edu/~shmat/shmat_oak08netflix.pdf

29. www.wired.com/threatlevel/2010/03/netflix-cancels-contest/

30. epic.org/privacy/reidentification/

31. www.wired.com/threatlevel/2012/06/wmw-arvind-narayanan

32. www.ncvhs.hhs.gov/071221lt.pdf

33. www.srh.noaa.gov/jetstream/lightning/lightning_faq.htm

34. www.mailman.columbia.edu/our-faculty/profile?uni=db2431

35. www.concurringopinions.com/archives/2012/09/re-identification-risks-and -myths-superusers-and-super-stories-part-ii-superusers-and-super-stories .html

36. www.techpolicyinstitute.org/files/the%20illusory%20privacy%20problem %20in%20sorrell1.pdf

37. lawweb.colorado.edu/profiles/profile.jsp?id=180

38. papers.ssrn.com/sol3/papers.cfm?abstract_id=967372

39. www.computerworld.com/s/article/9231566/Facebook_to_delete_all
    _European_facial_recognition_data
40. www.slate.com/articles/health_and_science/science/2010/02/dont_touch
    _that_dial.single.html
41. Blair, Ann. 2003. "Reading Strategies for Coping with Information Overload
    ca. 1550–1700," *Journal of the History of Ideas*, 64(1), 11–28.
42. thebreakthrough.org/index.php/journal/issue-3/dont-blame-the-internet
    -for-political-polarization/
43. www.minnpost.com/second-opinion/2010/02/socrates-would-probably
    -have-hated-facebook
44. books.google.com/books?id=9i-gAAAAMAAJ&pg=PA258
45. www.princeton.edu/futureofchildren/publications/journals/article/index
    .xml?journalid=45&articleid=201&sectionid=1310
46. edition.cnn.com/2005/WORLD/europe/04/22/text.iq/
47. www.telegraph.co.uk/science/science-news/5149195/Twitter-and-Facebook
    -could-harm-moral-values-scientists-warn.html
48. www.dailymail.co.uk/health/article-1149207/How-using-Facebook-raise
    -risk-cancer.html
49. www.danah.org/papers/talks/2013/ASTD2013.html
50. www.tkconference.org/
51. www.aclu.org/technology-and-liberty/modernizing-electronic-communications
    -privacy-act-ecpa
52. www.huffingtonpost.com/2012/07/31/aclu-privacy-act_n_1724764.html
53. www.privacy-europe.com/blog/dutch-government-to-reduce-cookie-consent
    -requirements/
54. www.instructables.com/index
55. www.cbpweb.nl/downloads_rapporten/rap_2013-patientendossiers-binnen
    -zorginstellingen.pdf
56. runkeeper.com/
57. www.sleepcycle.com/
58. foodzy.com/
59. www.zdnet.com/blog/igeneration/facebook-does-not-erase-user-deleted
    -content/4808
60. www.guardian.co.uk/money/2011/may/11/terms-conditions-small-print
    -big-problems
61. dataportability.org/
62. www.linkedin.com/in/korddavis/
63. www.amazon.com/Ethics-Big-Data-Balancing-Innovation/dp/1449311792
64. www.privacy.org.au/Resources/PLawsWorld.html
65. www.urbandictionary.com/define.php?term=digital%20immigrant
66. www.nytimes.com/2010/05/13/technology/personaltech/13basics.html
67. gizmodo.com/5984666/facebook-got-hacked-last-month-and-is-just-telling
    -you-now

68. edition.cnn.com/2013/03/04/tech/web/evernote-hacked
69. www.pcworld.com/article/257045/6_5m_linkedin_passwords_posted _online_after_apparent_hack.html
70. www.spookmag.com/2009/11/23/why-terrorists-should-buy-life-insurance/
71. www.amazon.com/SuperFreakonomics-Cooling-Patriotic-Prostitutes -Insurance/dp/0060889578/ref=sr_1_1?ie=UTF8&s=books&qid=1255494 800&sr=1-1
72. www.sis.gov.uk/
73. www.guardian.co.uk/world/2013/jun/18/nsa-chief-house-hearing-surveillance -live
74. www.guardian.co.uk/world/2013/jun/06/us-tech-giants-nsa-data
75. www.rsaconference.com/
76. www.linkedin.com/pub/ramin-safai/1/686/910/
77. jefferies.com/
78. www.emc.com/collateral/analyst-reports/security-analytics-esg-ar.pdf
79. www.iii.org/
80. it.slashdot.org/story/13/03/09/0234252/dns-hijack-leads-to-bitcoin-heist
81. www.emc.com/collateral/industry-overview/big-data-fuels-intelligence -driven-security-io.pdf
82. www.weforum.org/
83. www.microsoft.com/government/ww/safety-defense/blog/Pages/post.aspx ?postID=74&aID=23
84. www.weforum.org/sessions/summary/risks-hyperconnected-world
85. www.icann.org/en/groups/board/beckstrom.htm
86. www.icann.org/
87. www.eff.org/deeplinks/2012/09/freedom-not-fear-cctv-surveillance -cameras-focus
88. www.dailymail.co.uk/news/article-1205607/Shock-figures-reveal-Britain -CCTV-camera-14-people—China.html
89. www.cameramanager.com/fin/en/cameramanager-about-us/cameramanager -press/the-video-surveillance-industry—market-size
90. www.cameramanager.com/fin/en/cameramanager-about-us/cameramanager -press/the-video-surveillance-industry—market-size
91. www.electronics-eetimes.com/en/over-50-of-video-surveillance-cameras -will-be-megapixel-and-hd-by-2014.html?cmp_id=7&news_id=222903390
92. www.bbc.co.uk/news/technology-19812385
93. www.bbc.co.uk/news/technology-14629058
94. www.crimmigrationcontrol.com/content/news/Presentations/%255B Presentation%2042%255D%20Maartje%20van%20der%20Woude.pdf
95. Interview with Wilma van Raalte - Program Manager of the Safety Region Twente, The Netherlands.
96. twitcident.com/
97. agtinternational.com/press/1419

98. bluemark-innovations.com/

99. seriousrequest.3fm.nl/

CHAPTER 6 BIG DATA IN YOUR ORGANIZATION

1. sites.tcs.com/big-data-study/big-data-study-key-findings/

2. www.sas.com/resources/whitepaper/wp_58466.pdf

3. www.cisco.com/en/US/solutions/ns340/ns517/ns224/big_data_wp.pdf

4. Mckinsey.com/insights/mgi/research/technology_and_innovation/big_data
_the_next_frontier_for_innovation

5. www.bbc.co.uk/news/business-19969588

6. www.business2community.com/marketing/walmartlabs-taking-big-data
-into-retail-0176299

7. www.tomtom.com/

8. www.engadget.com/2012/06/11/apple-tomtom-ios-6-maps/

9. www.apple.com/ios/maps/

10. corporate.tomtom.com/releasedetail.cfm?ReleaseID=739428

11. www.tomtom.com/services/tomtom-home/

12. www.tomtom.com/en_gb/products/car-navigation/tomtom-navigation-for
-iphone-ipad/navigation-app/index.jsp

13. www.tomtom.com/en_us/products/built-in-car-navigation/

14. business.tomtom.com/

15. technopundit.com/tom-tom-connected-pnd/

16. www.tomtom.com/en_us/maps/map-share/

17. www.infowars.com/dutch-cops-using-tomtom-data-to-position-speed
-cams/

18. www.stuff.co.nz/technology/digital-living/7959302/TomTom-opens-up
-maps-to-developers

19. www.deere.com/wps/dcom/en_INT/our_company/news_and_media/press
_releases/2011/nov/farm_sight.page

20. www.forbes.com/sites/kashmirhill/2012/02/16/how-target-figured-out-a
-teen-girl-was-pregnant-before-her-father-did/

21. tech.fortune.cnn.com/2012/07/30/amazon-5/

22. www.engadget.com/2012/10/25/amazon-announces-q3-2012-earnings
-13-18-billion-revenue/

23. www.fico.com/en/Company/News/Pages/11-20-2012-Europe-Bankers
-Rank-Analyzing-Big-Data-on-Customers-Among-Top-2013-Priorities
-FICO-EfmaSurvey.aspx

24. online.wsj.com/article/SB10001424052702304458604577488822667325882
.html

25. www.constructionbusinessowner.com/topics/equipment/construction
-equipment-management/how-telematics-systems-guide-operations-managers

26. opendatachallenge.org/

27. openglam.org/tag/apps-for-the-netherlands/

28. nationaleappprijs.nl/

29. www.smartplanet.com/blog/ideas-insights/how-to-use-big-data-to-transform
    -your-company/122

30. www.smartplanet.com/blog/bulletin/how-open-source-big-data-can-improve
    -supply-chains/4833

31. www.telecomtv.com/comspace_videoDetail.aspx?v=6273&id=e9381817
    -0593-417a-8639-c4c53e2a2a10

32. www.mckinsey.com/insights/mgi/research/technology_and_innovation/big
    _data_the_next_frontier_for_innovation

33. wikibon.org/wiki/v/Enterprises_Struggling_to_Derive_Maximum_Value
    _from_Big_Data

34. www.iab.net/media/file/2012-BRITE-NYAMA-Marketing-ROI-Study.pdf

35. www.techrepublic.com/blog/big-data-analytics/defining-an-roi-for-big
    -data/194

36. lunchpail.knotice.com/2012/04/23/fun-facts-on-big-data/

37. www.sas.com/offices/europe/uk/press_office/press_releases/Big-data-on
    -balance-sheets.html

38. www.att.com/Common/about_us/files/pdf/ar2011_annual_report.pdf

39. www.wired.com/threatlevel/2011/09/diginotar-bankruptcy/

40. www.computing.co.uk/ctg/news/2123215/putting-value-key-getting-ceos
    -board

41. www.crmsolution.com/top10failure.html

42. www.ihgplc.com/index.asp?pageid=375&section=Factsheets

43. www.ihg.com/hotels/us/en/reservation

44. www.ihg.com/priorityclub/hotels/us/en/home

45. online.wsj.com/article/SB10001424127887324178904578340071261396666
    .html?mod=WSJ_hpp_sections_tech

46. ftp://ftp.software.ibm.com/software/emea/de/rational/IntercontntlHotels
    _CS.pdf

47. www.linkedin.com/pub/manish-shah/0/440/722

48. blog.anametrix.com/hotel-marketing-strategy-digital-analytics-ihg
    -hospitality/

49. www.linkedin.com/in/daschmitt

50. www.allanalytics.com/document.asp?doc_id=236772

51. lithosphere.lithium.com/t5/science-of-social-blog/Finding-the-Influencers
    -Influence-Analytics-2/ba-p/570952.

52. www.prdaily.com/Main/Articles/Taming_PRs_latest_trend_Big_Data
    _11647.aspx

53. www.waxingunlyrical.com/2013/01/24/harnessing-the-power-of-big-data
    -for-public-relations/

54. online.wsj.com/article/SB10001424127887324034804578344303429080
    678.html

55. online.wsj.com/article/SB100014241278873240348045783443034290080678.html

56. www.cubist.com/

57. www.businessweek.com/articles/2013-05-16/the-next-big-thing-in-big-data-people-analytics

58. www.gladwell.com/tippingpoint/guide/chapter2.html

59. www.nytimes.com/2013/04/28/technology/how-big-data-is-playing-recruiter-for-specialized-workers.html?pagewanted=all&_r=0

60. www.catalystitservices.com/

61. www.linkedin.com/pub/michael-rosenbaum/3/288/b8

62. online.wsj.com/article/SB10001424127887324178904578340071261396666.html?mod=WSJ_hpp_sections_tech

63. online.wsj.com/article/SB10001424127887324178904578340071261396666.html?mod=WSJ_hpp_sections_tech

64. www.catalystitservices.com/sites/default/files/Content/images/Catalyst_IT_Services_Overview%20FINAL.pdf

65. www.cio.com/article/719764/How_to_Use_a_Moneyball_Approach_to_Build_a_Better_IT_Team?page=3&taxonomyId=3123

66. www-01.ibm.com/software/data/bigdata/

67. www.emc.com/collateral/about/news/idc-emc-digital-universe-2011-infographic.pdf

68. www.computerweekly.com/news/2240180815/Bank-legacy-systems-will-remain-until-CIO-life-expectancy-increases

69. www.computerweekly.com/contributor/Karl-Flinders

70. www.mis-asia.com/tech/applications/big-data-legacy-system-refresh-and-mobility-drive-banks-transformational-projects/

71. www.computerworlduk.com/news/applications/3425725/deutsche-bank-big-data-plans-held-back-by-legacy-systems/

72. www.datanami.com/datanami/2013-03-18/legacy_systems_a_challenge_for_big_automakers.html

73. www.mckinsey.com/insights/health_systems_and_services/how_big_data_can_revolutionize_pharmaceutical_r_and_d

74. www.computerweekly.com/feature/Legacy-systems-continue-to-have-a-place-in-the-enterprise

75. www.computerweekly.com/news/2240180815/Bank-legacy-systems-will-remain-until-CIO-life-expectancy-increases

76. thefinanser.co.uk/fsclub/2013/03/commonwealth-bank-of-australias-cio-the-four-million-dollar-man.html

77. www.computerweekly.com/news/2240180815/Bank-legacy-systems-will-remain-until-CIO-life-expectancy-increases

78. marketsmedia.com/unlocking-big-data/

79. www.indigobio.com/blog/?p=169

80. www.bigdata-startups.com/big-data-job-descriptions/

81. research.microsoft.com/pubs/163083/hotcbp12%20final.pdf
82. www.youtube.com/watch?feature=player_embedded&v=EsVy28pDsYo
83. www.youtube.com/watch?v=EsVy28pDsYo
84. www.bigdata-startups.com/BigData-startup/ayasdi/
85. www.bigdata-startups.com/BigData-startup/synerscope/
86. www.sap.com/corporate-en/news.epx?PressID=19188
87. www.linkedin.com/in/nstevenlucas
88. www.sap.com/corporate-en/news.epx?PressID=19188
89. www.ibmbigdatahub.com/infographic/taming-big-data-small-data-vs
   -big-data
90. www.bigdata-startups.com/BigData-startup/the-nike-gamification
   -platform-delivers-valuable-big-data-insights/
91. realbusiness.co.uk/article/19203-big-data-big-problem-for-smes
92. www.nytimes.com/2004/08/20/national/20flight.html
93. Vicktor Mayer-Schönberger and Kenneth Cukier, *Big Data: A Revolution That Will Transform How We Live, Work, and Think.* New York: Eamon Dolan/Houghton Mifflin Harcourt,
94. www.cisco.com/en/US/solutions/ns340/ns517/ns224/big_data_wp.pdf

CHAPTER 7 BIG DATA BY INDUSTRY

1. www.xtimeline.com/timeline/History-of-agriculture-1
2. cdn.intechopen.com/pdfs/15910/InTech-Sensor_fusion_for_precision
   _agriculture.pdf
3. siliconangle.com/blog/2012/09/07/building-big-data-farming-big-data-goes
   -to-the-cows/
4. 12most.com/2012/03/12/advanced-agricultural-technologies/
5. www.slideshare.net/RevolutionAnalytics/order-fulfillment-forecasting-at
   -john-deere-how-r-facilitates-creativity-and-flexibility?ref=www.revolution
   analytics.com/news-events/free-webinars/2012/order-fulfillment-forecasting
   -at-john-deere/
6. www.deere.com/wps/dcom/en_US/campaigns/ag_turf/farmsight/farmsight
   .page
7. myjohndeere.deere.com/
8. www.deere.com/wps/dcom/en_US/products/equipment/ag_management
   _solutions/information_management/john_deere_mobile_farm_manager/
   john_deere_mobile_farm_manager.page?
9. www.bigdata-startups.com/BigData-startup/tomtom-big-data/
10. www.kurzweilai.net/googles-self-driving-car-gathers-nearly-1-gbsec
11. www.ask.com/question/average-time-spent-in-a-car
12. www.huffingtonpost.ca/2011/08/23/car-population_n_934291.html?just
   _reloaded=1

13. infocus.emc.com/william_schmarzo/big-data-in-automotive-and-machinery
    -using-analytics-to-deliver-better-products-and-a-more-fulfilling-driver
    -experience/
14. www.cio.com/article/718053/GM_Bets_on_Insourcing_Brings_Back_10
    _000_IT_Jobs
15. mailto:www-01.ibm.com/software/ebusiness/jstart/
16. www.mshare.net/
17. www.oracle.com/us/corporate/profit/opinion/011813-cmoren-1899118
    .html
18. blogs.forrester.com/michael_barnes/13-02-15-big_data_adoption_in_asia
    _pacific_clear_use_cases_drive_growing_demand
19. www.marketingweek.co.uk/big-data-embracing-the-elephant-in-the-room/
    3030939.article
20. www.engadget.com/2013/10/22/apple-ios-7-downloaded-over-200-million
    -times-in-5-days/
21. www.youtube.com/watch?v=6h-r_sofp0E
22. wikibon.org/
23. gigaom.com/2013/03/27/why-apple-ebay-and-walmart-have-some-of-the
    -biggest-data-warehouses-youve-ever-seen/
24. www.forbes.com/sites/netapp/2012/10/03/google-apple-maps-big-data
    -cloud/
25. www.datasciencecentral.com/profiles/blogs/apple-big-data-big-design
26. www.wired.com/wiredenterprise/2013/04/siri-two-years/
27. nccs.ed.gov/
28. www.ed.gov/
29. hortonworks.com/blog/big-data-in-education-part-2-of-2/
30. ai.stanford.edu/~ang/
31. www.coursera.org/course/ml
32. www.coursera.org/
33. hortonworks.com/blog/data-in-education-part-i/
34. www.purdue.edu/
35. www.prweb.com/releases/2012/7/prweb9664003.htm
36. www.educause.edu/annual-conference/2011/course-signals-student-success
    -systemstoplights-student-success
37. www.noellevitz.com/case-studies/student-retention-case-studies/retention
    -excellence-awards
38. www.blackboard.com/
39. www.itap.purdue.edu/newsroom/detail.cfm?newsId=2601
40. www.itap.purdue.edu/learning/tools/signals/
41. siliconangle.com/blog/2012/07/09/emc-partners-with-purdue-university-to
    -solve-big-data-problems/
42. www.emc.com/index.htm
43. www.purdue.edu/ethics/oie/OfficeofInstitutionalEquity002826-2013.html

44. www.scientificamerican.com/article.cfm?id=electricity-gap-developing
    -countries-energy-wood-charcoal
45. www.forbes.com/sites/tomgroenfeldt/2012/05/09/big-data-meets-the-smart
    -electrical-grid/
46. bit.ly/YgrbH1
47. www.selinc.com/synchrophasors/
48. bit.ly/Y3Imvz
49. www.forbes.com/sites/tomgroenfeldt/2012/05/09/big-data-meets-the-smart
    -electrical-grid/
50. ftp://public.dhe.ibm.com/software/pdf/industry/IMW14628USEN.pdf
51. ibm.co/YoLIv0
52. ftp://public.dhe.ibm.com/software/pdf/industry/IMW14628USEN.pdf
53. www.youtube.com/watch?v=BF_BjQ25t8Y
54. ibm.co/12ZZUt2
55. www.vattenfall.com/en/index.htm
56. ibm.co/YoJM5H
57. www-03.ibm.com/press/us/en/pressrelease/35737.wss
58. science.time.com/2013/03/26/smart-power-why-more-bytes-will-mean
    -fewer-and-cleaner-electrons/
59. www.ibmbigdatahub.com/blog/driving-down-price-risk
60. www.analyticbridge.com/forum/topics/the-big-data-tidal-wave-how
    -technology-is-shaping-tthe-way
61. blogs.wsj.com/cio/2013/03/11/visa-says-big-data-identifies-billions-of
    -dollars-in-fraud/
62. blogs.wsj.com/cio/2013/03/11/visa-says-big-data-identifies-billions-of
    -dollars-in-fraud/
63. www.dutchnews.nl/news/archives/2013/05/direct_debit_processor_plans_t
    .php
64. www.forbes.com/sites/tomgroenfeldt/2012/05/30/morgan-stanley-takes-on
    -big-data-with-hadoop/"
65. www.forbes.com/sites/tomgroenfeldt/2012/05/30/morgan-stanley-takes-on
    -big-data-with-hadoop/"
66. www.linkedin.com/in/bhattacharjee/
67. www.datanami.com/datanami/2012-07-09/how_four_financial_giants
    _crunch_big_data.html?page=2"
68. www.forbes.com/sites/tomgroenfeldt/2012/05/30/morgan-stanley-takes-on
    -big-data-with-hadoop/"
69. blogs.wsj.com/cio/2012/09/16/morgan-stanley-smith-barney-betting-big
    -on-analytics/"
70. www.wallstreetandtech.com/data-management/morgan-stanley-turns-to
    -wire-data/240162551"
71. www.extrahop.com/" ExtraHop
72. blog.revolutionanalytics.com/2013/03/big-data-in-video-games.html

73. slashdot.org/topic/bi/game-studios-at-the-forefront-of-bigdata-and-cloud/
74. www.mpaa.org/resources/3037b7a4-58a2-4109-8012-58fca3abdf1b.pdf
75. www.sand.com/zynga-big-data-game/
76. company.zynga.com/es/news/engineering-blog/what-powers-play-zynga
77. www.dbms2.com/2011/09/05/zynga-linkedin-data-warehous/
78. www.industrygamers.com/news/zynga-rallies-against-criticism-of-metrics
    -approach/
79. www.industrygamers.com/news/zynga-rallies-against-criticism-of-metrics
    -approach/
80. zettanalytics.blogspot.nl/2011/09/zyngas-analytics-philosophy.html
81. online.wsj.com/article/SB100014241278873241789045783400712613966
    666.html?mod=WSJ_hpp_sections_tech
82. www-conf.slac.stanford.edu/xldb2012/talks/xldb2012_wed_1125_Daniel
    Mccaffrey.pdf
83. www-conf.slac.stanford.edu/xldb2012/talks/xldb2012_wed_1125_Daniel
    Mccaffrey.pdf
84. www.splunk.com/
85. www.codefutures.com/database-sharding/
86. gigaom.com/2012/01/23/as-genomics-pushes-big-data-limits-cloud-could
    -save-the-day/
87. www.pwc.com/us/en/healthcare/publications/the-price-of-excess.jhtml
88. practicalanalytics.wordpress.com/2011/12/12/big-data-analytics-use-cases/
89. healthcare.dmagazine.com/2013/06/13/health-systems-use-big-data-to-cut
    -costs-improve-quality/
90. blog.fluturasolutions.com/2012/12/5-disruptive-big-data-use-cases-in.html
91. www.informationweek.com/software/business-intelligence/ibm-big-data
    -monitors-patients-for-brain/240150671
92. blog.fluturasolutions.com/2012/12/5-disruptive-big-data-use-cases-in.html
93. www-01.ibm.com/software/data/bigdata/industry-healthcare.html
94. online.wsj.com/article/SB10000872396390443884104577645783975993
    656.html
95. www.guardian.co.uk/science/2013/jun/08/genome-sequenced
96. blog.gopivotal.com/case-studies-2/data-science-labs-predictive-modeling
    -to-detect-healthcare-fraud-waste-and-abuse
97. www.govhealthit.com/news/part-3-9-fraud-and-abuse-areas-big-data-can
    -target
98. www.forbes.com/sites/tomgroenfeldt/2012/04/20/aurora-health-uses-big
    -data-to-reduce-risk-in-outcomes-based-pay/
99. www.slideshare.net/sanderklous/big-data-in-healthcare
100. www.forbes.com/sites/tomgroenfeldt/2012/04/20/aurora-health-uses-big
    -data-to-reduce-risk-in-outcomes-based-pay/2/
101. staging.asterdata.com/aurora-health-care-video.php

102. www.allanalytics.com/author.asp?section_id=1411&doc_id=246903
103. www.oracle.com/us/products/applications/health-sciences/network/over view/index.html
104. www.informationweek.com/smb/hardware-software/how-a-boutique-law -firm-handles-big-data/240145916
105. www.tkhr.com/
106. www.informationweek.com/smb/hardware-software/how-a-boutique-law -firm-handles-big-data/240145916
107. www.abajournal.com/magazine/article/the_dawn_of_big_data/?utm _source=feedburner&utm_medium=feed&utm_campaign=ABA+Journal +Magazine+Stories
108. tymetrix.com/products/legal-analytics/
109. www.abajournal.com/magazine/article/the_dawn_of_big_data/?utm _source=feedburner&utm_medium=feed&utm_campaign=ABA+Journal +Magazine+Stories
110. www.skyanalytics.com/
111. itunes.apple.com/us/app/ratedriver/id400465980?mt=8
112. www.forbes.com/sites/netapp/2012/10/31/big-data-law-cloud-analytics/
113. www.proskauer.com/files/News/b6c4d609-61e2-4557-ab5f-1e22744f685a/ Presentation/NewsAttachment/1c0d50f9-f52b-4b60-8e49-1fd042cfaeab/ Proskauer%20041111%20NLJ%20-%20Goldberg%20(Big%20Data _BYLINE_POSTED%20VERSION).pdf
114. www.youtube.com/watch?v=hrhoXMEAA14
115. spectrum.ieee.org/podcast/at-work/start-ups/can-big-data-win-your-next -court-case
116. juristat.com/
117. allthingsd.com/20130618/ready-for-the-industrial-internet-ge-announces -predictivity-platform-new-partnership-with-amazon-web-services/
118. www.grtcorp.com/content/coming-industrial-internet-means-analytics -security-challenges
119. allthingsd.com/20130529/ge-ceo-jeff-immelts-big-data-bet/
120. blogs.wsj.com/cio/2012/06/20/ford-gets-smarter-about-marketing-and-design/
121. www.greencarcongress.com/2012/12/ford-20121222.html
122. www.usatoday.com/story/tech/2013/04/29/data-ford-gigaom/2120481/
123. gigaom.com/2013/04/26/how-data-is-changing-the-car-game-for-ford/
124. www.theinquirer.net/inquirer/news/1015284/aston-martin-gets-neural -network
125. gigaom.com/2013/04/26/how-data-is-changing-the-car-game-for-ford/
126. gigaom.com/2013/04/26/how-data-is-changing-the-car-game-for-ford/
127. www.zdnet.com/fords-big-data-chief-sees-massive-possibilities-but-the -tools-need-work-7000000322/
128. www.usatoday.com/story/tech/2013/04/29/data-ford-gigaom/2120481/

129. www.unglobalpulse.org/
130. www3.weforum.org/docs/WEF_TC_MFS_BigDataBigImpact_Briefing _2012.pdf
131. blogs.worldbank.org/category/tags/big-data
132. maps.worldbank.org/
133. www.aidtransparency.net/
134. www.linkedin.com/in/artatevossian
135. www.devex.com/en/news/big-data-for-development-what-is-it-and-why -you/81453
136. www.smartinsights.com/mobile-marketing/mobile-marketing-analytics/ mobile-marketing-statistics/
137. www.bigdata-startups.com/BigData-startup/cignifi/
138. www.developmentprogress.org/blog/2013/06/11/could-big-data-provide -alternative-measures-poverty-and-welfare
139. www.facebook.com/f4ep
140. www.hsph.harvard.edu/ess/bigdata.html
141. www3.weforum.org/docs/WEF_TC_MFS_BigDataBigImpact_Briefing _2012.pdf
142. blogs.worldbank.org/psd/big-data-for-development-beyond-transparency
143. www.rbm.who.int/psm/smsWhatIsIt.html
144. www3.weforum.org/docs/WEF_TC_MFS_BigDataBigImpact_Briefing _2012.pdf
145. www.bigdata-startups.com/BigData-startup/the-nike-gamification-platform -delivers-valuable-big-data-insights/
146. www3.weforum.org/docs/WEF_TC_MFS_BigDataBigImpact_Briefing _2012.pdf
147. opendata.go.ke/
148. blogs.worldbank.org/psd/big-data-for-development-beyond-transparency
149. pooreconomics.com/
150. blogs.worldbank.org/psd/big-data-for-development-beyond-transparency
151. allthingsd.com/20130520/in-media-big-data-is-booming-but-big-results -are-lacking/
152. nyti.ms/17pDsiJ
153. allthingsd.com/20130520/in-media-big-data-is-booming-but-big-results -are-lacking/
154. allthingsd.com/20130520/in-media-big-data-is-booming-but-big-results -are-lacking/
155. www.businessinsider.com/the-film-industry-needs-big-data-2013-5
156. www-05.ibm.com/innovation/uk/wimbledon/index.html
157. www.fairfaxcountyeda.org/companies/time-warner-cable
158. www.fastcompany.com/3004619/how-big-data-keeps-cable-tv-watchers -hooked

159. www.fastcompany.com/3004619/how-big-data-keeps-cable-tv-watchers
     -hooked

160. www.fastcompany.com/3004619/how-big-data-keeps-cable-tv-watchers
     -hooked

161. www.slideshare.net/blaurent/twc-20275998

162. www.slideshare.net/blaurent/twc-20275998

163. blog.vanspall.com/2012/12/oil-and-gas-twins-meets-two-other-big.html

164. www.hds.com/assets/pdf/hitachi-webtech-educational-series-big-data-in-oil
     -and-gas.pdf

165. bit.ly/14PJdAF

166. www.computerworld.com/s/article/9225827/Shell_Oil_targets_hybrid
     _cloud_as_fix_for_energy_saving_agile_IT

167. www-950.ibm.com/events/wwe/grp/grp037.nsf/vLookupPDFs/RICK%20
     -%20IDC_Calgary_Big_Data_Oil_and-Gas/$file/RICK%20-%20IDC
     _Calgary_Big_Data_Oil_and-Gas.pdf

168. blogs.wsj.com/cio/2013/01/02/big-oils-big-data-push-changing-the-future
     -of-energy/

169. fd.nl/ondernemen/topics/innovatie/349154-1303/shell-wil-hardware-delen
     -maar-data-niet

170. www.computerworlduk.com/news/public-sector/3367938/government
     -could-save-33bn-a-year-using-big-data-says-think-tank/

171. www.mckinsey.com/insights/mgi/research/technology_and_innovation/big
     _data_the_next_frontier_for_innovation

172. www.mckinsey.com/insights/business_technology/big_data_the_next
     _frontier_for_innovation

173. innovategov.org/2013/05/22/potential-savings-in-the-public-sector-from
     -effective-use-of-big-data/

174. accumulo.apache.org/

175. www.oracle.com/us/industries/public-sector/public-sector-big-data-br
     -1676649.pdf

176. www.statetechmagazine.com/article/2013/05/8-benefits-big-data-state-and
     -local-governments

177. www.applieddatalabs.com/content/big-data-and-government-transparency

178. www.zdnet.com/30-big-data-project-takeaways-7000005499/

179. www.greenplum.com/sites/default/files/the_big_data_opportunity.pdf

180. www.oracle.com/us/industries/public-sector/public-sector-big-data-br
     -1676649.pdf

181. www.emc.com/collateral/service-overview/h11653-svo-emc-big-data-solutions
     -public-sector.pdf

182. www.oracle.com/us/industries/public-sector/public-sector-big-data-br
     -1676649.pdf

183. www.informatica.com/us/solutions/industry-solutions/public-sector/us
     -federal-civilian/improper-payments/

184. strata.oreilly.com/2012/11/3-big-ideas-for-big-data-in-the-public-sector.html
185. www.deltares.nl/en/project/108270/the-smart-dike/108272
186. www.ijkdijk.nl/nl/livedijken
187. www.google.org/flutrends/about/how.html
188. www.oracle.com/us/industries/public-sector/public-sector-big-data-br-1676649.pdf
189. www.nytimes.com/2012/11/17/opinion/beware-the-big-data-campaign.html?_r=0
190. www.linkedin.com/pub/chris-wegrzyn/1/902/95a
191. whatis.techtarget.com/definition/MPP-massively-parallel-processing
192. www.mckinsey.com/insights/mgi/research/technology_and_innovation/big_data_the_next_frontier_for_innovation
193. www.youtube.com/watch?v=aZXVWOAcXjA
194. retail-fit.com/2013/07/01/big-data-analytics-and-kpis-in-e-commerce-and-retail-industry/
195. siliconangle.com/blog/2013/05/02/3-ways-big-data-has-changed-retail-analytics-forever/
196. retail-fit.com/2013/07/01/big-data-analytics-and-kpis-in-e-commerce-and-retail-industry/
197. gigaom.com/2012/03/23/walmart-labs-is-building-big-data-tools-and-will-then-open-source-them/
198. www.walmartlabs.com/
199. www.walmartlabs.com/social/social-genome/
200. www.facebook.com/Shopycat
201. dl.acm.org/citation.cfm?id=2367520
202. www.walmartlabs.com/social/
203. walmartlabs.github.com/thorax/
204. walmartlabs.github.com/lumbar/
205. www-01.ibm.com/software/data/bigdata/industry-telco.html
206. www.booz.com/global/home/what-we-think/reports-white-papers/article-display/benefiting-big-data
207. www.booz.com/global/home/what-we-think/reports-white-papers/article-display/benefiting-big-data
208. news.softpedia.com/news/Dutch-Law-Prohibits-Traffic-Throttling-3-Strikes-Disconnecting-Deep-Packet-Inspection-268557.shtml
209. www.booz.com/global/home/what-we-think/reports-white-papers/article-display/benefiting-big-data
210. www.booz.com/global/home/what-we-think/reports-white-papers/article-display/benefiting-big-data
211. www.t-mobile.com/
212. www.informatica.com/products_services/powercenter/Pages/index.aspx
213. www.splunk.com/
214. www.bigdata-startups.com/BigData-startup/tableau-software/

215. public.dhe.ibm.com/common/ssi/ecm/en/gbw03168usen/GBW03168 USEN.PDF

216. ibm.co/14mDbKU

217. www8.hp.com/h20195/v2/GetDocument.aspx?docname=4AA4-3942ENW

218. public.dhe.ibm.com/common/ssi/ecm/en/gbw03168usen/GBW03168USEN .PDF

219. public.dhe.ibm.com/common/ssi/ecm/en/xbl03022usen/XBL03022USEN .PDF

220. public.dhe.ibm.com/common/ssi/ecm/en/imc14725usen/IMC14725USEN .PDF

221. www.usxpress.com/

222. www.cio.com/article/670113/Big_Data_How_a_Trucking_Firm_Drove _Out_Big_Errors?page=1&taxonomyId=3028

223. www.computerweekly.com/news/2240146943/Case-Study-US-Xpress -deploys-hybrid-big-data-with-Informatica

224. searchbusinessanalytics.techtarget.com/video/Big-data-analytics-mobile-BI -apps-help-US-Xpress-truck-more-data

225. www.usxpress.com/Innovation-and-Technology/Technology-Awards.aspx

226. www.ventanaresearch.com/resources/resources.aspx?id=508

227. www.wttc.org/site_media/uploads/downloads/world2012.pdf

228. www.businessinsider.com/big-datas-role-in-business-travel-2013-1

229. www.qubitproducts.com/the-official-company-blog/big-data-tavel/

230. www.operasolutions.com/wp-content/uploads/2013/06/global-travel-case -study_final.pdf?submissionGuid=eececc59-de5b-4570-8b81-0f99b08b4402

231. www.forbes.com/sites/tomgroenfeldt/2012/01/23/big-data-meets-online -travel-20-billion-offers-one-second-response-time/

232. bits.blogs.nytimes.com/2013/06/26/why-the-airline-industry-needs-another -data-revolution/?_r=1

233. www.caesars.com/

234. www.totalrewards.com/

235. www.linkedin.com/in/joshuakanter/

236. loyalty360.org/resources/article/big-data-means-big-benefits-for-entertainment -caesers-exec1

237. online.wsj.com/article/SB10001424127887324178904578340071261396 666.html?mod=WSJ_hpp_sections_tech

238. loyalty360.org/resources/article/big-data-means-big-benefits-for-entertainment -caesers-exec1

CHAPTER 8 THE FUTURE OF BIG DATA

1. www.w3.org/DesignIssues/Semantic.html

2. blog.xo.com/industry-trends/semantic-web-from-data-silos-to-web-of-data/

3. www.google.com/insidesearch/features/search/knowledge.html

4. venturebeat.com/2013/01/22/larry-page-on-googles-knowledge-graph
   -were-still-at-1-of-where-we-want-to-be/

5. tsensors.org/

6. gigaom.com/2013/06/19/joyent-cto-the-convergence-of-data-and-compute
   -will-disrupt-global-profits/2/

7. www.joyent.com/blog/the-future-of-big-data-is-asking-dumb-questions

8. www.analytics.northwestern.edu/analytics-examples/descriptive-analytics
   .html

9. www.bigdata-startups.com/gartner-tempers-the-expectations-of-big-data/

10. Big Data Can Help Construction Companies Deliver Projects On Time.docx

11. gizmodo.com/how-prescriptive-analytics-could-harness-big-data-to-se
    -512396683

12. gizmodo.com/how-prescriptive-analytics-could-harness-big-data-to-se
    -512396683

13. www.youtube.com/watch?feature=player_embedded&v=VtETirgVn9c

Index

About the Author

Mark van Rijmenam is founder of the online Big Data knowledge platform BigData-Startups.com, which aims to become the central point for Big Data on the web. BigData-Startups.com is a platform that offers trends, best practices, information, open-source tools, and Big Data startups for organizations developing a Big Data strategy. The objective is to help organizations develop a Big Data strategy and find the right Big Data technology vendor for that strategy. The platform attracts an important niche of consumers, job seekers, organizations, and governments interested in Big Data. BigData-Startups developed the Big Data Strategy Model, which is is a valuable new tool in the ever-growing Big Data ecosystem, and one that helps organizations take the first steps toward their Big Data strategy.

Mark van Rijmenam advises organizations on how to develop their Big Data strategies. He is aware of the latest trends in the world. Next to blogging on BigData-Startups, he also blogs on SmartData-Collective.com, which is a platform with the world's best thinkers on Big Data. As such, he is a well sought after speaker on this topic. He has lectured to the International MBA Class and Executive Class at Business University Nyenrode, as well as at other events. He is co-founder of Data Donderdag a bimonthly (networking) event in The Netherlands that helps organizations better understand Big Data.